Civil War Savannah

Derek Smith

Civil War
Savannah

Frederic C. Beil
Savannah

Published in the United States by
Frederic C. Beil, Publisher, Inc.,
609 Whitaker Street,
Savannah, Ga. 31401

Library of Congress Cataloging-in-Publication Data
Smith, Derek, 1956 Nov. 3–
Civil War Savannah / by Derek Smith
p.   cm.
Includes bibliographical references (p.   ) and index.
ISBN 0-913720-93-3 (hardcover)
ISBN 1-929490-00-3 (softcover)
1. Savannah (Ga.)—History.
2. Georgia—History—Civil War, 1861–1865.
I. Title
F294.S2S65   1997   975.8´72403—dc21   97-27568

Beil website address: http://www.beil.com

This book was typeset by SkidType, Savannah, Georgia;
printed on acid-free paper; and sewn in signatures.

Printed in the United States of America

For
Helen

anchored, St. Patrick's Day revelers jam River Street during the annual March bacchanalia.

Along Bay Street, now choked with the noise and dust of heavy traffic, Sherman's veterans once paraded in victory before the Yankee Caesar.

Savannah's history dates to colonial times when Yamacraw tribesmen first met English soldier and explorer James Oglethorpe on the Savannah River bluffs in 1733. While many historic homes and sites have been preserved, others were doomed by the perpetual growth of the city, a lack of vision, or simple greed.

Groups such as the Historic Savannah Foundation and the Historic Review Board have done a commendable job in preservation efforts, but not everything was or could be saved. Before these organizations were established, many buildings that withstood hurricanes, fire, and war became victims of the wrecking ball.

Virtually nothing remains of the 1779 battlefield and siege lines where British and Loyalists held Savannah against American and French forces in some of the Revolutionary War's bloodiest fighting. Many of Savannah's Civil War sites have disappeared in similar fashion. Because Chatham County is a latticework of snaking rivers, creeks, and branches, the Confederates built a strong web of forts and batteries to keep the Federals out of these waterways.

Unfortunately for the historian, many of these works occupied "prime waterfront property" or had a wonderful marsh view, making them choice real estate. Developers bulldozed earthworks for their subdivisions and condominiums. Rifle pits manned by blue or gray have been leveled for mini-malls and strips of fast-food restaurants.

Certainly Savannah has done a better job of remembering its Civil War history than other cities, such as Atlanta, which has sprawled over most of its many battlefields and even lowered itself to rename streets that once honored Confederate heroes. Everywhere, North and South, Civil War battlefields and landmarks are constantly under attack from this new front—urban development at the cost of heritage.

Savannah has a wealth of encounters between Rebs and Yanks, famous and infamous, which rarely surface. Incidents like the Confederates' buccaneer-style capture of the USS *Water Witch* or the suspicious fire that destroyed much of downtown Savannah days after Sherman's departure gain little more than a footnote in most books on the conflict.

The roles of black Savannahians also have been overlooked. Some, like Moses Dallas, gave their lives for the Confederacy. Others put themselves

Preface

With a little imagination it's not hard to visualize Savannah, Georgia, during the war years of 1861–1865. To stroll the city's oak-shaded streets today is to walk in the footsteps of men such as Robert E. Lee, William T. Sherman, Jefferson Davis, Edwin Stanton, and P. G. T. Beauregard.

Most Civil War enthusiasts know that Sherman ended his "March to the Sea" after a brief but desperate battle at nearby Fort McAllister. The shell-scarred brick walls of Fort Pulaski still offer grim evidence of the April 1862 bombardment that revolutionized warfare. And who hasn't heard of Sherman presenting Savannah as a stocking stuffer for President Lincoln's Christmas in 1864?

Yet other than narratives about Fort Pulaski or Sherman's exploits, the "Hostess City of the South" receives scant attention in most general histories of the war. Confederate Savannah and the Federal occupation that followed don't garner the widespread popularity of the Historic District's architectural treasures or the city's natural Southern charm.

Today giant container ships from around the globe ply the Savannah River, once the realm of Rebel leviathans like the CSS *Savannah* and CSS *Atlanta*. Downtown office-workers lunch in the serenity of Johnson Square, where torch-lit secession rallies stirred war fever in 1860.

With cargoes of foreign-made rifles, ammunition, cloth, and other supplies, rakish blockade-runners docked at the city wharves after slipping the Union naval net off the coast. Where these oceanic greyhounds

Contents

at great risk by escaping or secretly learning to read and write, prohibited by state law at the time. Hundreds of slaves brought in from area plantations worked in the construction of Savannah's Confederate defenses.

The Reverend Garrison Frazier probably was the most eloquent of Savannah's freedmen. He spoke for a delegation of black leaders who met with U.S. Secretary of War Edwin Stanton to discuss Sherman's treatment of former slaves and their race in general.

Even the Fifty-fourth Massachusetts, whose story is depicted in the 1989 film *Glory*, figured in Savannah's war saga. As occupation troops, the Fifty-fourth came ashore not far from where some of the movie's scenes were shot on River Street.

In *Civil War Savannah* I have tried to provide a glimpse into the lives of the women and men who will forever be associated with the city through their wartime deeds. Some, like Lee, left Savannah and rode into legend. Others fought and died in obscurity, whether in battle along the Georgia coast or on distant fields—such as the six Sunday school mates from Savannah who marched to their deaths at First Bull Run.

This is also the saga of the most terrifying military technology of the age—the ironclad behemoths, the rifled cannon, and the buried or submerged "torpedoes," forerunners of modern land and sea mines. All were used with hard efficiency by men with dead aims and dead-earnest causes, fighting for their countries.

The ghosts of pirates, patriots, cavaliers, and their ladies will forever dance about Savannah—creaking an occasional staircase or flitting through a fog-shrouded cemetery, maybe even strolling the riverfront ballast stones after the tour buses leave.

In this realm ring the echoes of cannon fire, the vistas of men in gray or blue marching in splendid columns, or slaves humming a soothing cadence while digging entrenchments or toiling in the fields. Yank or Reb, man or woman, free or slave, this is their story.

Acknowledgments

The people who experienced the turbulent times of the War Between the States and wrote about this American cataclysm are the true authors of this work. They are the chroniclers who braved the bullets, made the speeches, dug the trenches, or fanned the home fires. It is my honor and privilege to weave their stories and exploits into this effort.

Many thanks go to Steve Bisson, chief photographer for the *Savannah Morning News*. A fellow Civil War buff, Steve helped me immensely with my first book, *Glory Yards*, and spent many hours working on illustrations for this project.

Also, thanks to Deric and Mary Ann Beil for their interest and encouragement regarding this endeavor since the time when it was only an idea. They were friends before they were business associates and remain so.

I also owe a debt to a man I never had the opportunity to know. Dr. Edgar J. Filson was a respected Savannah physician and a colleague in the study of "the late unpleasantness" before his death several years ago. His gracious wife, Kate, knew of our similar interests and honored me with some of Dr. Filson's Civil War literary collection. Thank you, Kate.

Retired Lieutenant Colonel Curtis L. Smart of the Jasper County Historical Society has my lasting gratitude for his assistance, as does my twelfth grade English teacher, Virginia Warr, who gave a shy teenager some badly needed confidence in his writing.

Thanks also to Dale K. Hooks and Cody, who helped me through a difficult summer.

The staffs of the Georgia Historical Society and the Chatham-Effingham Regional Public Library also provided invaluable help in the creation of this book.

At my parents' home in Bishopville, South Carolina, volume six of *Collier's Encyclopedia* has a thumb-worn binder from when I, even as a first grader, was fascinated by the engravings and photographs of its Civil War entry. Much love to Gordon and Willene Smith for buying that set of encyclopedias, as well as being wonderful and supportive parents.

Heroine worship is reserved for my wife, Helen Pitts Smith, who has always encouraged my writing and passion for history. Nothing I have ever done as a writer could have been accomplished without her.

Introduction

The cacophony of a people at war is a perpetual chronicle of Savannah's history. In the 1700's James Oglethorpe mustered his Englishmen for raids on the Spanish who threatened from outposts in Florida. Colonial children darted into the streets to collect sizzling cannonballs during Revolutionary War bombardments. Recruits flocked to join the Cuban relief effort in the Spanish-American War. Railcars of Abrams tanks trundled to the port and flag-waving civilians lined the riverfront to say good-bye to soldiers who won their glory in the Persian Gulf War.

Transports lifting into the night sky probably mean the elite Army Rangers are on a mission to a distant trouble spot. Savannah has always known the anxiety, excitement, pride, and grief of its finest headed for a hostile front.

Yet at no time in its history was Savannah as completely immersed in a war effort as it was during the bloody schism between South and North. Support for secession, states' rights, and John Breckinridge were the rage in 1860, a wildfire of ideology burning through the city as it did most of the South. The 127-year-old city was a rebellion hotbed already steeped in history—a former colonial capital of the Crown, and Georgia's main seaport. Her chronicle began when Oglethorpe and a small group of English colonists sailed up the Savannah River and established a camp on the river bluffs in February 1733. Oglethorpe's campsite, some seventeen miles inland from the Atlantic, marked the genesis of Savannah and what would become the colony of Georgia.

During the American Revolution the British captured the city from an inept patriot force in December 1778. The redcoats withstood probably the war's most brutal siege in autumn 1779, when French and American forces failed to retake Savannah after weeks of shelling and a climatic, disastrous assault. The allies' failure was due in great part to a crack regiment of Scottish Highlanders from Beaufort, South Carolina, who reinforced the British garrison. These British troops rowed to Savannah through a maze of coastal creeks and rivers that would prove just as important to Rebels and Yanks in the next century.

In 1860 Savannah was a town of about 14,000 whites and some 8,400 blacks, including freedmen and slaves. The city limits stretched south to Gaston Street, which bordered Forsyth Place, a large park with a three-year-old majestic fountain that was a popular spot for socializing.

The city had the sinewy toughness of an old port where stevedores loaded countless bales of cotton and other cargo aboard merchant ships sailing to the globe's far reaches. It bustled as a railroad hub fed by the Central of Georgia, the Charleston & Savannah, the Augusta & Savannah, and the Savannah, Albany & Gulf railroads. The Atlantic & Gulf line, linking Savannah with the southern portion of the state, was under construction.

Two shipyards, saw mills, iron works, and lesser industries stamped the city as a commercial center—one whose life blood was the meandering river. Flatboats also eased into port from the sixteen-mile Savannah and Ogeechee Canal, linking the inland Ogeechee River with the Savannah.

Three other major waterways also accessed the city. A few miles to the south the Wilmington River wound inland from Wassaw Sound, eventually joining the Savannah. Also to the south was Ossabaw Sound, fed by the Vernon River and the Great Ogeechee River. The French used the Vernon to land infantry prior to the 1779 siege. General Sherman would utilize the Ogeechee to great effect in 1864. Most of these rivers and creeks were relatively shallow, which would hinder both navies in the war.

Savannah's main exports were rice and lumber, but her fortune was certainly made by "King Cotton." Shipping agents and cotton brokers ignored the war rhetoric to make Savannah the nation's third largest cotton exporter, even as the fragile Union cracked. Barges and steamers ladened with the white harvest glided down the Savannah River from Augusta while trains brought in the crop from Georgia's interior counties.

Amid the sweat of commerce and industry and the courtly elegance of the Old South, Savannah girded for bloodshed in 1860. Hot words and hotter tempers were about to thrust her into the maelstrom of a nation at war with itself.

Savannah was a city that would seethe with defiance, bristling defenses, and, eventually, gaunt, shallow-eyed hope in the war years. Her fate was cast in the crusade borne by the grand design for a new country—a confederacy ground underfoot by a Northern war machine of dominant technology and vaster resources and manpower.

Today the central feature of Savannah's Chippewa Square is a bronze statue of General Oglethorpe standing eternally vigilant. Sword in hand, he gazes south down Bull Street, perennially poised to meet a Spanish attack from Florida that will never come.

Just as stern and forever alert, a Rebel infantryman atop the Confederate monument in Forsyth Park is ever watchful, facing north. The statue was created with Hamilton Branch, a Savannah Confederate, serving as the model. Now it stands over ground where jaunty militia units like the Irish Jasper Greens, the Republican Blues, and the Georgia Hussars drilled to the delight of local belles before heading to the front. Like soldiers and sailors in every war, most quickly learned that the brass band send-off and rousing oratory of politicians couldn't prepare them for the indescribable nightmare of battle.

Oglethorpe and the unnamed Rebel in the park both are sentinels for bygone, tumultuous ages in which their human predecessors each held domain with an iron will, gunpowder, and cold steel.

The Confederate guards a time when the Stars and Bars fluttered defiantly in the wind and Savannah was an Atlantic coastal jewel of the infant southern republic.

Four years later the fate of Savannah, as well as the nation, had been forged on the anvil of total war, unbending politics, and the reality that the Confederacy's cause was indeed lost.

I

Secession Fever—1860

"While no one could have seen the magnitude of the convulsion that was to soon to shake the land, still there was grave foreboding everywhere, a feeling that we were upon the edge of a volcano." With these words Charles H. Olmstead described the disunion fire engulfing Savannah in the summer of 1860. "Differences between the Northern and Southern sections of the country had reached an acute state."[1]

"There was an eager restlessness that filled every soul," Charles C. Jones, Jr., wrote, "and while the older citizens may have felt some forebodings for the future, there can be no doubt that the great mass of the people thought the time for argument had passed and were ready to maintain what they believed to be their rights at the hazard of their lives."[2]

Fervent secessionists like Francis S. Bartow fanned the blaze of Southern unrest from Savannah to Atlanta to Charleston. "If the storm is to come, and it seems to me as though it must, be its fury ever so great, I court it now in the day of my vigor and strength," Bartow said in a September 17 speech in Savannah. "If any man is to peril life, fortune and honor in defense of our rights, I claim to be one of those men."[3]

The dominoes of support for the Union had been toppling for years as event after momentous event rocked the disunited democracy sired by Washington and Jefferson. Yet the animosity brewing between the "slave" and "free" states was not a poison concocted overnight. As the country sprawled westward, sectionalism had been become a natural outgrowth of the republic's evolution.

Charles C. Jones, Jr., an officer in the Chatham Artillery, was Savannah's mayor in 1860–1861 before going to war. (Courtesy of the Georgia Historical Society.)

The Missouri Compromise of 1820 was an attempt to equalize the numbers of free, or nonslave, states and those in the South that supported the ownership of blacks. At the same time, the compromise was designed to limit the spread of slavery in the west.

The 1852 publication of Harriet Beecher Stowe's *Uncle Tom's Cabin* deepened the resolve of abolitionist factions and pushed the South further toward separatism. Politicians like William L. Yancey of Alabama and Charles Sumner of Massachusetts railed at each other with brimstone and desolation speeches on Capitol Hill, and antislavery men in Wisconsin met in early 1854 to form the Republican Party.

On the Missouri-Kansas border the debating was done with butcher knives and long rifles. In late May 1856, a proslavery band of Missourians raided Lawrence, Kansas, a hotbed of abolitionist settlers. A fire and sword abolitionist named John Brown retaliated by leading a small band of followers who killed proslavery men on nearby Pottawatomie Creek. Guerrilla attacks and deadly ambushes increased on the frontier in the years to come.

The Supreme Court's decision in the Dred Scott case of 1857 was a setback to the Unionists when the court ruled that the runaway slave did not have the right to sue for his freedom because he was "property."

With the zeal of an Old Testament prophet, John Brown resurfaced on a cold Virginia night in October 1859. Charged with a flame to incite a

Francis S. Bartow, Savannah attorney and secession firebrand

slave insurrection across the South, Brown and a raiding party tried to take a federal arsenal at Harpers Ferry. The attack failed and Brown was captured. Convicted of criminal conspiracy and treason, he was hanged on December 2, 1859.

The Savannah *Daily Morning News* spoke for most Southerners in its edition the next day. In being executed, "the notorious horsethief, murderer, insurrectionist and traitor, expiated his guilt. Would that his might be the fate of the craven-hearted instigators and plotters of the treason which he so recklessly endeavored to execute—There are thousands of white-cravated necks in New England and the Northern States to-day, that are as well deserving of John Brown's hempen tie."[4]

For thousands in the North, however, Brown became an instant martyr the moment the hangman's rope snapped taut.

The first weeks of 1860 found Savannahians excited about an Italian opera company appearing at the Athenaeum theater. Newspapers carried lists of ships departing or arriving from New York, Liverpool, Boston, and Baltimore. Even while Bartow and others spoke out against the Union, Savannah thrived as the country's second major commercial port on the south Atlantic behind Charleston. The Central Railroad published schedules of trains headed to Macon, Augusta, and Milledgeville.

At the corner of Congress and Whitaker, merchant Charles Cannon offered "a choice lot" of smoked salmon and mackerel. Sundries were the specialty of Gaut & Remshart on Bay Street, where everything from baker's flour to corn meal to "prime eastern hay" was available.

Just as much a sign of the times in the South was this brief article in the February 4 *Daily Morning News*: "We have been unable to procure the particulars of the sale of negroes by J. Bryan & Son on Wednesday last. We learn that the lot of 138 (not considered prime negroes) sold at an average of $625 each."[5]

Across the Savannah River from the city docks stretched the wide rice fields and sea marshes of South Carolina. The view was one of bucolic wild beauty—a dominion crowned with nature's many blessings. In 1860 this land also was fertile earth for the seeds of secession, which the Carolinians flung to the wind, rooting in Georgia and across the entire South.

The Democratic National Convention convened in Charleston in the last week of April to try to decide on a candidate in the 1861 presidential election, but the party was badly split along sectional lines. Delegates from eight Southern states walked out of the convention after the party officially refused to endorse slavery.

The *Daily Morning News* strongly backed the Southern delegates, stating they "patriotically and nobly contended for a recognition of Southern rights and Southern equality."[6]

The newspaper reflected the mood of many Savannahians a few weeks later as the cries for secession grew louder: "The people of the South have been too long dependent on their Northern neighbors for every conceivable thing, from a clothes-pin to a fancy buggy," the June 15 edition said, "and any enterprise which proposes to relieve them from this state of bondage deserves well at the hands of a Southern public. We have talent and industry, and capital enough at the South to render us independent of those who would rob us of our property, and we bid God-speed to every effort at 'Southern independence,' whether 'the result of Northern aggression' or not."

By September 1860 the presidential election was two months away, but Dixie was readying for war if the damnable Republicans won out.

John C. Breckinridge of Kentucky was the choice of Southern Democrats to carry their banner in the election. He was the champion who might thwart the chances of Republican Abraham Lincoln's gaining the presidency.

Lincoln, himself a Kentuckian, proposed a compromise on the complex issue of slavery. Yet most Southerners felt his election would herald the end of states' rights, personal freedom, and respect for private property, including slaves owned by a small percentage of the Southern white population.

Also in the race was the Democratic Party's official candidate, Stephen Douglas of Illinois, and Tennessee's John Bell, of the new and moderate National Constitution Union Party.

While orators like Bartow backed Breckinridge, they also urged their countrymen to prepare for action if Lincoln was elected. To this end, Savannah was electric with the states' rights current coursing through the South.

The Republican Party "was absolutely and entirely sectional and by its acts really waged a quasi warfare against the South," Olmstead wrote. He added that Lincoln's election would tighten the grip of Republican control over the government, meaning there was "no longer safety for the South in the Union."[7]

Cheering crowds hoisting torches and banners marched through the streets almost nightly, igniting bonfires and listening to speakers who stoked their enthusiasm for revolution against "Yankee tyranny." One of the favorite rally sites was Johnson Square, where secession flags were draped over the Nathaniel Greene Monument.

During the first week of October, Charles Jones, a twenty-eight-year-old Savannah attorney, was elected the city's mayor. Jones's father, the Reverend Dr. Charles C. Jones, was a well-known minister who had been pastor of Savannah's Independent Presbyterian Church and had also devoted much of his career to the spread of religion among slaves in Liberty County. The Jones family history was deeply rooted in coastal Georgia. One of their ancestors, Major John Jones, had been among the patriots killed in the siege of Savannah in 1779.

"The election of Lincoln seems now almost a fixed fact," the new mayor wrote to his father on October 18. "Should Lincoln be elected, the action of a single state, such as South Carolina or Alabama, may precipitate us into all the terrors of . . . war."[8]

In spite of garnering only forty percent of the popular vote, Lincoln won the presidency on November 6, taking 180 electoral votes out of 303, and carrying the eighteen anti-slavery states. His vice-presidential running mate, Hannibal Hamlin of Maine, also was elected.

There was little, if any, despondency in Savannah about Lincoln's triumph. On the contrary, the city was a scene of "intense excitement" and in "perfect turmoil," one observer wrote.

"The telegrams announce the fact of Lincoln's election," Mayor Jones penned to his parents on November 7. "South Carolina today has virtually seceded. . . . We are on the verge of Heaven knows what."[9]

Some three thousand Savannahians turned out for a public hearing at the Masonic Hall on November 8 to endorse anti-Union resolutions, including one by Bartow that the "election of Abraham Lincoln and Hannibal Hamlin . . . ought not to be submitted to." The resolutions were eventually forwarded to the state legislature.

This night, however, the crowds reveled in the revolutionary spirit. "Brass bands were playing, rockets soaring, bonfires blazing; in fact the old town seemed to have gone crazy," Olmstead wrote.

"With the exception of eight or ten citizens here, all are in favor of secession," a *New York Times* correspondent said in a dispatch from Savannah on November 21.

"The feeling here is noisy and deep," Savannah physician Richard Arnold, who would be one of the city's wartime mayors, wrote to a Northern friend in early December. "With the fanatics who rule you and would rule us, we are ready for war to the knife and the knife to the handle."

Georgia heightened its war preparations, and the General Assembly appropriated $1 million for the state's defense. The post of adjutant and inspector general also was created and offered to Savannah's Henry C. Wayne, a longtime army officer.

Wayne, whose father was a justice of the U.S. Supreme Court, accepted the commission. The decision forced him to resign from the U.S. Army, which he had served for more than twenty years. An 1838 West Point graduate, Wayne had fought with distinction in the Mexican War. In the 1850's he was involved in the army's experiment of bringing African camels to the American Southwest as a possible means of transportation for the military. He also published a book, *Sword Exercises Arranged for Military Instruction*, in 1850.

All eyes were on South Carolina, where the powderkeg of secession was expected to explode at any time. "Our citizens are anxiously awaiting the action of the South Carolina convention, but as yet we have no news," Mayor Jones wrote to his parents in Liberty County on December 17. "I sincerely trust that there will be no hesitancy or faltering on their part."[10]

Savannah's rebellion frenzy intensified when South Carolina seceded on December 20, the first Southern state to take such an audacious step.

Henry C. Wayne, the first adjutant general and inspector general of Georgia troops

A spectacular rally to honor Carolina was held in Savannah on the night of December 26. Practically every house was illuminated, and bonfires flared as cheering processions descended on Johnson Square. Of the flags displayed, one showed an American eagle about to strike a woman (symbolizing South Carolina) while another female intervened for defense. The inscription read "Touch Her If You Dare," signifying Georgia's close ties with the Palmetto State. Another rebellion banner unfurled bore "the representation of a large rattlesnake, with the inscription, 'Don't Tread On Me.'" Savannah's newspapers were filled with calls for Georgia to "ratify the course of South Carolina."

Savannah's oldest volunteer militia companies—the Chatham Artillery, Savannah Volunteer Guards, Republican Blues, Georgia Hussars, Phoenix Riflemen, Irish Jasper Greens, Oglethorpe Light Infantry, De Kalb Riflemen, and the German Volunteers—"promptly tendered their services for any duty that might be required of them."

News that U.S. troops stationed at Fort Moultrie, South Carolina, had evacuated their post and moved to previously unoccupied Fort Sumter in Charleston Harbor pushed Georgians closer to the brink.

Bartow was in Atlanta addressing a pro-secession crowd on December 28, when he received word of Fort Sumter's occupation. The message fueled the fire of his speech, particularly against anyone in the audience considering anything short of war: "While you talk of cooperation, you hear the thunder of the cannon, and the clash of sabres . . . from South Carolina," he shouted to the cheering masses.[11]

"It was the theater of exciting events," Jones wrote of South Carolina, "and even local affairs were lost sight of in view of the contest between that State and the Federal authorities."[12]

If the Carolinians were taking aim on Fort Sumter, Georgians, especially Savannahians, were taking a hard look at Fort Pulaski. The menacing brick stronghold was located at the mouth of the Savannah River about seventeen miles east of the city. Pulaski was not occupied other than a caretaker and an ordnance sergeant, but the Southerners believed the volatile state of affairs might result in U.S. troops being sent there.

"The abolitionists are defiant and in consequence, Fort Pulaski is in danger," Georgia Senator Robert Toombs said in a December 31 telegram to Alexander Stephens, future vice-president of the Confederacy. "The time has come for action."[13]

Toombs' dispatch was leaked to the press and published in the *Savannah Republican*, sparking calls for the fort's seizure.

II

1861—"Our Flag Victorious!"

The first days of 1861 were a rush of rebellious action and decisions in Savannah. Citizens appeared ready to take matters into their own hands and march on Fort Pulaski. Fearing a riot, General Wayne and Colonel Alexander R. Lawton, commander of state troops at Savannah, wired Governor Joseph E. Brown to come and regain control of the city. Brown also had a telegram from Toombs warning of the threat of Pulaski being garrisoned by federal forces.

The governor arrived in Savannah about 9 p.m. on January 1 and appeared ready to show his mettle and commitment to the Southern cause. He conferred with Wayne, Lawton, and civilian leaders, none of whom was sure that taking the fort was the best decision.

"One of them said to me: 'If you take possession of the Fort, and there is one spark of vitality left in the Federal Government, it will shell you out in ten days,'" Brown wrote of the civilian representatives.[1]

After some reflection and discussion, the governor made his decision: "I take responsibility, and I direct the immediate occupation of the fort."[2] On Brown's authority, Alexander Lawton would orchestrate the first major act of rebellion in Georgia—the capture of Fort Pulaski.

Lawton and his adjutant, Charles Olmstead, had been busy organizing the First Volunteer Regiment of Georgia. The First Georgia initially was composed of Savannah's nine original volunteer companies.

A South Carolinian born near Beaufort in 1818, Lawton was an 1839 West Point graduate who attended Harvard Law School, earning his degree

Georgians drilling at Fort Pulaski in 1861. (*Harper's Weekly*, Dec. 28, 1861, courtesy of the Georgia Historical Society.)

in 1842. A practicing attorney in Savannah before the war, Lawton also served as president of the Augusta & Savannah Railroad and as a state legislator.

The governor's instructions were for Lawton to "take possession of Fort Pulaski" and to "hold it against all persons, to be abandoned only under orders from me or under compulsion by an overpowering hostile force." In the event abolitionist sympathizers or spies had infiltrated the Georgians, Brown added that, "If circumstances should require it the telegraph will be placed under surveillance."[3]

Brown officially issued his order on January 2, and Lawton spent the rest of the day organizing a strike force composed of 134 men and six artillery pieces. Most of the militiamen belonged to the Savannah Volunteer Guards, Chatham Artillery, Georgia Hussars, and the Oglethorpe Light Infantry.

Among them was Bartow, a captain of the "Oglethorpes." That same day he and two other Savannahians, John W. Anderson and Augustus S. Jones, were unanimously elected to represent Chatham County at a state convention to be held later in the month.

In addition to orders given to Lawton and Wayne, Brown sent dispatches to the governors of Alabama, Florida, Louisiana, and Mississippi informing them of his intent to take the fort.

The plan to seize Pulaski would not be a military secret—the Georgians virtually made it a holiday. "With high gratification we are enabled to announce that [Brown] has directed the occupation of Fort Pulaski by State troops and that early this morning a detachment will descend the river for that purpose," Savannahians awoke to read in the *Daily Morning News* on January 3.[4]

Brown's order left Savannah "in a fever of excitement," wrote Jones. "Here at last was the first step in actual war—a step that placed State and central government in open antagonism, the beginning whose ending no man could foretell. There may have been faint hearts that trembled in view of resulting possibilities, but among the military of Savannah the order was received with unbounded enthusiasm."[5]

Politics were forgotten in the martial splendor of that rainy Thursday as the militia units proudly marched to the city wharves and boarded the steamer *Ida* for their downriver trip to the fort. Because of the masses who turned out to see them off, the men had some difficulty moving through the streets to the docks.

Unknown to most, the fort had been scouted hours earlier by a lone Georgian on Brown's staff. Henry Rootes Jackson already was well known for a varied and colorful career and was one of Savannah's most influential secession advocates. An Athens native, Jackson graduated from Yale law school in 1839 and opened his practice in Savannah. He was appointed a federal district attorney before he was twenty-four years old. Jackson was colonel of a Georgia volunteer regiment during the Mexican War and later served as a newspaper editor, superior court judge, and U.S. minister to Austria—all before the Civil War.

Sent to see if Pulaski was defended, Jackson headed down the river in a rowboat. He was drenched by a rain storm, but found the fort virtually unoccupied. He later wrote proudly of being "the first rebel . . . actively engaged upon land or water, at the South."

The Savannah militia took the fort without firing a shot. The men exultantly raised a flag representing Georgia, a banner with a lone red star on a white background, over the ramparts.

"I can shut my eyes and see it all now, the proud step of officers and men, the colors snapping in the strong breeze from the ocean; the bright sunlight of the parade as we emerged from the shadow of the archway; the first glimpse of a gun through an open casement door; one and all they were photographed on my mind," Olmstead recalled of the day.[6]

More than three months before the firing on Fort Sumter, Savannah had struck the first major military blow of the war.

Among the troops who marched into Pulaski was Gilbert Moxley Sorrel, a young private in the Georgia Hussars. This was great fun for Sorrel, who by day was a bank clerk for the Central of Georgia Railroad. He was destined to become one of the Confederacy's best staff officers.

The Georgians found Fort Pulaski in poor shape. The parade ground was overgrown, her few guns were rusting, and their wooden carriages were rotting. Under the direction of Bartow and Olmstead, the men began the task of transforming the neglected fort into the coastal bastion her designers envisioned when she was completed in 1847. "The work of repairing the imperfect gun carriages is vigorously progressing, timber and mechanics for that purpose having been taken down by the *Sampson,*" the *Daily Morning News* said on January 5.[7]

Toombs's warning of Union troops being sent to Pulaski remained a possible threat for impending bloodshed. "A few days must determine whether we are to have use for [the guns], in which event His Excellency Governor Brown . . . will be prepared to send any amount of reinforcements to hold the fortress," the newspaper stated.

Mayor Jones, himself a member of the Chatham Artillery, was maternally released from any ties to the Union in a January 3 letter from his mother, Mary. Writing from Montevideo, the family's winter home near Riceboro, Georgia, Mrs. Jones said: "When your brother and yourself were very little fellows, we took you into old Independence Hall; and at the foot of Washington's statue I pledged you both to support and defend the Union. That Union has passed away, and you are free from your mother's vow."[8]

A Georgian who arrived at Pulaski on January 11 waxed satirical in a letter to his sister: "Thinking you would like to have a few lines from the seat of war, I have concluded to write them, not withstanding the horrible din that penetrates my retreat. You must know then that we arrived here safely yesterday, fully armed and equipped with empty stomachs and canteens. After two perilous expeditions to the dock for our baggage and brandy, from which I returned sober, I led a forlorn troop upon the quartermaster's department and put to the knife several defunct swine."

The garrison soldiers bedded down on fresh hay spread in the casemates and adjusted to the discipline of life in the military.

Bartow was not long on the scene at Pulaski. The state convention convened in Milledgeville on January 16; and the fire-eating attorney, joined by Chatham's two other delegates, would be there to determine Georgia's course.

There was little doubt about the outcome. Mississippi joined South Carolina in secession on Wednesday, January 9, Florida the next day, and Alabama on Friday.

The January 12 *Daily Morning News* trumpeted these actions as a chain of events in which Georgia's secession was the next link: "The Rubicon is passed—a new nation is born!"[9]

Georgia's convention made it official on January 19 with a majority voting for secession. It was a Saturday night long to be remembered as the city's populace "kicked up a big noise generally" in celebration.

On February 1 a Georgia flag was unfurled to the breeze over the U.S. Customs House on Bay Street. John Boston, the federal collector of customs, had nervously resigned the previous day, anxious to leave the city. The state banner went up to the "hearty cheers of Custom House officers and citizens in the streets," the *Daily Morning News* said.[10]

"Won't it be glorious to meet once more in the Republic of Georgia to fight for our Altars and our fires, God and our native land!!!," Savannahian Eddie Neufville, a student at Princeton University in New Jersey, wrote to a relative. "By God that's bully!! If those infernal Yankees don't get more hot lead than they can digest in a year, then I don't know anything about Southern pluck and shooting!"

Savannah troops also occupied Fort Jackson in the last week of January. A small brick work built before the War of 1812, Fort Jackson stood on the cityside of the Savannah River and about three miles downstream.

Early February also saw Governor Brown make another daring maneuver that sharpened the strain between North and South. New York authorities in January had seized thirty-eight boxes of muskets bought by a Macon company and set for shipment to Savannah aboard the steamer *Monticello*.

Brown fired off a "sharp remonstrance," which was ignored by the Northerners. In retaliation he ordered Georgia troops to seize and hold any ships in Savannah that were owned or operated by New Yorkers. On February 8 platoons of the Phoenix Riflemen boarded and held five merchant vessels. Brown received word three days later that the muskets were to be shipped, and the ships were released.

A delay in shipment of the guns, however, caused Brown to seize three other vessels at Savannah. Two of these ships were being advertised for sale when the cases of muskets finally were sent South, possibly averting a crisis that quickly might have escalated into war. History would have to wait until Fort Sumter.

News of Brown's aggressiveness quickly spread across the South. "What do you think of Governor Brown?," John Elliott, a Georgian attending South Carolina College, wrote his mother from Columbia, South Carolina, on February 12. "Hasn't he fixed the New Yorkers? You regret to hear how quiet the South Carolinians are keeping when the action of the two states are brought into comparison, and I have heard a great many wish that they had a Brown at the head of their affairs. Georgia has really acted splendidly."[11]

The Georgians also seized the Oglethorpe Barracks, which housed some U.S. Army personnel. U.S. Captain William H. C. Whiting was in charge of Fort Pulaski and other government property about Savannah. Quartered at the barracks, he was away on an inspection of Fort Clinch near Jacksonville when Pulaski was occupied. Upon his return, he reported that he was treated with "great civility" by the Georgians. Colonel Lawton graciously allowed him to stay in the barracks while Whiting closed up his "business."

Whiting, a Mississippi native, did not wear the Union blue much longer. Before the end of the month he accepted a commission as a major of engineers in the provisional Confederate army. Whiting fought at First Manassas, Seven Pines, in "Stonewall" Jackson's Valley Campaign, and the Seven Days battles near Richmond. His major wartime achievement was the development of Fort Fisher defending Wilmington, North Carolina, as possibly the "strongest fortress in the Confederacy."

Savannahians donated four old ships to the citizens of Charleston to help that city prepare its sea defenses. The hulks were loaded with stone and sunk in Charleston's main shipping channel to prevent deep-draft enemy warships from attacking. Because of these obstacles, many larger merchant vessels were diverted from Charleston to Savannah, prompting one wag to declare that Savannah was eager to offer other derelicts to clog Charleston's harbor.[12]

General Wayne was busy working on coastal defenses and also in trying to establish a Georgia navy at Savannah. In February, Josiah Tattnall, who had served in the U.S. Navy for almost a half-century, was chosen senior flag officer of the state navy. "No man in the old federal navy had attained higher honors or wore them more gracefully than Commodore Tattnall," the *Daily Morning News* reported on February 20.[13]

The son of a state governor, Tattnall was born in 1795 on his family's

Flag Officer Josiah Tattnall, one of the luckless commanders of the Savannah River Squadron. (Courtesy of the Georgia Historical Society.)

plantation near Savannah. Educated in England, he joined the navy as a midshipman and fought the British in the War of 1812. Tattnall rose steadily through the ranks, seeing action in the Algerine War and against pirates in the West Indies. He was wounded in the Mexican War and was appointed flag officer and commander of the U.S. East India Squadron in 1857.

Nearing retirement, Tattnall personally opposed disunion, but went with his state when Georgia seceded. At age sixty-five he had the daunting task of creating a naval force from scratch.

Indeed, the chest-thumping rhetoric of Savannah's secessionists dimmed somewhat amid the reality of wholesale war without a navy in 1861. The sudden break with the United States left the Confederacy with no sea force and an enemy whose navy had been evolving in power, pride, and tradition since the Revolutionary War. Like Memphis, New Orleans, Charleston, and other Rebel cities vulnerable to enemy naval assault, Savannah had to find some warships immediately.

The first steps to establish the navy were taken before Tattnall arrived. A young officer named John McIntosh Kell had been one of the first to resign from the U.S. Navy when Georgia seceded. On orders from Governor Brown, he had come to Savannah in late January with orders to procure a steamer, take command, and ready her for war. After weeks of negotiating, Kell settled on the river steamer *Everglade*.

"The *Everglade* returned here today and I believe now has all her papers correct so that the purchase will probably be closed tomorrow," he wrote to his wife on February 24.[14]

The state paid $40,000 for the paddlewheeler, which was renamed the

Lieutenant John N. Maffitt, CSN. (Courtesy of the Georgia Historical Society.)

GS *Savannah*—the Georgia navy's new flagship. A thirty-two-pounder cannon was soon mounted on her deck.

Tattnall established headquarters in Savannah in February. He immediately set about the recruitment of crews and the arming of harbor craft, including tugboats, with deck guns to fashion a ragtag squadron.

On February 28 Lieutenant Kell stepped aboard the *Savannah* as her new skipper. "I took command of the steamer *Savannah* this afternoon, with officers and men numbering 45," he wrote his wife.[15]

A native of Darien, Georgia, Kell would later be best known as first officer for Captain Raphael Semmes aboard the renowned raiders *Sumter* and *Alabama*. In early spring 1861, however, his reputation was yet to be earned.

Kell drilled the *Savannah*'s crew and on March 7 proudly embarked on the steamer's first cruise along the Georgia coast. He described his seamen as "a formidable body of men when I get them well drilled to their arms. The arms consist of two 12-pound Howitzers, fifty Maynard rifles, cutlasses, pikes, and Colt's revolvers."[16]

The *Savannah* saw no combat during this time, and when she entered Confederate service in May, Kell relinquished command to Lieutenant John N. Maffitt. Maffitt was far from impressed with the *Savannah*, describing her thusly: "A more absurd abortion for a man of war was rarely witnessed." He was equally unimpressed by the rest of Tattnall's force: "I unhesitatingly condemned the whole squadron, save as provisional guard-boats, and urged that proper vessels should at once be built and purchased."[17]

Kell's stay in Georgia was brief. That summer he was ordered to New Orleans at the request of Semmes, who was captain of the newly fitted CSS *Sumter*. Tattnall was not quick to lose Kell, "giving him up very reluctantly," Semmes wrote.

Maffitt too earned Confederate glory on the high seas at the helm of the raider CSS *Florida* and as a blockade runner. His time in Savannah, however, would raise early questions about his leadership abilities.

Tattnall was appointed a Confederate Navy captain in March, but still faced a herculean ordeal in forming a force able to oppose the U.S. Navy.

Within weeks of Georgia's exodus from the Union, Savannah became a marshaling point for hundreds of state troops. Governor Brown and his military advisers logically reasoned that the port or other points on the Georgia shore were the most likely to be attacked and that forces should be concentrated there.

Trains huffed in from all over the state bringing in young recruits, many of whom had never before been away from home. Men who had been in camp for a few days needled the new arrivals, telling them they would believe they were "in Hades or the penitentiary instead of the army before night," a Georgian wrote. Bivouacs were set up all over the city and its outskirts. Units drilled from before dawn until the moon was high in the sky or worked on bolstering the city's defenses.

Much of the military activity centered on the Oglethorpe Barracks, located where the DeSoto Hilton Hotel now stands at Bull and Liberty streets. The two-story building would be used as a hospital and headquarters for the Confederates until December 1864. Many of the Southerners coming in to Savannah found themselves standing in line to undergo physicals at the barracks before being accepted for service. The shaggier Rebels also had to face regimental barbers.

One young "Southron" described the bustle of Savannah's riverfront: "While not on drill we get passes out in the city, the wharf being of the most interest, where the flags of all civilized nations are thrown to the breeze. All kinds of sailing craft, from the magnificent *R. R. Cuyler* to the smallest of sailboats. Everybody seems to be in a hurry. The stevedores with their merry gangs loading and unloading vessels. The drays are almost impassable on the wharfs, hauling to and from the city . . . Savannah's entire [water] front is full of crafts, and don't look like there is room for another."[18]

This narrative would offer a sharp contrast to the scene several months later when the Union blockade was showing its effects.

The State Convention reconvened at Savannah on March 7, three days after the first flag of the Confederate States of America was raised in the new capital of Montgomery, Alabama. Georgia legislators ratified the Confederate constitution on March 16 and officially joined the Southern republic.

Savannah now had fourteen militia companies, which were consolidated into the First Georgia. The regiment, over a thousand strong, held a triumphant review on March 21 with Colonel Lawton riding at its head. The *Daily Morning News* described the march as "the most imposing and gratifying military display we have seen in Savannah."

The regiment was composed of the Georgia Hussars, Chatham Artillery, Mounted Rifles, Blue Caps, Phoenix Riflemen, Republican Blues, Irish Jasper Greens, Savannah Volunteer Guards (two independent companies), Oglethorpe Light Infantry, Pulaski Guards, Irish Fusiliers, German Volunteers, and the De Kalb Riflemen.

"In their fatigue dress the companies made a very soldier-like appearance in passing in review for the Convention politicians on the parade route through the city."[19]

That night Alexander H. Stephens, the Georgian newly elected vice-president of the Confederacy, strode to a podium in the Athenaeum. The frail Stephens had been persuaded to make a state-of-the-new-nation address, and hundreds of Savannahians jammed the theater. On the street outside the building, crowds pushed as close as they could to the open doors and police officers had to quiet them when Stephens began to speak. In what would be known as his Cornerstone Speech, Stephens described the patriotism of the Confederate Congress and the democratic nobility of the new Constitution it had adopted. He also outlined what he felt were the basic convictions of the Southern government and its people.

"A fundamental error in the old government had been corrected in the new," the *Daily Morning News* paraphrased Stephens in its March 22 issue. "The old government was formed on the false theory of the equality of the races—that what God had made unequal was equal. Ours was based on the inequality of the races. The old structure was built on a false foundation and when the storm came and the wind blew, it fell."[20]

The Confederacy was founded on "exactly the opposite idea" of racial

Confederate Vice-President Alexander H. Stephens delivered his famous "Cornerstone Speech" in Savannah on March 21, 1861. (Courtesy of the Georgia Historical Society.)

equality. "Its foundations are laid, its cornerstone rests upon the great truth that the negro is not equal to the white man; that slavery—subordination to the superior race—is his natural and moral condition."[21]

When units of the First Georgia were ordered to Fort Pulaski in March, work there was progressing rapidly. Pulaski soon would become the linchpin of defenses along the Savannah River. Huge guns were lifted into emplacements by hundreds of soldiers using ropes, pulleys, and blocks and tackles. Riverboats brought supplies and ammunition. Gun crews began drilling with the heavy artillery.

The Georgians also posted a few troops on Tybee Island, less than a mile east of the fort. This little outpost on the Atlantic likely would be the first to see or encounter enemy forces approaching the coast.

Savannah joined the Rebel ecstasy when Southern batteries opened fire on Fort Sumter in Charleston Harbor early on the morning of Friday, April 12, 1861. A newspaper correspondent was among Savannahians who hurried to Charleston by train to watch the historic fireworks. His account appeared in the April 15th *Daily Morning News* under the headline "Our Flag Victorious!"

News of the fort's April 13 surrender touched off celebrations throughout Savannah—a furor that intensified when wire reports reached the city five days later that Virginia had seceded. Virginia had escaped "the foul

Lincolnhood of Abolitionism," the April 19 *Daily Morning News* said.

On Bay Street near the City Exchange, Savannahian William Hone fired an eight-shot salute with his "little Russian cannon," honoring the Old Dominion State.

"Crowds of people were gathered in the street," the newspaper said. "Joy beamed in every countenance, and words of congratulation and exultation were on every lip. Hurra(h) for Virginia! The Mother State is with us and the South is a unit!"[22]

In mid-April, Alexander Lawton was commissioned a brigadier general in the provisional Confederate army and given command of the Savannah district. While Lawton earned some laurels by his promotion, Francis Bartow remained, by far, the most active and visible Savannah Rebel during this period. Elected to the provisional Confederate Congress, he had been in the capital at Montgomery since February, helping shape the destiny of the new nation. He served briefly as chairman of the Congressional Committee on Military Affairs.

Born in Savannah in September 1816, Bartow was the son of respected local physician Theodosius Bartow. He attended Franklin College in Athens, Georgia, where he and another student tied for top graduating honors in 1835. He also went to Yale Law School and returned south to open a law practice in Bryan County, Georgia. During this time he studied law under Senator John Berrien and later married Berrien's daughter.

As a Whig, Bartow campaigned for William Henry Harrison before the 1840 presidential election, which Harrison won. In the prewar years Bartow served in the state legislature, where he was known for his "sound states-manship and ability to debate." While fanning the secession whirlwind, Bartow and his family lived in a large, three-story house on Pulaski Square.

Some historians credit Bartow with deciding the color of the uniform for the Confederacy's fighting men. With war appearing imminent, the Savannah Volunteer Guards exchanged their dapper dress uniforms for coarse gray tunics and pants, better suited for field duty. Bartow admired the uniforms so much that he lobbied strongly in Congress to adopt gray as the color of the Confederate military.

There was a flurry of excitement in Savannah during the first week of May, when two U.S. Army officers were discovered staying at the Pulaski House hotel on Johnson Square. "Alert" Savannahians noticed the names of officers Hook and Miller on the hotel register, "and an excited number of citizens soon assembled there." Were they Yankee spies?

The mob grew and the talk grew louder. Mayor Jones arrived and asked to see the officers, who agreed to an audience. Jones soon found himself talking to two young lieutenants, fresh from West Point, who were "far gone in consumption." On leave for several months, they had been trying to "recruit their enfeebled constitutions" in Florida and were accompanied by ladies with the same affliction. Jones determined that the lieutenants "were returning home to die" and had no espionage plans. He informed the crowd of the situation and the officers were told they could head north the next day if they were physically able to do so.[23]

London *Times* correspondent William Howard Russell was sent to America that spring to cover the war. He arrived in Savannah by train on April 20 and provides a unique look at the city during this period. Noting that it had "the deepest sand in the streets I have ever seen," Russell wrote that the "streets were composed of the most odd, quaint green-windowed, many-colored little houses I ever beheld, with an odd population of lean, sallow, ill-dressed, unwholesome-looking whites, lounging about the exchanges and corners, and a busy, well-clad, gaily-attired race of Negroes."[24]

If not impressed with the Rebel citizenry, Russell appeared enchanted with Savannah's beauty: "The fringe of green and the height attained by the live oak, Pride of India and magnolia give a delicious freshness and novelty to the streets of Savannah, which is increased by the great number of squares.... The wealthier classes have houses of the New York Fifth Avenue character."

Russell also described "the shady park with its cool fountains" and discovered that the "mosquitoes were very keen and numerous."[25]

Accompanied by Tattnall and Lawton, Russell was taken on a May 1 inspection of Fort Pulaski. Going ashore at Cockspur Island, Russell wrote: "A guard was on duty at the landing—tall, stout young fellows in various uniforms, in which the red shirt and felt slouched hats predominated. They were armed with smooth-bore muskets, quite new, and their bayonets, barrels and locks were bright and clean. The officer on duty was dressed in blue frock coat with brass buttons, emblazoned with the arms of the state, a red silk sash and glazed kepi and straw-colored gauntlets.... Men were busy clearing out the casemates, rolling away stores and casks of ammunition and provisions, others were at work at the gin and shears, others building sandbag traverses to guard the magazine doors, as though expecting an immediate attack."

Russell admired the discipline and spirit of the Rebel garrison. But he

Colonel Francis S. Bartow of the Oglethorpe Light Infantry left his home on Pulaski Square on May 21, 1861. He would never return, falling in battle at First Bull Run.

pointed out to Lawton that the fort was on low ground, accessible to naval assault, and open to attack from the rear. "What I saw did not satisfy me that Pulaski was strong or Savannah very safe," the Irishman wrote.[26]

At Montgomery the Confederate Congress in May authorized troop enlistments for the war's duration. Bartow quickly conferred by telegraph with his beloved Oglethorpes in Savannah and offered their services to President Jefferson Davis. Within days he was back in Savannah with orders for the company to join Southern forces marshaling in Virginia.

The May 21 departure of the Oglethorpe Light Infantry's Company A was among Savannah's grandest spectacles of the war. With a brass band blaring "Bold Soldier Boy" and other martial airs, the Oglethorpes assembled at their parade ground and crisply fell into line for the march to the railroad depot. Smartly-uniformed militiamen from Savannah's other military units lined the streets, saluting Bartow and his men as they passed. Two other companies of Oglethorpes, who were to remain in Savannah for a time, were among them.

Sweethearts and other admiring women blew kisses and waved handkerchiefs. Many of these ladies already were busy with their own war effort, making clothing and bandages and gathering items for the soldiers to make their camp life more convenient and comfortable.

Before Bartow's troops boarded a 2 P.M. train for the trip north, the company was presented a silk Confederate flag donated by some of Savannah's belles.

The departing Oglethorpes included the three Branch brothers—Hamilton, John, and Sanford, affectionately nicknamed "Santy." Their story would be among Savannah's first war tragedies.

Bartow, with his usual eloquence, assured the ladies that the Oglethorpes would not dishonor the banner: "I pledge to you this day in their behalf that should they fail to bring back to you this flag it will be because there is not one arm left among them to bear it aloft."[27]

The city's fairest may have swooned or hidden behind fluttering fans at these words, but they were soon back at their war work. If knitting and sewing circles were abundant to supply the soldiers' clothing needs, so were groups with a deadlier intent. These women chatted while preparing thousands of rifle and cannon cartridges, stacking them in their homes before they were gathered to be shipped to the front.

William Russell called at Lawton's home and found the general "just setting out to inspect a band of volunteers, whose drums we heard in the distance and whose bayonets were gleaming through the clouds of Savannah dust" near the Pulaski Monument. On a tour of the house Russell saw a "hall filled with little round rolls of flannel. 'These,' said (Lawton), 'are cartridges for cannon of various calibres made by the ladies of Mrs. Lawton's 'cartridge class.' There were more cartridges in the back parlor, so that the house was not quite a safe place to smoke a cigar in!"[28]

"The ladies of Savannah are not idle," Mayor Jones wrote on April 17. "They are daily engaged singly and in concert in the preparation of cartridges both for muskets and cannon. Thousands have been already made by them, and the labor is just begun. Others are cutting out and sewing flannel shirts. Others still are making bandages and preparing lint. Their interest and patriotic efforts in this our cause are worthy of all admiration."[29]

Seamstresses were a prime commodity, needed to make uniforms for the troops. Women nurses soon would be just as essential in a role usually dominated by men.

While serving in a Savannah hospital, nurse Marie R. de la Coste was so moved by the suffering and death that she wrote a poem about her experiences. The verses eventually were sent to renowned Southern composer John H. Hewitt, who used them to create "Somebody's Darling," one of the popular, if somber, songs of the war.

Savannah was still aglow with the Oglethorpes' departure when a hostile sail appeared off Tybee Island during the last week in May 1861. As was the military custom of the day, Union authorities sent word to the Rebels in Savannah on May 28 that the blockade had commenced. A grace period of fifteen days was given for neutral vessels to leave the port. The USS *Union* was the first U.S. vessel to begin blockade operations off Savannah. She would soon be joined by many others.

III

"Never Give Up the Fight"

Even as he basked in the adulation of Savannah's farewell, Bartow knew that he was openly defying Joseph Brown. The governor was adamant that state troops equipped with state money should remain in Georgia and defend their native soil. He issued orders on May 14 prohibiting any company from taking state equipment beyond Georgia's borders without his consent.

Bartow ignored the mandate, telling Brown in a dispatch sent on the day of the Oglethorpes' departure that he was under orders from President Davis to proceed to Virginia, where a Union offensive appeared certain.

"I go to illustrate, if I can, my native State, at all events to be true to her interests and her character," Bartow wrote. Customizing the quote as "I go to illustrate Georgia," the phrase soon appeared in newspapers across the South and personified Bartow's fighting spirit for the Confederacy.[1]

After a journey of several days, Bartow's men arrived in Virginia and were assigned to the Georgia Regiment of Volunteers, of which Bartow was elected colonel.

Angered by Bartow's insolence, Brown fired off a May 29 letter to the colonel: "Should [Savannah] be attacked or destroyed in your absence, I fear you would not receive the commendation of these mothers and sisters, whose sons and brothers you took from that city to fill places in Virginia, which thousands of others would gladly have occupied."[2]

At Harpers Ferry, Virginia, Bartow bristled when he read Brown's message and penned a fiery reply: "I assure you, in passing, that I shall never think it necessary to obtain your consent to enter the service of my country.

God forbid that I should ever fall so low. I trust, if God spares my life, I shall set foot again upon the soil of Georgia and be well assured that I no more fear to meet my enemies at home than I do now to meet the enemies of my country abroad."[3]

Within a few weeks Bartow was appointed commander of the Second Brigade of General Joseph E. Johnston's Army of the Shenandoah operating in the Shenandoah Valley. Among his five regiments was the Eighth Georgia, which included the Oglethorpe Light Infantry. Brigadier generals Barnard E. Bee of South Carolina and Thomas J. Jackson of Virginia headed Johnston's other brigades.

On July 18 Johnston received a frantic call for reinforcements from Brigadier General P. G. T. Beauregard, who had a force of about 23,000 Rebels near Manassas Junction in north-central Virginia. Beauregard was facing imminent attack from some 35,000 Federals under Brigadier General Irvin McDowell. Driven by cries of "On to Richmond," these Yankees were ready to end the war before the summer was over.

Marching at times on the dead run and traveling by train, a portion of Bartow's exhausted brigade was among reinforcements reaching Beauregard's positions south of Bull Run Creek on July 20. On the dust-choked road leading to the trains to take them to Manassas, Bartow's sweating men saw their colonel galloping toward them along the line of march. Lieutenant A. O. Bacon of the Ninth Georgia recalled that Bartow, "as he reached the head of each regiment, waved his hat and shouted to them say[ing] in an excited manner that now they would be put to the test and their manhood proved for that they were marching to the assistance of Beauregard who that morning had been attacked by the enemy in overwhelming number. What a shout greeted the announcement! Their eyes brightened, their cheeks flushed and with a tighter grasp upon their guns the brave fellows quickened their steps. . . . To some extent it was a march to glorious victory, but a march to the grave for many of that noble band."

Not all of Bartow's brigade made it to Bull Run because there were not enough trains to accommodate them when they reached the junction at Piedmont, Virginia. Bartow took the first train bound for Manassas, but the cars could only hold two of his five regiments. The Seventh and Eighth Georgia piled into them. Bacon recalled that the last time he ever saw Bartow, the colonel "was sitting on the tender of the engine as it sailed off." On account of the railroad's problems, Bacon's regiment didn't reach Beauregard's forces to participate in the coming battle.

As his weary men bedded down along Bull Run Creek that night,

Bartow walked among them, stopping to talk with the Oglethorpes. Some of these soldiers had been nicknamed "Bartow's Beardless Boys" because they were teenagers and few were married.

"Our captain (God bless him!) treats us more like his children than like soldiers," a Savannahian wrote before the Manassas battle.

Bartow told the men he had Beauregard's promise that they would be among the first Southerners to fight in the battle expected to erupt before dawn. He added a grim reminder: "But remember boys, battle and fighting means death, and probably before sunrise some of us will be dead."

Just before daybreak on July 21, McDowell launched two divisions in a surprise attack on the Rebels' left flank, Beauregard's weakest point.

Bartow's brigade was among units sent to reinforce the endangered left on Matthews Hill. The furious battle in this sector raged through the morning, but the Rebels were outnumbered and pushed back as more and more Federal units joined the attack. By noon, half of McDowell's force was poised to break Beauregard's flank and roll over the rest of the Rebel army.

Jackson's brigade had arrived on the scene about 11:30 A.M. and taken positions on Henry Hill behind which many of the disorganized Southern units were milling in confusion. Bartow's men were among these demoralized Rebels gathered in the gullies and rolling fields, their commander trying to rally them.

In desperation, General Bee led a forlorn charge, but not before kindling a controversy that would sear the name of "Stonewall" Jackson into American history. Preparing for his attack, Bee shouted to his men that Jackson's brigade was standing "as a stone wall." Minutes later, Bee lay dying from a wound, his charge crumpled.

The question remains whether Bee meant Jackson was not doing enough to help the shattered Southern brigades or that his troops were stalwart fighters who could be relied upon. Whatever the implication, "Stonewall" Jackson had gained a nickname that would make him a legend.

Beauregard and Johnston galloped onto the field to direct the battle and save the remains of the Confederate flank. Bartow's Eighth Georgia had been badly chewed up, but about sixty men assembled on their own and began to march back to the battle. Beauregard dashed by them and yelled, "I salute the gallant 8th Georgia Regiment!"

These Georgians, along with what could be assembled of Bee's command and the brigade of Colonel N. G. "Shanks" Evans, formed a battle line on the left of Jackson's position.

Bartow and Colonel Lucius J. Gartrell of the Seventh Georgia were able to rally most of Gartrell's troops. Riding to Beauregard, Bartow asked, "What shall I do, tell me, and if in the power of man, I will do it." Beauregard ordered Bartow to post the Seventh on Jackson's right along Henry Hill's crest.

When Gartrell asked where his soldiers should advance, Bartow grabbed the regimental flag from its bearer and shouted, "Follow me and I will show you where!" Bartow positioned the Seventh Georgia on the hill next to Jackson's Thirty-third Virginia.

"General Beauregard says you must hold this position and Georgians, I appeal to you to hold it," the Savannahian exhorted his men.

Heavy artillery fire and musketry tore the Confederate line as a mass of yelling Union infantry came up the slope.

Still carrying the flag, Bartow was wounded in the lower leg and knocked from the saddle. His horse was killed, but he was quickly given another mount. Waving his sword, Bartow shouted to his troops to prepare to charge. Riding among soldiers stationed near a fence, he handed the Seventh's banner back to its bearer.

Almost immediately he was hit by an enemy bullet that wounded him in or near the heart. Bartow swayed and tumbled from the saddle, clutching his chest with both hands. Gartrell caught him in his arms, breaking his fall. The dying colonel was laid in the trampled, bloody grass as some of his officers and men surrounded him.

The August 1 Savannah *Daily Morning News* offered a colorful account of Bartow's last minutes: "With both hands clasped over his breast, he raised his head with a God like effort, his eye glittering in its last gleam with a blazing light."

Struggling to speak, Bartow gasped, "They have killed me, but never give up the fight." Carried from the field, he died shortly afterward.[4]

In spite of his death, the remnants of his brigade fought desperately in the patchwork Rebel line anchored by Jackson on Henry Hill. The battle swirled over the hills for several hours. By late afternoon, however, more reinforcements had been received from Johnston's army and the tide of battle shifted. Staving off disaster, the Confederates pounded McDowell until his once-proud army fled in rout toward Washington.

President Davis arrived on the battlefield sometime during the day and visited Rebel wounded in the field hospitals. He grieved in particular over the deaths of Bartow and Bee. Davis had the bodies of both officers placed aboard his special train. They were taken to Richmond and lay in state at the Confederate capitol for several days. "Colonel Bartow died a noble and brave death," the *Richmond Dispatch* said. The Savannahian was "waving his sword and cheering his gallant band on to the fight when some miscreant's ball pierced his brave heart."

In the hours after the battle someone had to assume the grim chore of informing his widow of the tragedy. Mrs. Bartow had traveled to Richmond before the battle so that she could be near her husband.

The Confederacy's First Lady, Varina Davis, was told of Bartow's death and decided to inform Mrs. Bartow herself. Diarist Mary Chesnut of South Carolina was also in Richmond and described how "a woman from Mrs. Bartow's county was in a fury because they stopped her as she rushed to be the first to tell Mrs. Bartow that her husband was killed."

Mrs. Chesnut described the scene when Mrs. Davis went to see the unknowing widow: "There was something in Mrs. Davis's pale face that took the life right out of her. She stared at Mrs. Davis and then sank back and covered her face with a shawl. 'Is it bad news for me?' Mrs. Davis did not speak. 'Is he killed?' Today she [Mrs. Bartow] told me: 'As soon as I saw Mrs. Davis's face, I knew.'"[5]

Savannah received the news from Manassas with a mixture of jubilation and woe. In addition to Bartow, the other Oglethorpes suffered heavy casualties, including six killed. The July 24 *Daily Morning News* mirrored the emotional extremes: "In the midst of the strains of victory the wail of woe rises from every hill and valley in the South at the death of heroes fallen in the strife," the newspaper said. "Georgia laments the death of the chivalrous Bartow, a Bayard of gallantry and honor of whom it may emphatically be said that he was a knight without fear and without reproach."[6]

For the first time in the war some of Savannah's women were seen wearing mourning black, grieving over loved ones slain in faraway Virginia. Perhaps the most lamented slain were six young soldiers from the same Sunday school class killed at Bull Run while serving in the Oglethorpes. They were among troops who jubilantly followed Bartow to Virginia in the spring and were in the thick of the fiercest fighting at Manassas. Among them was John L. Branch, one of the three Branch brothers.

"My dear, dear Mother," Hamilton Branch wrote home on July 23, "I wrote you last from Manassas. We were then one mile from the junction. Since then the cold hand of death has been in our family. John, our beloved, has been killed, poor fellow."

Brother "Santy" Branch had been closer to John during the fighting on the Confederate flank and saw John suffer his death wound. Santy cradled his dying brother in his arms and was captured shortly afterward.

"I scarcely know how to begin this sad, sad letter," he wrote his mother from a prison compound in Washington on July 26. Sanford described how the Eighth Georgia had been ordered forward to support Bee's troops.

"We gained a small piece of woods, when I left the left of the company and advanced in front, discharged my gun and loaded, when I thought I would look behind me to see if any of my company had fallen. But Mother, just think of my horror to see John, dear John, reel and fall, I dropped my gun and ran to him. I got there just after Dr. West, who dear John asked whether there was any chance or not. When told he must die, he replied, Very well, he would die like a soldier and a man."

The Georgians carried John to the rear of the regiment where Santy stayed with him. "My poor brother lived about three-quarters [of] an hour. He was perfectly sensible about half the time. He died in my arms. His last words were about you and Hamilton. I cannot write any more now, as I was taken prisoner, standing by his body."

John Branch and the other slain Oglethorpes, Julius A. Ferrill, George M. Butler, William H. Crane, Ryan Morel, and Thomas Purse, Jr., were buried together on the battlefield.

Hamilton Branch, who was twice slightly wounded, sent lockets of John's hair to their mother. He also witnessed the death of Tom Purse.

"He was walking in front of me about ten feet, when he fell on his knees and stuck his head in the ground," Branch said in a July 26 letter. "I had seen men do the same dodging bomb shells, and I thought he was doing the same thing. As I passed him I thought I would stop and see who it was and tell him to come on, as the balls were raining all around us. I looked and saw that he was dead and that it was Tom."

The remains of these Oglethorpes were not returned to Savannah until February 1862, when a mass funeral was held for them at Independent Presbyterian Church.

"All young, all unmarried, all gentlemen," a news correspondent wrote, "there was not one of the killed who was not an ornament to his community and freighted with brilliant promise."

Bartow's body arrived in Savannah by train on the night of July 26 with an escort of the Oglethorpes. The body lay in state at the City Exchange until two days later when his funeral was held, a week after he was killed.

"Colonel Bartow's remains have reached Savannah and will be buried tomorrow eve and his funeral preached," wrote S. A. Dickey, who was among troops from Thomas County arriving a few days earlier.

Hundreds of Savannahians wept or watched in somber silence as the black hearse drawn by four gray horses clip-clopped through the city. In accompaniment were detachments from Savannah's military units. Bells tolled and cannon salutes cracked as the column slowly marched to Christ Church, where the Right Reverend Bishop Stephen Elliott performed the funeral service. The procession then wound to Laurel Grove Cemetery, where Bartow was buried with military honors.

The *Daily Morning News* described the scene as "the most solemn and imposing spectacle we ever witnessed in Savannah" and said Bartow was "not less loved in life than honored in his glorious death."

The city had been bloodied, but Confederate arms, as expected, had won out over the vile Yankees. And Savannah, as well as the rest of Georgia, had its first Civil War hero in Bartow, "among the purest of patriots and most chivalrous men who ever served in council, or commanded in the field," the July 30 *Milledgeville Southern Recorder* stated. Before the year was out, Cass County, Georgia, was renamed Bartow County in honor of the fallen hero.

In spite of the losses at Bull Run, the war still was an unbridled adventure in 1861. The Savannah papers were filled with recruiting notices and ads for tents, forage caps, and other military accoutrements.

Tattnall tried to drum up recruits for his gunboats. "Wanted for The Navy of the Confederate States—200 Able Bodied Seamen, Ordinary Seamen and Landsmen," read a July 15 ad in the *Daily Morning News*. The men would be paid $18, $14, and $12 respectively with "Four cents per day allowed in addition for grog ration." The Southern navy, including the Savannah squadron, suffered from a lack of experienced seamen throughout the war.[7]

Union vessels hovered off the coast, but to this point they had had little effect on Savannah's shipping.

In the Confederate bivouacs in and around the city, the troops settled into the routines of daily life in the military. "Dear Father, Mother and Family: Seated out upon the grass in the middle of our camp, I now am whilst I write you," Henry Carlton of the Troup Artillery penned from Savannah on June 8. "The soldiers, having just [gotten] through their dinners, are now lying like sheep in the shade around the camp underneath the beautiful, wide, spreading oaks which adorn our camp."

"Well, now a little about our duties. In the morning at daylight the drum and fife is heard. We all bounce from our pallets, form in the center of our camp and answer to roll call. Then half an hour is given to washing, cleaning up tents, &c. Then the drum beats again. We assemble for drill [and] drill one hour. Then dismissed, we prepare to satisfy an appetite produced by exercise before breakfast and by no means a small one, I assure you. This over, we then have what we term guard mounting, viz. relieving the guard of the day before and appointing a new guard for duty for twenty-four hours to serve. This through, we then rest an hour or so. Then another drill for an hour or an hour and half, governed of course as to length by the heat of the day. When this drill is through, we then devote ourselves to the general duties of the camp until 5:30 P.M. Then another drill of [the] same length. This over, we prepare for supper. After this, all make their preparations for a comfortable night's lodging. At 9 o'clock the drum beats tattoo, all fall in line, the roll is called. Then all report to tents. Twenty minutes thereafter the drum beats taps, and all lights are extinguished. Then all is still and quiet in our camp 'till morning, naught heard save the rattling of the guards' swords as they pass the tents up and down their lines and their calls to the officer of the guard.... Thus the day and night is passed."

S. A. Dickey, the Rebel from Thomas County, was impressed with Savannah after his unit came in from Thomasville by train. In a letter to his brother he wrote: "We are encamped on the parade ground and a beautiful place it is, about 60 to 70 acres paled in and grown up in Bermuda grass, hard and a mighty level and good place to drill.... The Savannah boys say we are [as] fine-looking as have passed through yet."

Excitement reigned in Savannah on September 18, when the screw steamer *Bermuda* reached the city loaded with a cargo of goods and munitions purchased by Confederate agents in Great Britain. Her captain, Eugene L. Tessier, reported that the *Bermuda* was not sighted by any of the Union blockaders before reaching Savannah.

Among the Southern emissaries operating covertly in Britain was Edward C. Anderson, a former Savannah mayor. Anderson had been a U.S. Navy officer, but resigned his commission before the war and come home. He was not as hell-bent for disunion as many others in the city, but when Georgia seceded, he went with the South.

"I had been reared under the U.S. flag in the Navy and was to the innermost recess of my nature, attached to its folds, yet the die was cast &

my lot as a Southern man with it," he remembered, adding bitterly that "Georgia especially had been led by the nose by South Carolina."

By May 1861 Anderson had been promoted to major of artillery and was on his way to Great Britain on a mission to obtain arms and ammunition for the Confederacy. His assignment was due, at least in some part, to his friendship with President Davis. Anderson described his position as "the Secretary of War in England."

He and fellow Georgian James D. Bulloch also negotiated with the British for the sale of warships and blockade-runners to the South. In Liverpool, when he heard the news of the Southern victory at First Bull Run, Anderson rode to a friend's home and ran up a Confederate flag on the rooftop.

Anderson, Bulloch, and their colleagues did their undercover work in spite of a proclamation by Queen Victoria that her subjects should not break the legally constituted Union blockade.

The *Bermuda* brought in at least eighteen rifled cannon, four heavy siege guns, 6,500 Enfield rifles, and some 20,000 Enfield cartridges. Many of these weapons had been bought by Wade Hampton of South Carolina to outfit his cavalry legion. General Lawton secured 3,000 of the Enfields for distribution to Georgia regiments posted in and around the city. The ship's cargo also included medical and quartermaster supplies, revolvers, and swords.

The *Bermuda* remained in Savannah until October 29, when she set a course for England with 2,000 bales of Georgia cotton. Again evading Northern warships, she reached Liverpool in mid-November. The success of the mission and the profits realized by the venture prompted other British shipping firms to begin blockade-running efforts.

Work on Savannah's defenses along the coast, the Savannah River, and salt marsh islands proceeded through the summer. A strong battery was erected on Wassaw Island to protect the entrance to Wassaw Sound. Several miles upriver from the sound a large earthen fort was built on a bluff overlooking the Wilmington River.

To watch over Ossabaw Sound, the Rebels constructed a ten-gun battery on Green Island to guard the Vernon River. A Rebel teenager stationed there in September wrote his sister: "If they try us I think they will be barking up the wrong tree for I do not believe there is one man ... who would not die before surrender."[8]

Also at Ossabaw, construction began in June on an earthwork on the south bank of the Great Ogeechee River. This fort would not only protect the river entrance but also the crucial Atlantic & Gulf Railroad bridge over the Ogeechee several miles upstream. Fort McAllister would come to symbolize Rebel defiance throughout the war.

"There is no mistake about the spirit of these people," William Russell wrote. "They seize upon every spot of vantage ground and prepare it for defense."[9]

The first week of October saw the Confederates concentrating on the defenses closest to the city in "anticipation of a land attack," one observer wrote. Captain Jeremy F. Gilmer, who would become one of the Confederacy's best engineers, was in Savannah and assisted Lawton in planning these lines.

Charles Jones's term as mayor expired in October, and he donned a uniform as a lieutenant in the Chatham Artillery. He joined the unit at Camp Claghorne on the Isle of Hope.

"Our pure white tents contrast beautifully with the dark, overhanging foliage ..." he wrote to his parents, "and our burnished battery gleams brightly in the morning sun. Our garrison flag is floating freely in the quick air."

Jones's successor as mayor was Thomas Purse, whose son had been killed with Bartow at Manassas.

In reporting the overall strength of the coastal defenses in 1861, Ordnance Officer W. G. Gill noted that some of the regiments were "armed with shotguns and sporting rifles. They have little or no ammunition for them."[10]

The Southerners along the Carolina and Georgia coast would need more than squirrel guns to weather the hurricane of Union naval might bearing down on them that autumn.

On October 29, a seventy-nine-vessel force of warships, troop transports, supply vessels, and support craft left Hampton Roads, Virginia, on a thrust at Port Royal, South Carolina, a deep-water port about twenty-five miles north of Savannah. This array of ships, including some 12,000 assault troops, was the most powerful American fleet assembled to that time.

The expedition had been in the planning stages for months. "A superior naval force must command the whole division of the coast," the commander, Flag Officer Samuel F. Du Pont, had written the previous July. The strike was supposed to be top secret. But Northern newspapers discovered and printed Du Pont's destination, alerting the Confederates in the process. Indeed, C.S. Acting Secretary of War Judah P. Benjamin telegraphed South Carolina Governor Francis Pickens on November 1 warning that "the enemy's expedition is intended for Port Royal." A smaller Union flotilla made a feint off Tybee Island, but the Rebels weren't fooled. Their only problem was that they were virtually powerless to stop Du Pont.

At Savannah, Josiah Tattnall worked vigorously through the fall to refit steamboats and other river craft into fighting vessels. Most of the time this meant mounting a cannon on deck and issuing carbines, revolvers, and cutlasses to his crews.

His command was augmented in late September by the arrival of a company of about seventy Confederate marines from Pensacola under the command of Captain George Holmes. In addition to the flagship *Savannah*, two tenders, the *Sampson* and the *Resolute*, had been armed with thirty-two-pounder deck guns. The side-wheeler *Huntress* also was fitted with a cannon. Like most of Tattnall's vessels, she was especially vulnerable to enemy shellfire because her engine and boiler were above deck as well.

William Russell gave this description of Tattnall in 1861: "I was much interested in the fine, white-headed, blue-eyed, ruddy-cheeked old man who suddenly found himself blown into the air by a great political explosion and in doubt and wonderment was floating to shore under a strange flag in unknown waters. He had served the stars-and-stripes for three-fourths of a long life. His friends are in the North, his wife's kindred are there, and so are all his best associations. But his state has gone out [of the Union]. How could he fight against the country that gave him birth! It was strange to look at such a man as the Commodore, quietly preparing to meet his old comrades and friends, if needs be, on the battlefield, his long service flung away, his old ties and connections severed. He is not now, nor has he been for years, a slave-owner."[11]

Tattnall had no illusions that his pretend navy could battle the enemy on anything close to equal terms. Knowing the naval opposition he faced, Tattnall had expressed his frustration to Russell during the tour of coastal defenses in May: "I have no fleet. Long before the Southern Confederacy has a fleet that can cope with the stars-and-stripes, my bones will be white in the grave"[12]

As the Federal armada threatened the coast, however, Tattnall showed that he was full of fight despite his lack of ships, guns, and sailors. He would be facing Du Pont, whom he had served with in the old navy.

With his makeshift "Mosquito Fleet," Tattnall steamed to Port Royal to assist in the ensuing clash. The Rebel naval force included the flagship CSS

Savannah, commanded by Lieutenant Maffitt; the *Sampson*, skippered by Lieutenant J. S. Kennard; and the *Resolute* of Lieutenant J. Pembroke Jones. Also accompanying Tattnall were the steamers *Huntress* and the *Lady Davis*, obtained by the Confederate government in Charleston.

As Tattnall readied his guns, the common soldiers in Savannah's coastal defenses knew little or nothing of the approaching blue menace. William W. Head was a member of the "Monroe Crowders," which had been incorporated into the Thirty-first Georgia Infantry. Head's company was at Camp Adams on Skidaway Island when he wrote his wife, Fannie, on November 3. The men were on picket duty, armed with a mix of Enfield rifles and double-barrel shotguns.

"Our provisions are plentiful though plain, consisting of sea bread, corn meal, rice, coffee, sugar, bacon, fresh beef, etc.," Head wrote. "Fish and oysters too plentiful to be good. I have not eaten any of either yet.... Vessels of various kinds are passing regularly all of which are hailed by our sentinals and friendly signals exchanged.... Like Robinson Cruso[e] we are monarchs of all we survey. Seldom seeing any landsmen except our own men."

While Head was collecting his thoughts for his letter, Du Pont's expedition began assembling off Port Royal Sound after it was scattered by severe storms along the North Carolina coast.

The Union ships still were arriving the next day when Tattnall boldly attacked with his little navy just before twilight, opening fire from long range.

"His [Tattnall's] vessels were river boats; as men-of-war they were in every respect of the most vulnerable class," a Union naval officer wrote.

The bigger, heavier-armed U.S. vessels easily drove off the Confederates, Tattnall wisely retreating in to Skull Creek before his mosquitoes were swatted. When Tattnall fell back, the *Huntress* became separated and made for Charleston. She would later aid in that city's defense.

Tattnall tried to attack again just after sunrise on November 5, but Union gunboats quickly drove him away, drawing fire from Confederate batteries ashore in the process.

At one point during the sea engagements, Tattnall's vessel came within range of Du Pont's flagship, the USS *Wabash*. In a sign of respect for his old friend, Tattnall ordered his flag dipped three times. Du Pont, however, did not notice the salute. He instead replied with his guns.

Tattnall was little more than a nuisance for the rest of the battle, although his marines and some seamen went ashore to aid in the land defense. Du Pont bombarded forts Walker and Beauregard, which were protecting the sound, and then launched a successful amphibious assault on November 7.

The struggle for Port Royal typified a war pitting brother against brother. Confederate Brigadier General Thomas F. Drayton commanded the Rebel defenders. His brother, Percival Drayton, was captain of the USS *Pocahontas*, one of the attacking vessels.

Port Royal's fall meant that the Yankees now had a deep South foothold for their blockade of the south Atlantic coast and that Savannah would suffer dearly because of it. Tattnall's fleet limped back to the city, but not before one of the old commodore's officers had sailed into hot waters. Tattnall was ashore for a conference on November 5, when Maffitt brashly took the *Savannah* too close to some of Du Pont's gunboats, which opened fire. An eleven-inch shell from the USS *Seneca* ripped into the vessel's starboard side near the wheelhouse. The result was substantial damage to the pride of the Savannah fleet.

An irate Tattnall had Maffitt arrested for his alleged rashness and misconduct, in spite of the lieutenant's protests. Tempers and the controversy soon cooled, however, and Maffitt resumed his duties.

"The boasted armada of Lincoln is now upon our coast, and we know not at what hour, or where, the attempted invasion may begin," Lieutenant Jones wrote from Camp Claghorne on November 5. "We have an inhuman enemy to meet, and in great force in all probability." Jones described the Yankees as "in the main cowards.... Either that, or they are inhuman fanatics, to be classed with mad dogs and shot accordingly."[13]

Savannah had been confident of victory and went wild in panic when word of Port Royal's fall reached the city. Those residents who didn't flee by wagon or packed trains eyed the coast, expecting to see the ugly smoke of Du Pont's approaching warships at any moment.

"Savannah is thus placed in a perilous position, and many of our people are removing their families and valuables," Confederate Lieutenant George A. Mercer wrote in his November 10 diary entry. "The banks, courts, &c. are transporting their papers, records, &c. to places of safety.... Several officers went so far as to declare that if Savannah was attacked it should at once capitulate, and many old women in breeches were in utter alarm and despair!"[14]

Sherard Roberts was among Southern troops who retreated from the Port Royal vicinity to Savannah on the night of November 7. He and his regiment reached the city by steamer the next morning. "I lost my overcoat and one of my blankets and knapsack and haversack," he wrote his wife that day. "Our whole regiment left everything they carried but their guns and ammunitions ... the Savannah folks give us plenty of cooked provisions today, and I felt very well this afternoon."

Roberts added that he expected to be in battle in the next few days "for they will try Georgia soon, I think."

Rumors raged that the Federals had landed at White Bluff, south of the city, "causing great excitement," but no Yankees were found.

"The [enemy] fleet was hourly expected & the decision with most was to burn their dwellings & let the Yankees have smoking ruins to welcome them," Mrs. George Anderson of Savannah wrote to a relative on November 11.

"It would be useless to attempt to disguise the fact that there has been much excitement in our city during the past few days," the *Daily Morning News* understated on November 11. "The danger has been greatly magnified by absurd and startling rumors that have been put into circulation by panicists." The writer added that "many families have left the city. This is proper enough, as there is no necessity to subject our women and children to the dangers and inconvenience of a siege."[15]

If many Savannahians were leaving, refugees from coastal South Carolina were streaming into the city to escape the Yankee menace. "It was a sad sight for me on Friday last to meet on the road ladies and children flying from Beaufort and Bluffton," Mercer recalled.[16]

"Today has been a gloomy one for us," Lieutenant Jones wrote to his father on November 8. "Each hour fresh advices arrive of our disaster at Port Royal.... A crushing responsibility rests upon the heads of those highest in military authority for the present helpless posture of affairs."[17]

"If the Yankees will only leave the cover of their ships' guns they will have bush fighting and guerrilla warfare to their hearts' content," Mercer wrote on November 11. "Their immense naval armament and success has thoroughly alarmed some nervous people, and an overweening confidence in sand batteries has given place to a timid faith in the resistless power of the Yankee ships."[18]

Jones correctly guessed the Union strategy even though most Savannahians believed otherwise: "I cannot think Savannah in immediate danger. My impression is that they will securely entrench themselves at Port Royal before advancing."

Indeed, Du Pont did not launch a strike in the following weeks or even try to besiege Savannah. Instead, he settled into Port Royal, intent on making it his base of operations for a naval blockade of the Rebel coast.

IV

R. E. Lee in Savannah

Even as Union troops were splashing ashore at Port Royal on November 7, a courtly officer in the gray uniform of a full Confederate general was riding to the front from Coosawhatchie, South Carolina, about fifty miles to the west.

General Robert E. Lee was the new commander of coastal defenses in Georgia, South Carolina, and eastern Florida. Finding Port Royal beyond help, Lee established headquarters at Coosawhatchie on the Charleston & Savannah Railroad. He would spend most of his time in both of those cities deploying troops and supervising construction of defenses.

"He would have been recognized any where in the world as a man of mark, one upon whom Nature had set the stamp of greatness," Charles Olmstead remembered of Lee in a winter inspection of Fort Pulaski. "Tall in stature, straight as an arrow, well knit and vigorous in frame yet graceful and easy in movement, a well shaped head just beginning to be touched with gray, and a face in which kindliness and sweetness of temper blended with firmness of purpose and a dignified and grave reserve; he met my highest conception of ideal manhood."[1]

Savannah was a homecoming of sorts for the Virginian, who had been stationed there and flirted with the local belles more than thirty years earlier. Born January 19, 1807, on the family estate of Stratford in West-moreland County, Virginia, Lee was the fifth child of Henry "Light Horse Harry" Lee, a famed cavalryman in the American Revolution. Henry Lee squandered the family fortune on poor land speculation deals, and the

Prewar portrait of Robert E. Lee. (Courtesy of the Georgia Historical Society.)

family was forced to move to a smaller home in Alexandria, where young Lee spent most of his childhood. There they lived on a trust fund established by his maternal grandfather. Robert was eleven when his father died, and he was raised primarily by his mother, Ann Hill Carter Lee. Attending school in Alexandria, Lee obtained a West Point appointment in 1825.

Lee graduated from West Point ranked second in the class of 1829 and did not accrue a single demerit at the Military Academy—an incredible record. Among his future Confederate classmates were generals Joseph E. Johnston, A. G. Blanchard, and Theophilus Holmes. Commissioned a brevet second lieutenant of engineers, Lee received orders in August 1829 to report to Cockspur Island in the Savannah River, where a fort (later named Pulaski) was to be built.

Lee had a Savannah connection even before he left West Point; Jack Mackay of Savannah was a fellow cadet and one of Lee's closest friends at the academy.

When Lee arrived in Savannah in the fall of 1829, he was welcomed as a son by Jack's family in their home on East Broughton Street. The three Mackay girls—Margaret, Catherine, and Eliza—made his visits there even more of a pleasure. He often stayed at the Mackay home overnight during his leaves.

It was quite a different story at Cockspur. Lee designed and helped build a dike system to support and drain the area where the fort was to stand.

45

Often he found himself in hip-deep water, battling insects, heat, and humidity and working like a field hand. Yet during this period, Lee wrote to Jack Mackay, describing Savannah as "That spot of spots! That place of places! That city of cities!!!"

Shortly afterward, Mackay was posted as an artilleryman to the small army garrison at Savannah. The old friends were reunited for a brief time before Mackay was reassigned to a post in Alabama. (Mackay did not live to be embroiled in the Civil War. Forced to resign from the army in 1846 on account of ill health, he died two years later.)

Whenever possible, Lee went upriver and enjoyed Savannah's social graces, especially those of the Mackays and the charms of two daughters in the Isaac Minis family. While he relished the attentions of Savannah's fairest, Lee could not forget his first love in Virginia. Since childhood he had known and grown increasingly closer to Mary Anne Randolph Custis. Distant relatives, she was twenty-one when Lee came home from West Point in the summer of 1829 and began their courtship. Mary's father was the adopted son of George Washington, and the family lived at Arlington, a fine mansion and estate on the outskirts of Washington, where Lee was a frequent visitor. Even while he was in Georgia, Lee spent his few furloughs in Virginia, wooing Mary.

In Savannah, however, the young officer obviously had his head turned by the local beauties, especially young Eliza Mackay. From his forlorn outpost on Cockspur Island, Lee once wrote Eliza: "It did grieve me to see the Boats coming down one after another, without any of those little comforts which are now so necessary to me. Oh me! ... But you will send me some sometimes, Will you not Sweet—? How I will besiege the P. Office."

Whatever their relationship, it never flowered—one reason being that Lee was transferred to Virginia in April 1831 to assist in the construction of Fort Monroe. The first phase of his Savannah adventure was over, and Lee married Mary Custis in June 1831.

The couple had seven children between 1832 and 1846. All three sons served in the Confederate army, two attaining the rank of major general.

Lee was a captain when the Mexican War erupted in 1846. He was sent to Texas and joined Lieutenant General Winfield Scott on the Vera Cruz expedition as a member of Scott's personal staff. Lee proved invaluable in scouting and advising the general during the march on Mexico City. He won Scott's everlasting admiration and was described by the general as "the very best soldier I ever saw in the field."

46

Lee emerged from the war with a slight wound, a sterling reputation, and a brevet colonelcy. He supervised the construction of Fort Carroll in Baltimore until 1852, when he was appointed superintendent of the Military Academy.

In 1855 he was promoted to lieutenant colonel and assigned to the newly formed Second Cavalry Regiment. He served on the Texas frontier until 1861.

Lee was on extended leave visiting his family in Virginia when John Brown's raiders descended on Harpers Ferry. He was sent to the village to command the combined force of marines and militia that overwhelmed Brown's band.

The nation was storming toward war, and Lee had to choose a side. Scott called him to Washington in February 1861 to try to persuade him to remain in the U. S. Army. Several Southern states already had seceded, but Lee's beloved Virginia had not yet acted.

Promoted to colonel of the First Cavalry in March, Lee wrestled with the question. He earlier wrote to one of his sons that "secession is nothing but revolution." Lee biographer Douglas Southall Freeman wrote that Lee's "mind was for the Union; his instinct was for his state. . . . As for his state, he looked on Virginia much as he did on his own family."

Lee apparently held no strong belief in slavery, having freed the blacks his family inherited after the death of his father-in-law in 1857. He was a Whig and firmly believed in the Constitution.

Less than a week after Fort Sumter's surrender, Lee learned that he was to be offered command of the U.S. forces assembling to end the rebellion. He refused, saying that although personally opposed to secession, he could not fight against the South. Scott would tell him that he had made "the greatest mistake of your life; but I feared it would be so."

The last straw came on April 19, when Lee learned that Virginia had seceded. Torn between allegiance to the Union or his state, Lee painfully chose the latter, submitting his resignation from the army the next day. He wrote Scott, stating that "Save in defense of my native State, I never desire again to draw my sword."

In this frame of mind Lee went to Richmond, and shortly afterward was placed in command of Virginia's land and naval forces. On May 14 he was appointed brigadier general in the Confederate army and promoted to full general on June 14.

Lee was sent to lead Rebel forces operating in the mountains of western Virginia in late July. It would be one of the lowest points of his career. A combination of bad weather, rough terrain, discord among his generals, and disease among his meager troops doomed all efforts in this pro-Union region. His forces were defeated in the Cheat Mountain campaign in September, and Lee came under some criticism.

Jefferson Davis, however, never lost confidence in him. In early November 1861 Lee was assigned to the southeastern coastal command that would bring him back to Savannah.

"All rejoice that General Lee has come—we hope in time to save us, under God," the Reverend C. C. Jones wrote to his son on November 14. "You know his reputation in the army: he checkmated Rosecrans in Western Virginia. And he is Miss Kitty Stiles's great friend. Should he make a progress through these regions I should be happy to know and to receive him at our house."[2]

Jones added, "A resignation of General Lawton, if not graceful at the present time, would certainly be altogether agreeable to the great body of our people civil and military."

In spite of Jones's praise, Lee's command abilities had yet to be proven, and critics called him "Granny." Some even blamed him for the debacle at Port Royal.

"It was utter defeat at Port Royal," Mary Boykin Chesnut wrote. "DeSaussure's and Dunavant's regiments were cut to pieces. General Lee sent them, they say. Preux chevalier, booted and bridled and gallant rode he, but so far his bonnie face has only brought us ill luck." [She referred to the Twelfth South Carolina of Colonel R. G. M. Dunovant and the Fifteenth South Carolina led by Colonel W. D. De Saussure. Both regiments sustained minor losses, and it is unlikely that Lee played any role in their direction during the battle.]

Lee himself was less than enthusiastic when first assigned to the coast, describing it as "another forlorn hope expedition" and "worse than western Virginia" in a letter to one of his daughters.[3]

Amid war preparations, Lee rekindled old friendships, especially among the Mackay family, whose daughters had enchanted the young lieutenant in the old days. Lee visited the home on Broughton Street, where he once had spent so much leisure time socializing with Eliza and her sisters.

Yet unlike the galas and festive dinners he enjoyed on leave from Pulaski's construction, Lee had little time for socializing in 1861. He found himself responsible for the defense of about three hundred miles of coastline with scant, scattered, and badly armed troops, few big guns, poor communications, and an aggressive U.S. fleet offshore.

While he never fought a battle in his four months in the coastal command, Lee's military engineering skills and ability to work with scarce resources would have a long-lasting influence on the Southern war effort.

He primarily divided his time between Savannah and Charleston, bolstering defenses, installing obstructions in the numerous coastal rivers and creeks, and consolidating his isolated units.

At Savannah, Lee was aided in his defensive preparations by Captain John McCrady, Georgia's chief engineer. McCrady was a professor of engineering and physics at the College of Charleston when the war began and had earlier worked on Charleston's fortifications.

John Maffitt, who had drawn Tattnall's ire at Port Royal, served as special naval aide to Lee for several weeks before being transferred to command the blockade-runner *Cecile* at Wilmington. Maffitt was well suited for his role with Lee. For fifteen years before the war he was in the United States Coastal Survey, where he became quite familiar with the southern coastline, harbors, and channels.

One of Lee's first goals was to strengthen Fort Pulaski. He visited Savannah and the fort on November 10–11. He also oversaw the construction of a defensive line running parallel to the South Carolina coast and designed to protect the railroad and other communication links between Savannah and Charleston.

On one inspection of Pulaski, Lee had an unexpected reunion with Francis Circoply, captain of the steamer *Ida*, whom he had known during his first assignment in Savannah. Circoply was the former coxswain whose boat had carried Lee to and from Savannah and Cockspur Island.

Lee, with other dignitaries, was coming up from the wharf as Circoply stood at attention amid the garrison soldiers near a bridge over the moat. Olmstead described the scene:

"The little procession was about to cross the bridge when General Lee saw him and came forward with both hands extended, a bright smile on his face and the exclamation 'Why Francis! Is that you?'

"'Just like I was one of his old friends,' said the old Captain.

"'You will tell it to your children,' I remarked.

"It was a little incident but one that showed the native kindliness of our great leader."[4]

Lee introduced Circoply to the other members of the gray entourage, including Governor Brown. The general also reviewed the Savannah Volunteer Guards manning Fort Screven, an earthwork on Green Island.

On parade, the Guards were ordered to march at double-quick time. A clumsy recruit near the front of the column stumbled and fell, tripping men on either side. Unable to stop, the units proceeded forward and many of the soldiers were sent sprawling. Lee apparently joined other officers in "inextinguishable laughter," but later praised the Guards, saying, "If I had ten thousand such troops, I would not hesitate to meet a very much greater force of the enemy."[5]

Before Lee left the Guards, the unit's officers brought out a bottle of genuine Holland gin to celebrate the occasion of his visit. Lee graciously declined to partake, as did his staff, although the latter "looked longingly at it," Savannahian William Basinger remembered.

Also during this time Lee bought a horse to help him cover the many miles of territory in his command. He first noticed Greenbrier, owned by another soldier, during the western Virginia campaign. When Greenbrier's master joined Lee's forces near Savannah, the general bought the young gray for $200. The horse's strength and stamina impressed Lee, who described him as a "fine traveller." The name fit and the legendary Traveller would carry Lee from Savannah to Chancellorsville, Gettysburg, Appomattox, and beyond. He would eventually outlive his master.

Lee cut a dashing figure riding his "Confederate gray" warhorse through Savannah's streets during the winter of 1861–1862.

V

"Repel the Invasion!"

The Federal naval blockade was slowly beginning to smother Savannah in the last weeks of 1861. Through the Confederacy's first summer, Savannahians had openly scoffed at "Abraham's blockade." Southern vessels and those of countries sympathetic to the South slipped in and out of Savannah, often never spying a Union ship of Commodore Silas H. Stringham's Atlantic Squadron. Blockade-runners took advantage of Great Britain's pro-South stance, seeking protection or refueling at Bermuda or in the Bahamas, both British possessions. From these havens they were within a few days' cruise of Savannah, Charleston, or Wilmington, the primary ports in the southeastern Confederacy.

By September, however, the U.S. government Blockade Board had reorganized its naval forces in the Atlantic, dividing them into two blockade squadrons. The South Atlantic Blockading Squadron, which covered the coasts of South Carolina, Georgia, and eastern Florida, was to be commanded by Du Pont.

Port Royal's capture in November was a crushing blow to blockade-runners plotting a course to or from Savannah. Du Pont quickly turned the harbor hamlet into a bustling Union navy yard and strung his warships along the southern coast.

Through his blockade Du Pont did more to hurt Savannah than any Union commander before William T. Sherman. Born in New Jersey in 1803, Du Pont began his long naval career as a midshipman in 1815, serving from the West Indies to the Far East. Promoted to captain in 1855, he oversaw the Philadelphia Navy Yard and was appointed chief of a naval board convened in Washington in June 1861 to plan U.S. military operations

Union Admiral Samuel F. Du Pont, shown in an 1863 drawing, was the scourge of Savannah, tightening the knot of the naval blockade. (*Harper's Weekly*, Apr. 25, 1863, courtesy of the Georgia Historical Society.)

at sea. Promoted to flag officer in September, he took aim at Port Royal a few weeks later.

Like the "Anaconda Plan" suggested by General Winfield Scott in the war's early days, the Union blockade began slowly strangling Savannah's naval commerce.

"I will cork up Savannah like a bottle," Du Pont wrote in late November.

The bottle was still open on November 12, 1861, however, when the merchant steamer *Fingal* eluded the blockade and arrived in Savannah from Greenock, Scotland, with an immense cargo of military hardware.

"Our city has been greatly excited and rejoiced today by the arrival of the steamer," George Mercer wrote. "Joy beamed on every countenance, and all declared that the safe arrival of this vessel, notwithstanding the fleet off Port Royal, and the receipt of arms just when they were most needed were wonderful instances of Divine interposition and favor!"[1]

Jubilant over the success of the *Bermuda* in slipping through the enemy blockade, Major Edward Anderson and Captain James Bulloch had negotiated with the British for the purchase of the *Fingal*, a new Scottish-built screw steamer that had attained speeds of thirteen knots in trial runs. Again they decided to try to puncture the Union blockade and reach Savannah. Bulloch and Anderson joined the primarily British crew for the voyage.

A partial bill of lading showed about 11,000 rifles (mostly Enfields),

24,000 pounds of gunpowder, 500 sabres, over a million percussion caps, and 500,000 cartridges. Also included were four artillery pieces, seven tons of shells, medicine, clothing, and blankets.

General Lee issued about 5,000 Enfields from the *Fingal* to Georgia and South Carolina troops stationed in the area. Two Blakely guns were sent to Fort Pulaski.

The *Fingal* did not reach Savannah without some difficulty. As she entered the Savannah River at daybreak that morning the *Fingal* had run aground on an oyster bar near Pulaski. Minutes earlier the crew had seen soldiers waving their caps in welcome from the fort's parapets. They were too distant to hear the garrison's cheers. Anderson came ashore and telegraphed Savannah for assistance. Several hours later Tattnall had three steamers on the scene to free the *Fingal* and escort her upriver to the city.

Bulloch and Anderson were mobbed by well-wishers when they disembarked after just over a month at sea. Bulloch left almost immediately for Richmond to continue his navy-building operations. Anderson also headed to the capital, intent on boosting the blockade-busting efforts. He met with the new Secretary of War, George W. Randolph, and also with Secretary of the Navy Stephen Mallory. Anderson proposed the establishment of an armed flying squadron under John Maffitt to escort blockade-runners to Southern ports. The idea, however, was lost in Richmond politics and disinterest. Mallory also resented what he perceived as Anderson's meddling in naval affairs.

Discouraged, Anderson returned to Savannah and was promoted to colonel on General Lee's staff. He was among the Confederate high command at Savannah until the end of the war.

Also aboard the *Fingal* was Lieutenant John Low of Savannah, an aide to Captain Bulloch. Low was a nephew of Andrew Low, one of the city's wealthiest citizens through his delvings into international banking, import-export trade, insurance, and cotton. John also was the son-in-law of Charles Green, a business partner of Andrew Low who would later become a very famous figure in Savannah's war story.

John Low was a private in the Georgia Hussars the previous summer when he received an appointment as acting master with the rank of lieutenant in the C.S. Navy. The promotion was largely due to his friendship with Bulloch, and he was ordered to report to the captain in Liverpool.

Bulloch arrived in Richmond from Savannah and conferred with Secretary Mallory about the most immediate needs of the Rebel fleet. They

Tybee Island lighthouse as it appeared in *Harper's Weekly*,
December 14, 1861. (Courtesy of the Georgia Historical Society.)

agreed that the *Fingal* should be loaded with a cargo of cotton and resin
and sail for England to obtain more military supplies as quickly as possible.

Bulloch hurried back to Savannah, where he and John Low readied the
Fingal for a return trip across the Atlantic. This process was delayed
because cotton shipments from upstate were slow in reaching Savannah.
Even though untouched by war, Georgia had a poor internal transportation
system in 1861. Not until December 20 would the *Fingal* be loaded and
prepared to again defy the Union blockade.

Savannah was rejuvenated by the safe arrival of the *Bermuda* and the *Fingal*.
Yet the good cheer was tempered two weeks after the *Fingal* made port,
when U.S. gunboats appeared off Tybee and opened a heavy bombardment
of the island.

Tybee was held by a light force of Confederates. Their comrades
were busily strengthening Fort Pulaski at the mouth of the Savannah
River on the island's north end. Anticipating an attack on Pulaski, the
Southerners had withdrawn most of their troops from Tybee back to the
fort. The most prominent Tybee features were a lighthouse and a structure
called the Spanish, or Martello, Tower, a forty-foot-high lookout post built

during the War of 1812. Both were located on the island's northern tip.

The enemy blockade had been in effect since late May, but the Rebels on Tybee, up to this point, had been bored by idleness and isolation, although they could see vessels of the Union fleet.

One Tybee Confederate wrote: "What a lonesome vigil at the wee hours of the night, tramping your lonely beat with nothing for company but the foamed capped waves as they break at your feet. You can imagine the waves capped with the enemy's small boats as they come rolling in, and how you wish to see again the light of day."[2]

These Rebels also were uncomfortable because of the merciless insects and the intense beach sun that cooked the "hot sands of Tybee." Still, the soldiers drilled, fished, and sunned themselves, waiting for action; it came on the night of November 24, 1861.

Three Union gunboats, the *Seneca, Augusta,* and *Pocahontas,* anchored off Tybee and opened a bombardment, driving the remaining graybacks off the island. About 3:45 P.M. on Sunday, November 25, Federal troops in thirteen "surf-boats" came ashore unopposed and planted the U.S. flag, a seaman from the *Augusta* doing the honors. Some of the Yanks ignited a number of camp fires to give the Rebels the impression that the island was held "in force."

From Fort Pulaski's ramparts, Confederates watched the bluecoats swarm from their boats and raise the Stars and Stripes on the beach. Few on either side considered at the time that Tybee's possession was key to the fate of Pulaski. Du Pont, however, was confident of victory: "By the fall of Tybee Island, the reduction of Fort Pulaski, which is within easy mortar distance, becomes only a question of time."

Brigadier General Thomas W. Sherman, who had Union army command in the Port Royal expedition, would oversee the troop build-up on Tybee, heading the new U.S. Department of the South.

"The Lincolnites ... landed on Tybee Island last Sabbath afternoon," a frustrated Charles Jones wrote to his family on November 27. "The Federal flag flies in sight of Fort Pulaski—and not more than two miles distant. Six thousand men are within less than a half hour of Savannah, ready and desirous of the liberty of attacking these vandals, and yet nothing is done."

Jones also took the opportunity to criticize the way General Lawton handled the developments: "[He] goes down in a steamboat, takes a look, returns home to a good dinner, and there the matter ends. The enemy meanwhile fortifies and reinforces, and flaunts his flag under our noses— and all forsooth because our general does not think it prudent to attack."

Union Brigadier General Thomas W. Sherman supervised the Federal troop buildup on Tybee Island. (Courtesy of the Georgia Historical Society.)

Jones added that there "exists a strange indifference or want of action on the part of those who are charged with the conduct of our military affairs. ... Idle troops are all about us; transportation sufficient can be had at any moment; and yet not the slightest effort is made to repel the invasion!"[3]

A few days later the Sandersville *Central Georgian* bristled at the notion of Yankees landing on the coast: "Shall one of Lincoln's vandals set foot upon Georgia's soil? Let it not be so."[4]

"The force on Tybee Island is reported to be large, but I am unable to state it," Lee wrote to Secretary of War Judah Benjamin on November 29. "No demonstration of their purpose has yet been made further than the occupation of the island."

With Tybee's capture, Du Pont reported that "Savannah is completely stopped up." And a *New York Tribune* reporter wrote that the city "is not only hermetically sealed, but is at our mercy."

To further infuriate and frustrate the Savannahians, the *Daily Morning News* ran a *New York Herald* dispatch dated November 29, stating "Savannah may be considered henceforth as of no importance to the South as a port."[5]

This was not much of an exaggeration. Du Pont posted warships off the Savannah River's mouth as well as in Ossabaw and Wassaw sounds, virtually closing off Savannah to the Atlantic.

Confederates stationed along the South Carolina coast were expecting to be sent to battle at Savannah, especially after they noticed the disappearance of Union ships in their vicinity. They presumed the vessels were heading south to join in an attack on the city. "Now that they have left we are looking hourly to march to Savannah for it is thought that we will have a tremendous fight there," Carolinian William Stevens wrote to his wife on November 29. "If they get the upper hand of us there it is thought that there will be a general revolution. If we can get them off the water we can whip them. . . . Our motto is 'To whip or die.'"

The Federals' landing on Tybee was a serious blow to Captain Bulloch's efforts to free the *Fingal* on the high seas. Within hours of the Yankee beachhead, Bulloch telegraphed Mallory about the developments, which effectively shut down any exit via the Savannah River due to the presence of the gunboats.

Her holds brimming with "King Cotton" and resin, the *Fingal* left Savannah on December 22 and slipped into a bight in Wilmington Island, hidden from the enemy's vessels. The next morning Lieutenant Low led a reconnaissance party to Wassaw Island and the surrounding area, looking for a way for the *Fingal* to escape the blockaders. The party consisted of sailors from the *Savannah, Sampson,* and *Fingal* as well as veteran pilot John H. Craig. Instead of finding an opening, Low's patrol saw that the Union gunboats were moving into positions to further tighten their control of the coast. After conferring with Tattnall, a frustrated Bulloch turned the *Fingal* back to Savannah.

Weeks later the *Fingal* remained in port, unable to slide past the blockade. Convinced there was nothing he could do, Bulloch wired Mallory for permission to return to Britain without the *Fingal* and continue his military efforts there. He also requested that Low accompany him. Mallory agreed to both requests, and Bulloch and Low left Savannah by northbound train on January 21, 1862. Arriving in Wilmington, North Carolina, they embarked for England aboard the blockade runner *Annie Childs.*

Low's wife, Eliza, Mr. and Mrs. Andrew Low, and Charles Green, John's brother-in-law, were involved in their own tale of intrigue and politics during this period. The Lows had accompanied John to Great Britain on his trip to first join Bulloch. Green already was in England on a visit. With John in military service, Eliza, the Lows, and Green returned to the U.S. On November 3 the Lows were arrested in Cincinnati while they were en route back to Savannah. The arrests were on a direct order from U.S. Secretary of State William H. Seward, who charged Low with being a Confederate collaborator and agent in England. Low was taken to Fort Warren Prison in Boston while his pregnant wife was held in Washington.

Also on Seward's order, Green and Eliza Low were taken into custody in Detroit. Both were charged with aiding the Confederacy through their overseas activities. Eliza Low was released eight days later after taking an oath that she would not enter any of the "States under insurrection" against the Union without Seward's permission and would engage in no hostile acts against the United States.

Andrew Low and his wife, meanwhile, remained in jail, but Low was an influential businessman with many Northern connections. Through these contacts he retained William M. Evarts of New York, one of the country's finest attorneys. Evarts vainly negotiated with Seward into December for the release of the prisoners. Mrs. Low, because of her pregnancy, had by this time been paroled to a home in Baltimore, but remained under arrest.

The weeks turned into the new year with no progress. Finally, through Evarts' vigorous efforts, Low was granted a sixty-day parole on February 8, 1862, to join his wife in Baltimore. Discussions continued with Low and Evarts, both strongly denying that Low had pro-South dealings on his agenda when he traveled to England. Their pleas paid off on March 14, when Low was issued a pass to take his wife south through the battle lines. Upon his honor, Low was sworn to render no aid "to the enemies of the United States" or "persons in insurrection against the authority" of the Union. Charles Green also was released and returned to Savannah.

Seward and his operatives were confused, perhaps intentionally, by the Lows and Green. They knew that a Confederate named Low had been sent to England as a CSA representative, but did not realize it was John, not Andrew. The who's-who relationship among the captives further clouded the picture, and the Lows and Green apparently did nothing to clear up the vagueness. While the Federals were sorting out the puzzle, John Low was performing valuable service to the Confederacy.

The Southerners at Savannah were not about to let the iron-hulled *Fingal* go to waste, especially at a time when they desperately needed vessels to defend the city. They decided to convert her into an ironclad warship. When completed in 1862, the CSS *Atlanta* was a Rebel poseidon considered one of the world's strongest battleships.

Du Pont further solidified his station in mid December 1861, sinking several stone-filled ships at the Savannah River entrance to block the channel.

Earlier the *Daily Morning News* reacted angrily when Northern newspapers first announced Du Pont's intent to sink the "stone fleet" and close the river: "The scheme is worthy of the vandal wretches," the November 6

A SHORT BLANKET.
OLD SECESH. "While I cover my Neck, I expose my Feet, and if I cover my Feet, I expose my Neck. Ugh!"

The *Harper's Weekly* cartoon of December 14, 1861, lampooned
Confederate efforts to cover Virginia and Savannah and Charleston
at the same time. (Courtesy of the Georgia Historical Society.)

edition said. "But it is not in the power of the Yankee nation to control the
currents of our rivers, nor the tides of the ocean."[6]

The Confederates firmly believed that Great Britain, France, or some
other European power might intervene on the side of the South. In this
vein, the newspaper continued its diatribe: "It remains to be seen how this
dastardly act of vandalism will be received by the nations of Europe. . . . Not
only would they be debarred from commercial intercourse with the southern
half of this continent, but their ships and the lives of their citizens would
be imperilled."[7]

In spite of the typically busy holiday season, some of Savannah's
downtown stores were closing by December, merchants already feeling the
sting of the enemy off the coast. The situation only worsened. Savannah's
blockade running was slowed to a trickle for the rest of the war on account
of the efficiency of Du Pont and Rear Admiral John A. Dahlgren, who
replaced him in July 1863.

Henry Rootes Jackson returned to Savannah during the winter. After his
adventure in Fort Pulaski's capture, he was appointed to a Confederate

judgeship and, when the war began, was named a brigadier general in the provisional Confederate army. Jackson fought under Lee in western Virginia, but resigned his Confederate commission on December 2, 1861, to accept a major generalship in command of Georgia state troops.

The post brought Jackson back to Savannah, where he boasted that if the city was attacked its defense would be as "famous as that of the success at New Orleans under the veritable Old Hicory[sic]." He was referring to General Andrew "Old Hickory" Jackson and the American victory over the British during the War of 1812.

Henry Wayne, Georgia's adjutant general, was appointed a brigadier in the Confederate army in December, but resigned his commission within weeks. By January he was back in Savannah in his previous post, a role he held until the war's end.

Early December also found Savannah responding to a plea from its own Georgia Hussars, who were among Confederate forces concentrated near Manassas, Virginia.

Like the other Rebels, the Hussars were suffering from the raw and rainy Virginia winter and were asking for "hospital stores and all kinds of comforts." The city quickly responded with a northbound shipment of supplies and food, including hams, smoked beef, hard biscuits, pickles, salmon, and preserves.

Winter also hit hard at the gray defenders of Savannah. "Our bivouac night before last was the first real taste of soldier's life," Charles Jones said in a Christmas Day letter to his parents. "Our caps were all frosted in the morning, and the canteens of the men sleeping around the fires had ice in them. It was quite cold, but clear, bracing; and no evil effects have been experienced by either men or horses."[8]

From Camp Jasper near Savannah, homesick Sergeant William Mosely of the Tenth Georgia Infantry Battalion sat down on Christmas Eve to finish a letter to his mother in Bibb County. He had just received a holiday cake she had sent to him: "Being as Christmas is close at hand the captain says he is going to give us all an egg nog so cake and egg nog will go pretty well together but it will not be as much of a Christmas here with both as it would be with egg nog by its self made of the eggs that Georgia [his 7-year-old sister] is saving for me."

Savannah's 1861 had been a miasma of celebration, grief, triumph, and tragedy. The enemy was a few miles downstream, his troops camped on Georgia soil, and his warships controlling the sea-lanes. The apparent lethargy of these Yankees, however, fueled defiance among the Southerners.

On December 30 the *Daily Morning News* fired a year-ending verbal volley at the Union forces menacing Savannah: "Our invaders seem to be so well satisfied with their first and only success during the war, the capture of the Port Royal sand batteries, and so well pleased with their settlement of the Carolina Islands that they are content to enjoy their honors in inglorious ease rather than venture upon new and more doubtful conquests. ... But as we have intimated, the time is close at hand when [the] issue must be tried."[9]

VI

"We Shall Soon Have Some Hard Fighting"—1862

The year 1862 dawned with Union forces toughening their foothold on Tybee Island to threaten Fort Pulaski. It also found Savannah's women praying or grieving over their sons, sweethearts, and husbands fighting and dying on faraway battlefields.

By early January General Lee was convinced that the Federals were planning some type of offensive in the Savannah sector. To his alarm a January 6 inspection of Pulaski and subsequent visits showed him that the fort was not ready to repel an assault or siege. He immediately stepped up efforts to provision and prepare the garrison for battle and transferred his headquarters to Savannah by February 3. Colonel Olmstead was now in command of the Pulaski garrison.

Lee, like most military experts, greatly underestimated the effect of the new rifled cannon, which the Yankees would use to decimate Pulaski. Lee visited the fort several times during this period, eyeing the enemy's progress on Tybee. Sizing up what was known of the Union positions, Lee told Olmstead, "They will make it pretty hot for you with shells but they cannot breach your walls at that distance."[1]

Olmstead admired Lee, but was forever haunted by the general's assessment on this occasion. "I have remembered his words particularly because of subsequent events which proved how mistaken they were."[2]

The consensus on both sides was that Pulaski could not be battered into submission by artillery. The Confederates were more fearful that light-draft Union gunboats would slip past the fort through the coastal rivers or creeks and bombard Savannah. One lady wrote Governor Brown with the bizarre idea of dumping 500 to 1,000 barrels of turpentine into the river and setting it afire to destroy the Federal fleet.

The Rebels' fears were almost realized in late January. By small boat Union Lieutenant James H. Wilson, chief topographical engineer, explored the inland waterways behind Pulaski.

Wilson found Wall's Cut, a man-made creek, which, after Confederate obstructions were removed, gave the Federals access to the river between Pulaski and Savannah. Wilson's efforts allowed the Yankees to mount batteries on several islands in the river and helped close off the fort's communications with the city. Even more important, the water channels through Wall's Cut and Mud Creek gave the navy a route for its gunboats to reach Savannah without testing Pulaski.

Lee knew of Union activity around Wall's Cut and rercognized the threat: "If the enemy succeed in removing the obstacles in Wall's Cut and Wilmington Narrows, there is nothing to prevent their reaching the Savannah River, and we have nothing afloat that can attend against them," he wrote on January 29.

At this time the Rebels still were building and strengthening their river batteries, and General Sherman conceivably could have moved troops upriver to these waterways to assault the city. Indeed by January, Sherman had devised a plan for a joint army-navy offensive against Savannah. But navy officials would not go along with the plan, stating that gunboats might be cut off in the river if tide conditions were unfavorable.

Still, Sherman came under criticism from the enemy as well as his own men. "Gen. Sherman seems to be pre-eminently endowed with one attribute at least of generalship—caution," the *Daily Morning News* said on January 10. A Union navy officer wrote in December that "If the general commanding were a man of vigor and genius, we would be in the city of Savannah in a fortnight."[3]

The criticism stung the Union commander, who had compiled an admirable service record prior to the war. Unrelated to the "other" Sherman who visited Savannah in 1864, Thomas Sherman was a Rhode Islander who had fought in the Seminole wars, the Mexican War, and on the frontier. As a youth of eighteen, he had walked to Washington from his hometown of Newport to personally accept a West Point appointment from President Andrew Jackson.

A brigade of state troops under Major General W. H. T. Walker was ordered to Savannah by General Jackson in early January, and Walker was

The Forsyth Park fountain was a popular gathering spot for
soldiers and civilians during the war.

appointed commandant of the city. Walker was a forty-five-year-old
Augusta native who had been a partner in a Savannah lumber and wood
pulping company before the war. An 1837 graduate of West Point, he had
been severely wounded in the Seminole and Mexican wars. One of his chief
concerns in cooperating with Lawton and Jackson was maintaining
discipline among the approximately 2,500 Georgia State Troops posted in
and around Savannah. Basically, this meant keeping the boys away from the
saloons and brothels. Both Walker and Jackson issued orders to check
disorderly conduct among soldiers. Walker's February 10 mandate minced
no words in dealing with Savannah's barkeepers: "Notice. It is hereby
ordered that any individual who shall sell, or furnish in any manner
whatever, liquors of any kind to any soldier within the limits of this city and
suburbs, will have his shop or store or barroom immediately closed, and his
liquors emptied into the street."

The orders apparently worked. A correspondent for the *Charleston Tri-
Weekly Mercury* reported that Savannahians "assured me they had never in
peace known their city kept in such perfect order and quiet. Such is the
spirit of one man," he wrote of Walker.

Some of Walker's boys were apparently armed with "Joe Brown Pikes,"
featuring an eighteen-inch, double-edged blade attached to a six-foot-long

staff. Governor Brown had authorized the production of these primitive weapons. Brown wrote that "one brave company was raised" and were "the favorites of the gallant Walker."

"I have been here twelve days, and it seems that I have been away from home nearly twelve weeks," Rebel J. H. Graham wrote to his wife on January 16. "You have no idea how much I want to see you and the children, to be at home once more.... The camp is a peculiar place [with] all sorts of men and dispositions of men. Now, while I write, there is a variety of amusements in hearing, one party playing at leap frog and singing spiritual songs, some dancing, some cursing, some reading the Bible, some drinking whiskey and all sorts and more evil than good."

Expecting the Yankees to attack Pulaski at any time, the Rebels on January 28 sent two transports downriver from Savannah with four months' provisions and ammunition for the garrison. The supply vessels were escorted by three of Tattnall's armed steamers. Two of the escorts, the *Savannah* and the *Resolute*, turned back on account of long-range shelling from Union gunboats. But the CSS *Sampson*, skippered by Lieutenant J. S. Kennard, refused to yield and shepherded the supply ships safely to the fort with no damage incurred.

The relief force came under fire again on the return trip to Savannah. The blue gunners were more accurate this time, hitting the *Sampson* four times. Two of the shells went completely through her. Sustaining no casualties, Kennard's little steamer limped back to the city and a hero's welcome.

"A truer, nobler, braver man does not breathe," Lieutenant Jones wrote of Tattnall in praising the expedition. "I love him almost as a father.... He stands in strange contrast with some others, high in military preferment, whose names it becomes me not to mention."[4]

By February 10, Union engineers had begun construction of a six-gun battery at Venus Point on Jones Island between Pulaski and Savannah. Within days Battery Vulcan, and Battery Hamilton, a six-gun emplacement on Bird Island, also between the city and the fort, were ready for action.

In addition, two U.S. infantry companies and three guns were placed aboard a hulk in Lazaretto Creek, an inland water route south of the fort, to try to cut off Rebel communications and supplies sent from the area of Wassaw Sound.

Lee, Lawton, and Tattnall briefly discussed an operation to retake Jones Island. The plan was quickly shelved because of the great risks involved.

General Walker proposed to send his Georgia brigade downriver, capture the Union batteries, and then attack Yankee gunboats venturing into the river narrows. His bold idea never came to fruition.

The Venus Point battery almost ambushed the steamer *Ida*, trying to reach the fort with some supplies on the morning of February 13. Chuffing down the river from Savannah, the *Ida* was surprised when enemy artillery blasted at her from Jones Island. Undaunted, Circoply's steamer reached Pulaski and was able to return to Savannah without being hit.

In firing nine shots at the *Ida*, all but one of the Venus Point guns recoiled off their platforms. The Yanks immediately doubled the size of the wooden supports.

Union troops mired on boggy Jones and Bird islands found themselves coping with few rations and the local wildlife. Amid their hardships, the boom of their guns disturbed the slumber of massive alligators basking in mud beds.

"We discovered the nose of one of these carnivorous reptiles near the cook's kettle," wrote Lieutenant Alonzo Williams of the Third Rhode Island Heavy Artillery. The New Englanders lassoed and subdued the gator, which turned out to be some ten feet long. "The boys have not forgotten what tender steaks he made, as this kind of meat was at a premium for a few days."[5]

Lee realized the danger of Pulaski being cut off from supplies and dispatches from the outside world. He tried to reassure Olmstead on February 18: "As far as possible, your safety will be anxiously cared for, and for the present your communication with the city will have to be by light boats over the marsh."[6]

Realistically, Lee also knew that a concentrated Federal offensive anywhere along his coastline could be disastrous and warned his superiors that Savannah and Brunswick might have to be abandoned. Governor Brown trusted Lee's judgment, but wrote that he should "leave [Savannah] in smoking ruins when driven from it." Brunswick was eventually evacuated by the Confederates to add troops to the Savannah defenses.

General Walker at Savannah was certainly in agreement with Brown, as suggested by a report in the March 11 edition of the *Charleston Tri-Weekly Mercury*. Asked about the possibility of surrender, Walker responded that he would "hang any man who makes such a proposition as soon as the rope can be adjusted around his neck." The dispatch also said Walker "openly announces his decision to burn the city rather than it shall fall into the enemy's hands."

At Camp Claghorne on the Isle of Hope, soldiers of the Chatham Artillery drilled and kept an eye on enemy troops on the nearby islands. Lieutenant Jones received a February 21 letter from his mother. Mrs. Jones had started a collection of war relics and treasured an autograph of Josiah Tattnall that her son had obtained for her. The letter described a more grisly souvenir given to her by her brother, a Presbyterian minister who explored the bloody fields at Manassas the day after the July battle. The minister had sent her a "portion of the nostril of [Colonel] Bartow's horse. It looks almost like a flake of isinglass," she wrote.

The Rebels at Pulaski traded shots with enemy vessels and professed confidence in their defenses despite the Union bustle around them.

"I think we shall soon have some hard fighting—it will be exclusively with cannon," Lieutenant Theodorick W. Montfort of the Macon County Wise Guards wrote to his wife when he joined the garrison on February 12. "I have no fear as to the result."[7]

By early spring the fort mounted almost fifty guns and had a garrison of about 385 men protected by Pulaski's 7½–foot thick brick walls.

The armament included eight- and ten-inch Columbiads, twenty thirty-two-pounder cannon, and two Blakely rifled guns. Some twenty of these pieces bore on Tybee.

Montfort, a peacetime lawyer in Oglethorpe, Georgia, could not ignore the extent of the enemy buildup around Pulaski, including the blockade: "You can see from the ramparts some 60 or 70 Yankee vessels. You can see their tents & hear their drums from an Island over on the SC side. We are almost surrounded by them."[8]

Even as Montfort was penning his letter, sweating bluecoats on Tybee Island were emplacing heavy guns among eleven batteries to pulverize the "Secesh" bastion. Most of the work was done at night so that the Rebels would not be able to pinpoint the Union positions.

The Yankees of engineer Captain Quincy A. Gillmore worked like army ants to point as many rifled guns, mortars, and other artillery as possible at Pulaski's red-brick walls.

Gillmore's men were emplacing a total of thirty-six rifled cannon, mortars, and other heavy guns to pound Pulaski into submission. Gillmore, a thirty-seven-year-old Ohioan who had been the chief engineer in the Port Royal campaign, was a firm proponent of the rifled guns even though they had never been tested against a masonry fort such as Pulaski.

Most military experts agreed, however, that heavy artillery was ineffective

Colonel Charles Olmstead, commander of Fort Pulaski's Confederate garrison in 1862. (Courtesy of the Georgia Historical Society.)

against such forts at more than 800 yards. The closest Union guns on Tybee were more than twice that distance from the fort. Indeed, General Joseph G. Totten, the Union Army's chief engineer, had stated that "the work could not be reduced in a month's firing with any number of guns of manageable calibers."

Sherman wrote that until the rifled cannon were fully tested, "All that can be done with guns is to shake the walls in a random manner."[9]

Gillmore, however, had examined Pulaski in late November 1861 to determine the "best method of reducing the fort." His recommendation went against the Union brass: "I deemed the reduction of the work practicable with batteries of mortars and rifled guns."[10]

Sherman's artillery chief, Captain John Hamilton, shared Gillmore's faith in the heavy guns. He predicted that Pulaski "would be reduced in three days from the time fire was opened."

On March 2 Lee wrote to one of his daughters about the condition of the coastal defenses: "I have been doing all I can with our small means and slow workmen to defend the cities and coast here. Against ordinary numbers we are pretty strong, but against the hosts our enemies seem able to bring everywhere, there is no calculating. But if our men will stand to their work, we shall give them trouble and damage them yet."[11]

Felix Gregory De Fontaine, the *Charleston Daily Courier* war correspondent better known to his readers as "Personne," was more optimistic in his assessment of Savannah's defenses: "The people of Savannah ... are now

Union Captain Quincy A. Gillmore oversaw the Federal bombardment of Fort Pulaski in April 1862. (Courtesy of the Georgia Historical Society.)

satisfied of their ability to hold the city against any odds," he wrote on March 1. "Yet the preparations for defence still continue. Fortifications against approaches by land are nearly, if not quite complete, and those protecting the water front are deemed equally efficient to resist an attack."[12]

William Head of the Thirty-first Georgia also believed Savannah was too strong to be taken: "Every thing in this country continues without any material change," he wrote to his wife in Milner, Georgia, on March 1. "The enemy stays at a safe distance, and our troops are in fine spirits. We are ready for them whenever they choose to land. Savannah is safe, I confidently believe."

Another Georgian, John Wood, was busy building breastworks outside Savannah during this time and was critical of the upper-class chivalry in the Rebel ranks: "You just ought to see the Savannah militia at work, especially these wealthy speculators who would [have] been a commissioned officer but could not be persuaded to be a private with their broadcloth coats, silk cravats, fine starched linen shirts, calf-skin boots on, half knee deep in mud and water, spade in hand, throwing sand and mud like a piney woods salamander, much to the amusement of our Newton [County] boys."

Lee was concentrating on the defense of Fort Pulaski on March 3 when he suddenly received orders to report to President Davis in Richmond. "If circumstances will, in your judgment, warrant your leaving, I wish to see you here with the least delay," Davis wrote.

Immediately heeding the call, Lee left Savannah by train that night after

Philadelphia-born Confederate Major General John C. Pemberton replaced Robert E. Lee as department commander in March 1862. (Courtesy of the Georgia Historical Society.)

conferring with General Lawton and leaving detailed instructions about Savannah's defenses.

"His loss will be severely felt by us," Lieutenant Jones wrote after reading of Lee's reassignment in the papers.

Lee would not see Savannah again during wartime, but the popular history of the Confederacy's premier soldier was about to begin. His defensive handiwork had paid off in making Savannah a bristling fortress.

"I doubt much if there is a stronger place in the Southern Confederacy," De Fontaine wrote from Savannah on March 14. "Nature has surrounded it with impassable marshes, and art has fortified every position that commands an approach."[13]

Also transferred about the time of Lee's departure was Captain Tattnall, who was sent to Norfolk, Virginia, to take charge of Confederate naval forces in the James River. This squadron included the famous ironclad CSS *Virginia*, which had fought its historic sea battle with the USS *Monitor* off Hampton Roads on March 9.

Tattnall made the *Virginia* his flagship less than two weeks later. He would be the author of her destruction before he returned to Savannah.

On March 14 Lee was replaced in the coastal command by Major General John C. Pemberton, a Pennsylvanian who had cast his lot with the Confederacy. Like Lee, Pemberton focused on strengthening Savannah and Charleston, where he established his headquarters. Also like the Virginian, Pemberton shared the belief in Pulaski's impregnability.

Pemberton was born in Philadelphia in August 1814. His childhood playmates included George B. McClellan and George G. Meade, both of whom would later command the Union Army of the Potomac. His allegiance to the South stemmed, in large part, from his 1848 marriage to Martha Thompson of Norfolk, Virginia, and to the strong friendships he developed with Southern cadets at the U.S. Military Academy. Pemberton graduated from West Point in 1837 with classmates Braxton Bragg and Jubal Early. He earned two brevet promotions during the Mexican War and resigned from the U.S. Army in April 1861 to join the Confederate cause.

March also saw the Rebels abandon their works on Skidaway and Green islands south of Pulaski on account of the strength and proximity of enemy forces. A landing party of bluecoats waded ashore and explored the empty fortifications. After raising a U.S. flag, they returned to their boats.

Southern troops continued to flood into Savannah. Strolling through the bivouacs, De Fontaine vividly described the Confederate soldier at Savannah in spring 1862: "In [Forsyth] Park, if a lady has an escort, it wears a uniform, while in the surroundings of the City where are encamped the various brigades you see the fine essence of soldierly esprit de corps. These regiments are just such as one might expect to find in Georgia—strong in numbers, and made up of all degrees of humanity from the wealthiest to the poorest and from the white haired veteran to the boy of thirteen. Their garments, it is true, represent every hue that the scriptural Joseph ever dreamed of in contemplating his own historic coat; some wear patched bed quilts that look like dilapidated rag carpets; some have hats without vizors; some red shirts, some white; (a few almost none at all); some wear coats, some don't."[14]

Based on De Fontaine's accounts, not all Savannahians were caught up in the patriotic fervor to don a uniform. "Personne" described a "draft" of recruits held in Forsyth Park:

"The Colonel now takes his place in the centre, and from the back of a magnificent horse in a few well timed remarks calls for volunteers. He said it was a shame that a Georgian should submit to be drafted, and dishonorable to a citizen of Savannah to be forced into the service of his country. He appealed to their patriotism, their pluck, and their-self. He told them of good clothes, good living and fifty dollars bounty, and on the strength of these eloquent considerations invited everybody to walk three paces in front. Nobody did it. An ugly pause ensued worse than the dead silence between the ticking of a conversation. The Colonel thought he might not have been heard or understood, and repeated his catalogue of persuasions. At this point, one of the sides of the square opened and in marched a company of about forty stalwart Irishmen, whom their Captain, in a loud and excited tone, announced as 'The Mitchell Guards—we volunteer, Colonel, in a body.' The Colonel was delighted. He proposed 'three cheers for the Mitchell Guards,' and the crowd indulged not inordinately in the pulmonary exercise. The requisite number did not seem to be forthcoming, however, and the Colonel made another little speech, winding up with an invitation to the black drummer and fifer to perambulate the quadrangle and play Dixie. Which they did, but they came as they went—solitary and alone, not the ghost of a volunteer being any where visible in the Ethiopian wake.

"As a dernier ressort, the Colonel directed all who had excuses to advance to the centre and submit them for examination. And then, for the first and only time during the occasion, there appeared to be the most wonderful unanimity of sentiment. . . . Every hand held its magical bit of paper, from a stable or foundry to the daintily gloved extremity of the dry goods clerk, just from his counter. Young and old, rich and poor, neat and nasty, Americans, Englishmen, Irishmen, Germans, Frenchmen, Italians, Israelites and Gentiles—all were to make up the motley mass. What a pretty lot of sick and disabled individuals there were to be sure! Swelled arms, limping legs, spine diseases, bad eyes, corns, toothaches, constitutional debility in the bread basket, eruptive diseases, deafness, rheumatism, not well generally—these and a thousand other complaints were represented as variously and heterogeneously as by any procession of pilgrims that ever visited the Holy Land."[15]

Any notion that Fort Pulaski's gunners were untrained was dispelled one afternoon when two soldiers of the Forty-sixth New York strolled down to a sand point to taunt the Confederates. According to Gillmore, the fort replied with a shot from a Blakely gun that cut one of the men in half. "The other retreated in disorder and could not be induced to return and pay the last offices to his ill-starred comrade till after dark," Gillmore wrote.

Olmstead himself aimed the gun. Seeing the enemy soldiers on the beach, he decided to get the range for one of his thirty-two-pounders by using them as markers. Olmstead recalled that he had "not the slightest thought that there would be anything more than a scare for the men. . . . It was an extraordinary shot."

Watching the Yankees close in from all sides, Montfort and his comrades soon realized they were hemmed in, with only occasional messengers slipping back and forth from the fort to Savannah. The lieutenant was in command of three big guns, his "pets." He called his sixty-four-pounder "Addie Elizabeth" after his mother, the fifty-three-pounder "Sarah" for Mrs. Samuel Hall, a Macon County neighbor. The thirty-two-pounder he named "Louisa" after his wife. Montfort obviously wanted to honor the ladies. Their reactions are not recorded.

Montfort's confidence in Pulaski's invincibility and the hope for reinforcements waned as the fort became more and more isolated. "I look more to Providence, sand flies, musquitoes [*sic*] & sickness relieving us than to any one else," he wrote on March 31. "If they don't do it, I think we will eventually perish out, compelled to surrender & land in some Yankee prison."[16]

"It seems that all [the garrison] is content in regard to us being cut off here," another Pulaski Confederate, Ricey Brooks, wrote to his wife on March 21. "I suppose in this time that the Yankees are as well fixed in their batteries as they can be, while our people, I suppose, are just living 'round Savannah, drinking whiskey and cursing the Yankees—like that would whip the river out. It is provoking!"

Brooks scoffed at any idea that Tattnall's squadron could deal with the Federal navy: "There was also a dispatch sent down requesting us not to give up the fort, that they would be down with the mosquito fleet in a few days. They [the Yankees] can bust that fleet into a thousand pieces at one time, so you see that it is no fleet at all. The Yankees have got some vessels that look almost as large as one side of this fort."

In late March, Major General David Hunter succeeded General Sherman in command of the Department of the South. He continued the Union concentration on Tybee. Hunter was an uncle by marriage of Savannah's Eleanor Kinzie Gordon, a native Chicagoan who was an ardent Rebel and whose husband was a Confederate officer.

A frustrated Ricey Brooks wrote to his wife about the industrious Yankees across the channel from Fort Pulaski: "They are at work while we sleep. I was out on guard duty and could hear them curse the Confederacy. They worked all the night, sleep in the day in order to keep us from firing on them. They are as cunning as a fox. It seems that we are defeated in all the fights that we undertake. We are becoming no match [and] inclined to give out."

Union Major General David Hunter commanded the U.S. Department of the South at the time of the Fort Pulaski bombardment.

The garrison had its daily routine despite the proximity of the enemy. "All the amusement we have is catching fish without a hook," Brooks said in a letter to his wife. "We can catch them as fast as we can drop our line over. . . . And on Sunday [we] have preaching. We also have Bible class of about two hundred. Saturday we have to scour the floors of the casemates. We also wash our clothes on that day. My health is better than it has ever been . . . I weigh about 150 pounds. If I continue to grow I will be as lazy as cousin Edward Brooks."

Enemy scouting parties clashed on Whitemarsh and Wilmington islands on March 30–31. General Lawton reported that elements of the Thirteenth Georgia under Captain J. T. Crawford skirmished with a Union force on both nights. Casualties were light on both sides, but the Rebels managed to take eighteen prisoners, a barge, and a six-pounder cannon.[17]

A patrol from the Forty-eighth New York was exploring Elba Island in the Savannah River about the same time, when they returned to camp to find a note written by unwelcome gray visitors: "The Glynn Guards have been in gunshot of you, you damned scoundrels, and examined your quarters. We invite you ashore; we have no navy."

VII

"Pulaski Fallen!"

By April 9 the Union batteries on Tybee were primed for action at ranges from 1,650 to 3,400 yards from Pulaski. Three years hence, the Union would be celebrating Lee's surrender at Appomattox, but on this spring day the blue-jacketed gunners were aching to test their aim. The batteries were named after Union heroes—Lincoln, Grant, Stanton, Lyon, Burnside, Sherman, McClellan, Scott, Halleck, Sigel, and, most ironically, Totten.

Construction of these batteries had been quite an achievement in itself. Getting the giant cannon from ships anchored off the east end of Tybee to the battery locations, a distance of more than two miles, was a monumental struggle through the mud marshes, miring sand, and saw grass. About 250 men, using ropes, carts, and timber skids, were needed to move one of the 17,000-pound mortars into position. Often the carts carrying the guns sank into the mud, forcing the soldiers to unload the mortar, roll it over planks to solid ground, and then reload it after the cart was freed.

Lieutenant Horace Porter was in charge of getting supplies and ordnance to the batteries, which were located on the northwest side of the island. Most of the work was done at night, the men disturbing the natural foliage as little as possible and camouflaging the positions with tree limbs and bushes. Swarms of gnats, mosquitoes, and sand flies were the constant foe of men on both sides.

"Up to the second week in March we could not see that the enemy on Tybee was making any demonstration towards us, but at that time I began noticing certain changes in the sand hills," Olmstead wrote a few months

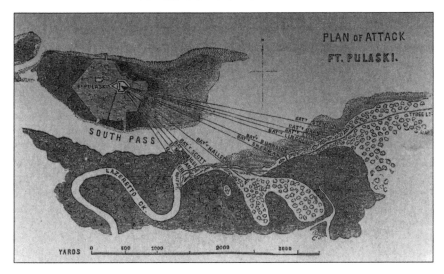

Plan of attack showing the position of Union batteries concentrated against Fort Pulaski. (Courtesy of the Georgia Historical Society.)

after the battle. "My pickets reported . . . nightly the noise of wagons and workmen. . . . I did not fire in the direction of noise at night for various reasons . . . our supply of powder . . . was far from being sufficient for the prolonged siege I thought before us."[1]

Gillmore's guns consisted of twelve heavy thirteen-inch mortars, six ten-inch Columbiads, five thirty-pounder Parrott rifles, four eight-inch Columbiads, four ten-inch siege mortars, and five James rifles. A shortage of fuse plugs for the ten-inch mortars resulted in soldiers, primarily from the Seventh Connecticut, being put to work whittling wooden fuse plugs.

On the afternoon of April 9 general orders were issued with each battery being instructed on the various points of attack, rate of fire, charges, and elevation. In spite of the Federal efforts to hide their positions, the Rebels sensed that they were about to be attacked.

In the fort Montfort watched with apprehension and sadness as soldiers spread sand around Pulaski's guns. Many also penned their wills and farewell letters. The garrison surgeon prepared for the expected assault in his own unnerving way.

"To see so many healthy men preparing for the worst by disposing of their property by Will, to see the surgeon sharping [sic] his instruments & whetting his saw to take off when necessary those members of our body that God has given us for our indespensable use, to see men engaged in carding up & preparing lint to stop the flow of human blood from cruel & inhuman wounds is awful to contemplate," Montfort wrote.[2]

"Yet there is still another preparation for battle, still more sickning [*sic*] ... the floor is covered around each gun with sand, not for health or cleanliness but to drink up human blood as it flows from the veins and hearts of noble men."[3]

Just before sunrise on April 10, Union Lieutenant James Wilson was rowed to the fort under a flag of truce. Wilson carried with him a surrender summons from General Hunter. Captain F. W. Sims of the garrison brought the note to Olmstead after meeting Wilson at the south wharf.

Olmstead did not hesitate in refusing the demand. His reply was brief: "I have to acknowledge receipt of your communication of this date demanding the unconditional surrender of Fort Pulaski. In reply I can only say that I am here to defend not to surrender it."

Excitement and anxiety mounted on both sides as Wilson returned to his lines with Olmstead's answer.

About 8:15 A.M. a Union mortar in Battery Halleck opened the cannonade, and by 9:30 A.M. all of the Union batteries had joined in the bombardment. Some accounts state that a New England cannoneer wrote "A nutmeg from Connecticut; can you furnish a grater?" on the first round fired.

The mortar crews were instructed to fire at fifteen-minute intervals with the other gunners firing two to three times faster, Gillmore recalled. The Rebel artillerymen commenced a vigorous return fire but were generally off target due to the careful concealment of the Union guns.

General Pemberton watched the battle from afar. At one point during the bombardment he remarked that Pulaski's defenders were wasting their shells in replying to the enemy fire. After all, wasn't the fort impregnable? Pemberton was so confident that he returned to his headquarters in Charleston that afternoon.

By 1 P.M., however, the work of the rifled guns had taken a toll on the fort's wall, particularly at the southeast angle.

Through field glasses Gillmore saw that "unless our guns should suffer seriously from the enemy's fire, a breach would be effected ... it could be seen that the rifled projectiles were surely eating their way into the scarp of the pan-coupé and adjacent south-east face."[4]

The shelling lasted for some nine hours before Gillmore ceased firing for the evening. Some Union guns, however, boomed through the night to disrupt Southern efforts to shore the damaged walls. Five Rebel cannon were silenced in the day's combat, Gillmore reported.

A Confederate captain on nearby Skidaway Island described the bombardment: "We were six miles off, but we could distinctly see the heavy columns of white smoke shooting up from the mortars on Tybee, and then see the immense shells bursting over the Fort. The enemy fired four and five times every minute, while the Fort replied slowly and coolly.... At night the sight was grand. The tongue of flame was seen to leap from the mortars."[5]

At Pulaski, weary Southerners not on watch sought the relative safety of the northwest corner casemates, but most got little rest due to the continued Yankee fire.

"I went to bed ... in my clothes but could not sleep, the excitement of the day, the heavy responsiblity resting upon me, and the many grave doubts I felt as to the ultimate result all combined to banish sleep from my eyelids," Olmstead later wrote.

The Union command briefly considered an amphibious assault, but the plan was quickly abandoned because no boats for such an operation were available. The Yankee mortars had been inaccurate and ineffective, but the obvious damage to the fort's walls inspired confidence in the Federal camps.

Shortly after sunrise on April 11, the blue cannoneers opened again, "puffs of yellow dust marking the effect of shot and shell," Gillmore wrote. At some point after the bombardment was renewed, Gillmore ordered preparations for an infantry attack despite his lack of boats. "It was plain that a few hours' work of this kind would clear away the scarp wall to a greater width than the small garrison could defend against assault," he recalled.[6]

A Union shell shattered Pulaski's flag staff. In moments Lieutenant Christopher Hussey of the Montgomery Guards and Private John Latham of the Washington Volunteers darted across the exposed parapet, disentangled the downed banner, and hoisted it on a temporary staff above a gun carriage on the northeast angle.

A Yankee corporal wrote that the Rebels hoisted the flag "under a perfect shower of shot and shell."

By noon the two casemates in the southeast face had been destroyed and Yankee rounds were roaring through the jagged brick hole, exploding dangerously close to the fort's magazine located in the northwest angle.

Part of the magazine wall also was blown away, exposing some of the 40,000 pounds of black powder stored there.

Olmstead later described the crisis to his wife: "The outer wall of two

Inside the breached casemate at Fort Pulaski

casements [*sic*] was entirely down while those terrible rifle projectiles had free access to the brick traverse protecting our magazine."[7]

Throughout the day thunderclaps of cannon rattled windows in Savannah. The acrid stench of black powder wafted upriver, mingling with the aroma of freshly bloomed azaleas and dogwood in the city's squares and parks. Like the military, Savannahians were confident that the fort could not be captured, but everyone was nervous.

Among those listening to the distant gunfire was the Georgia adjutant-general, Henry Wayne. An officer in the regular army before the war, Wayne could distinguish the sound of guns fired in opposite directions. He noted that the blasts of cannon aimed toward Pulaski were steadier and more numerous than those guns facing the Yankees, meaning the enemy was apparently winning the battle. Wayne's observations to this effect almost resulted in his being attacked by a band of civilians before the fate of the fort was known.

With the threat of an enemy shell ripping into the magazine at any moment and sparking an explosion that would likely kill most of his men, Olmstead in the early afternoon called a conference of his officers in one of the casemates. After a discussion about the situation, the officers voted unanimously to surrender "in order to save the garrison from utter destruction by an explosion, which was momentarily threatened," the April 12 *Savannah Republican* said.[8]

Extent of Union bombardment is still evident today.

About 2 P.M., the Confederates showed a white flag and Olmstead ordered a cease fire.

"Among the last guns fired were those on the parapet, and the men stood there exposed to a storm of iron hail to the last," the *Republican* noted.

"The colors, fluttering for a few minutes at half-mast, came slowly down," Gillmore said of the capitulation. In a whale boat, Gillmore and a number of other officers started across the channel to receive the surrender, but heavy seas delayed their progress.

Lieutenant Porter later wrote that "the effort [of the crossing] became rather ludicrous, and it looked for a time as if even the patience of a garrison waiting to surrender might become exhausted, and they be tempted to open fire again on their dilatory captors."

A *New York Times* correspondent wrote that Olmstead met Gillmore's party when they finally docked and asked that all except Gillmore remain outside the fort until surrender terms were negotiated.

The rival commanders talked for about an hour in Olmstead's quarters and finalized the agreement. Olmstead then gave Gillmore a tour of the fort as Yankees mingled with the captured Rebels.

"The best of feeling prevailed," Gillmore recalled of the fraternization.

"Many a jest and repartee passed between them." Porter encountered a Confederate officer who inquired about a civilian who came ashore with the Union entourage. The civilian was George W. Smalley, war correspondent for the *New York Tribune*, run by fire-eating abolitionist editor Horace Greeley. Porter wrote that when the Rebel learned of Smalley's identity, he said, "Well I could have stood the surrender, but this humiliation is too much!"[9]

Gillmore had departed by the time officers representing General Hunter arrived late in the afternoon. Hunter had written the original surrender note, but was not present during the battle. He was represented by his assistant adjutant-general, Major Charles G. Halpine, whom Olmstead escorted on another tour of the fort and introduced to his staff.

The surrender proceedings were held in Olmstead's quarters and described by the *Times* reporter: "The ceremony was performed in the colonel's headquarters, all standing. It was just at dark and the candles gave only a half-light."

In order of rank the garrison officers laid their swords on a table and nearly everyone made some statement, the reporter noted.

Addressing Halpine and his escort, Olmstead said, "I yield my sword, but I trust I have not disgraced it."[10]

Halpine told the Southerners that it was a painful duty "to receive the swords of men who had shown by their bravery that they deserved to wear them," the *Times* writer stated.

When the ceremony was over, Olmstead turned to speak to his officers and the Union men withdrew. Moments later the U.S. flag was hoisted on the ramparts.

Gillmore reported that sixteen of the twenty Rebel guns bearing on Tybee were silenced by his fire, whereas none of the Federal batteries sustained notable damage.

Fort Pulaski's defenders lost one man killed and twelve wounded. The only Union casualty was a private in the Third Rhode Island Artillery who was fatally wounded when a shell exploded in an embrasure of one of the batteries.

The Union artillery had been supplied ammunition for a week of siege operations but expended only about one-fifth of its shells. Gillmore reported that his men fired 5,275 rounds during the two-day cannonade.

He also recognized the significance of the bombardment: "The effect of our fire upon the walls of the fort is interesting, as the first example, in actual warfare, of the breaching power of rifled ordnance at long range."[11]

Hunter later noted that the performance of the rifled guns against Pulaski was a revolution in warfare that was just as significant as the sea battle between the USS *Monitor* and the CSS *Virginia*, the first clash of naval ironclads.

"The result of this bombardment must cause, I am convinced, a change in the construction of fortifications as radical as that foreshadowed in naval architecture by the conflict between the *Monitor* and *Merrimac* [*Virginia*]. No works of stone or brick can resist the impact of rifled artillery of heavy caliber," Hunter wrote.

In the surrender discussion with Olmstead, Gillmore had agreed that the Rebel sick and wounded would be allowed to enter the Confederate lines. Hunter, however, refused to ratify this agreement, and these men were sent to prisons in New York harbor with the rest of the garrison.

Olmstead disconsolately sat down to write a letter to his wife that evening. "I address you under circumstances of the most painful nature. Fort Pulaski has fallen and the whole garrison are prisoners.... Oh, my dear Wife, how can I describe to you the bitterness of that moment! It seemed as if my heart would break. I cannot write now all the details of our surrender, it pains me too much to think of them now.... Teach our little one all the pretty little ways that will endear her to my heart when I see her, and let us both pray God that the time may not be far distant when we may be again united.... Guns, such as have never before been brought to bear against any fortification, have overpowered me. But I trust to history to keep my name untarnished."

Among the Rebel prisoners was Father Peter Whelan, a Catholic priest whose compassion was colored neither blue nor gray. Born in County Wexford, Ireland, in 1802, Whelan came to America and was ordained as a priest in Charleston, South Carolina, in November 1830. He served in several North Carolina communities before becoming pastor of a Catholic church in Locust Grove, Georgia, in 1837. Located on the stage road between Washington and Sparta, Locust Grove was the first Catholic community in the state. In 1854 Whelan was summoned to the Savannah diocese, where he was stationed for the rest of his life.

After Georgia troops took Pulaski, Whelan volunteered to go there and serve the needs of the garrison's Catholic soldiers. As Union forces began closing in on the fort in late December 1861, Whelan found himself counseling men of all faiths who came to him for solace.

Whelan and others of the garrison were shipped north to Fort Columbus on Governor's Island, New York. Almost immediately he opened talks with Catholic officials in New York, negotiating for food, clothing, and other supplies for the needy Rebels. The New York Catholics sent Whelan a new uniform (based on a plea they received from the Rebel prisoners) and also persuaded Union authorities to release him, fearing that the hardships of imprisonment might kill him. Whelan refused, choosing to stay with the soldiers and continuing his daily morning Mass.

Whelan and a number of Confederate sick and wounded were released in August 1862. He returned to Savannah and was appointed vicar-general, but his war duties were far from over.

Southern reaction to Pulaski's fall was a mixture of shock, dismay, and defiance. News of the disaster first reached Savannah with the arrival of Corporal Charles T. Law of the Phoenix Riflemen stationed at Thunderbolt. Law was in the fort and was allowed to leave before the surrender because he had escorted a signalman to the fort on the night of the tenth and was not a member of the garrison.

"The favorable reports that reached us yesterday morning [April 11] from those who, from points below, watched the contest between the enemies [*sic*] batteries and ... Fort Pulaski, had not prepared us for the startling intelligence of the surrender," said the *Daily Morning News* on April 12. "The result has shown how little reliance is to be placed in brick walls against modern batteries."[12]

The April 15 *Republican* said "The capitulation ... after a brief defense of 32 hours has taken the whole country by surprise." Two days later the newspaper added, "Pulaski has fallen, and we are told with a boastful air that in a few days Savannah will also drop into his hand—Stand by your State in an hour of peril like this!"[13]

"Alas! our fort is gone," Rebel William Davidson wrote to his wife, Sarah, from Camp Claghorne on April 13. "I am indeed sick at heart, but, my dear, we must pray to our God fervently to look down upon us and help us in this our hours of need.... I think the Yankees will attack the city by next Sunday if not before."

In an April 15 entry, Mary Boykin Chesnut of South Carolina lamented in her famous wartime diary over this latest setback to Confederate arms: "Pulaski fallen! What more is there to fall?"[14]

General Lawton was roundly criticized for not being more active in preparing for the enemy assault, and Olmstead's judgment also came under attack.

"It does not seem to me, no matter how damaged the condition of the fort, that I never would have surrendered it with magazines well supplied," Lieutenant Jones wrote on April 14. "I am afraid Olmstead lacked nerve. . . . Had he perished in the ruins of Pulaski he would have lived a hero for all time. As it is, his reputation is at best questionable."[15]

In penning his memoirs years after the war, Olmstead stated: "I am still convinced that there was nothing else that could be done."

A few days after the surrender Montfort wrote an undated letter to his family, probably sent from Hilton Head Island, South Carolina, the Pulaski prisoners' first stop on their journey north: "Children, do not grieve or be disturbed about me. It may be months before you will hear from me again. Yet you all will be affectionately remembered by me every hour of the day."[16]

Montfort was among the Fort Columbus prisoners, but within two months he was transferred to a prison camp at Johnson's Island, Ohio. Montfort was exchanged in September, but was deathly ill due to the rigors of prison life. On September 27, three days after reaching his mother's home in Butler, Georgia, he died, surrounded by his wife and four children. His youngest daughter, eleven-month-old Laura, saw her father for the first time as he lay on his death bed.

VIII

"Mamma, It Was Terrible to Look At"

The disaster at Pulaski threw Savannah into a panic similar to the frenzy after Port Royal's capture in November. Roads leading out of town were soon clogged with overloaded wagons and carriages as droves of panicky citizens fled before the expected Union attack upriver. Hundreds of slaves were put to work bolstering the city's fortifications over the next few weeks.

State legislators passed a resolution stating that Savannah must not be surrendered and should be defended street by street and house by house. Again there was talk of burning the town rather than leaving it to the Yankees.

In a rage, General Walker barged into a hotel filled with a crowd of boisterous, distraught, and frustrated Savannahians. Many were ready to flee or capitulate. Based on a soldier's postwar account, the frail but volatile Walker railed at the citizens for their cowardice: "I'll never surrender anything more than the ashes of Savannah. I'll stay here and I'll keep you here till every shingle burns and every brick gets knocked into bits the size of my thumbnail and then I'll send the Yankees word that there isn't any Savannah to surrender. I've had a convenient limb trimmed up on the tree in front of my headquarters and I'll string up every man that dares say surrender."

General Pemberton telegraphed Richmond, asking for permission to declare martial law, but was refused.

The anticipated enemy advance, however, did not happen; the Federals were, for the moment, content to hold Pulaski. Aggressiveness on their part probably could have resulted in Savannah's capture, but the Union command was stymied by lack of information about the number of Rebels in Savannah, development of forts guarding the city upriver, and the unknown strength of the city's naval squadron.

Indeed, the "floating battery" CSS *Georgia* was launched in May 1862 and the CSS *Atlanta*, one of the most impressive ironclads built by the Confederacy, made her first trial run on the Savannah River in late July.

Neither warship was ready for battle, however. The *Georgia* lacked armament, armor, and vital machinery. She would not be ready for active service until October. "The iron is yet to be placed on the roof and the guns to be mounted," an officer noted.[1]

The *Atlanta* was in worse shape, still months away from being fit for combat. Both ships would have been floating targets if the Federals had attacked.

Yet other than a reconnaissance in force on April 16 which the Rebels repulsed on Whitemarsh Island, the blue "invaders" made no serious effort to attack Savannah from the coast. The thrust at Whitemarsh was led by Union Lieutenant Wilson, who had carried the surrender demand to Pulaski. Leading some four hundred troops of the Eighth Michigan Volunteers, Wilson experienced his first up-close combat in a tangle with about eight hundred Rebels east of the city.

Losses were minor, but Wilson gained little information about the island other than it was swarming with "Secesh." Wilson would go on to greater accomplishments as one of the Union's best young cavalry generals.

"It appears that late in the afternoon the enemy landed on the island from their barges, and attempted a reconnaissance in force," the *Savannah Republican* said on April 17. "They had not proceeded far before they encountered a large Confederate picket [from] the 13th Georgia. Our troops attacked them vigorously." The account added that the Yankees were driven back to their boats with casualties "said to be considerable."[2]

General Hunter believed he was outnumbered and called for reinforcements after Wilson's foray. Hunter, a vigorous abolitionist, appears to have been more preoccupied with political aspirations than battle honors at this time. A Union officer described him as a "fine, gallant, and manly old fellow more interested in abolishing slavery than in putting down the rebellion."

Two days after Pulaski's surrender, Hunter issued an order freeing all blacks who lived or worked on Cockspur Island, where the fort was located. On May 9, he extended his decree, declaring slaves in Georgia, Florida, and South Carolina "forever free."

Union troops in formation at Fort Pulaski. Other soldiers appear to be playing baseball in the background. (Courtesy of the Fort Pulaski National Monument.)

Abolitionists strongly backed the edict, but most of Hunter's officers and a majority of his troops opposed it. These Yanks were fighting to preserve the Union, not for an end to slavery. President Lincoln quickly revoked the order, apparently feeling the time was not yet right for such an extreme act.

Hunter also began recruiting a regiment of black troops, the First South Carolina, in and around Port Royal, a move that earned praise from Radical Republicans. But his extremist attitude and the belief that such an action would further unite the South resulted in Hunter being ordered to abandon the project. (One company of the First South Carolina was covertly kept together. It would later form the nucleus of the Thirty-third U.S. Colored Infantry.)

Hunter's efforts, however, made him a marked man in the South. Orders were issued that he was to be executed if taken prisoner.

The Confederate government also reached a landmark decision less than a week after the Pulaski debacle. The Conscription Act, authorizing a military draft, was passed by the C.S. Congress and approved by President Davis. This meant that Georgia state troops, like their comrades elsewhere

Map showing Fort Pulaski and approaches to Savannah. (*Harper's Weekly*, Apr. 19, 1862, courtesy of the Georgia Historical Society.)

in the South, passed into national service for the Confederacy. Indeed, the act required men between the ages of eighteen and thirty-five to serve in the military for three years or until the war ended. For many Rebels fighting for states' rights, this was an unpopular and controversial decision.

The armies dug in and built batteries on various islands while the U.S. Navy maintained its grip to blockade Savannah. Other than an occasional skirmish or naval shelling, men on both sides soon found common enemies: stinging swarms of bugs, the heat and humidity of coastal Georgia, and boredom.

"We are all more than anxious to be sent to the front, preferring an active campaign to remaining here doing coast duty and being ate up by the mosquitoes and sand flies," a Georgia infantryman wrote. "Besides, the heat of the noonday sun upon the sand is terribly distressing."[3]

"Affairs around Savannah are profoundly quiet," Mercer remembered. "The work of defence goes vigorously on. Old batteries are being strengthened and new ones made. The river is now quite effectually obstructed and soon will be thoroughly so. The work is, however, necessarily slow and difficult."[4]

According to Lieutenant Jones, the Federals were using the earliest form of aerial reconnaissance to spy on the Rebels: "The Lincolnites from below were yesterday taking observations from a balloon," he wrote on May 9. "I presume wishing to verify these observations they today adopted the ruse of a flag of truce."[5]

Indeed, the Savannah Rebels themselves were experimenting with balloon warfare. Captain Langdon Cheves constructed a balloon at one of the Savannah armories that spring. His creation was patched together from swatches of multicolored dress silk, although no Savannah belles actually had to sacrifice their dresses for the cause.

The Confederates' seaward and Savannah River defenses were either in place or nearing completion by the time of Pulaski's fall. If the Yankees decided to send gunboats upstream, they would have to run a crossfire of shot and shell from Rebel batteries and forts.

The most powerful of these works were forts Jackson and Bartow, both on the Georgia side of the river. Fort Bartow, named for the fallen hero, was a massive earthwork guarding the Savannah at a point where it joined the Wilmington River about ten miles inland from Fort Pulaski. Covering some seventeen acres, the fort was erected on Causton Bluff.

Robert E. Lee narrowly escaped an untimely death while on an inspection tour of Bartow and other river forts in early 1862. Lee was on hand as gunners were test firing a large-caliber cannon supposed to be able to hurl shells some five miles distant. On the first shot the big gun exploded, killing and wounding several men. A section of the barrel whirled close over Lee's head and thudded into a marsh, but the general was unscathed.

After Fort Pulaski's surrender, a Union officer derisively described Fort Jackson as "a little brick fort that would have been knocked down by half a dozen heavy shells." Fort Jackson would become the Confederate headquarters for the Savannah River defenses, including the navy.

Colonel Edward Anderson, who had brought the *Fingal* to Savannah, was given command at Jackson and over her supporting river batteries.

To support Fort Jackson, the Rebels built Battery Lee just to the east. A Rebel officer who visited Lee in early 1862 described it as "the mud valley." The Southerners linked it to Savannah by railroad, and Fort Lee soon became a formidable outpost.

The Confederates also erected batteries Cheves and Lawton across the river from Fort Jackson.

On the Wilmington River, Fort Thunderbolt, another big earthwork, was constructed to guard against enemy intrusion from Wassaw Sound. Other strongpoints included batteries on Rose Dhu Island, Beaulieu, and the Isle of Hope.

Communications among these scattered outposts were maintained by telegraph and semaphore flag signaling.

The interior crescent of defenses also was being bulwarked. Captain

Captain William R. Boggs, later a
Confederate general, was instrumental in
designing Savannah's defensive network.

William R. Boggs, a military engineer and future Confederate general, was
the principle architect of this secondary line based on the earlier work of
Captain Gilmer.

A native of Augusta, Boggs graduated from West Point in 1853. Serving
as an ordnance lieutenant, he resigned his commission in February 1861 and
was immediately appointed captain and ordnance officer to General
Beauregard at Charleston.

Within a few months he was transferred to Pensacola and assigned as
chief of engineers and artillery for General Braxton Bragg. He came to
Savannah on temporary duty as Georgia's chief military engineer.

Equipped with a hatchet, nails, and a good map, Boggs personally
surveyed the land, riding through the pine woods, swamps, and marshes to
find the best locations for forts and rifle pits. The line ran in a half moon
from the Savannah River on the east, around the city to Laurel Grove
Cemetery on the west.

Fort Boggs was the cornerstone of these defenses—a large stronghold
situated on Brewton Hill a few hundred yards from the river and east of the
city. Another Rebel officer described Fort Boggs as "one of the finest field

works constructed on either side during the war." The fort incorporated some of the grounds of the Savannah Golf Club, established in the late 1700's.

Although never tested in combat, Boggs's handiwork greatly enhanced Savannah's fortifications.

The Southerners employed in building this line went about their spade work with patriotic vigor, but the sabre-rattling attitudes of a few months back were more subdued.

April had been an awful month for Confederate arms on all fronts. In addition to Fort Pulaski, the Rebels lost a major battle at Shiloh, or Pittsburg Landing, in southern Tennessee on April 6–7. And New Orleans fell to an enemy naval squadron on April 25.

In Virginia the Union Army of the Potomac, composed of more than 100,000 men under General George B. McClellan, was advancing on Yorktown, a prelude to an anticipated strike against Richmond.

By early June this Federal army was camped a few miles from the Confederate capital in spite of desperate battles at Fair Oaks and Seven Pines.

Weighing the news, Lieutenant Jones wrote, "We have a chapter of evil tidings which it is almost impossible to consider with composure."[6]

Lee was now in command of the greatly outnumbered Rebel army facing McClellan. He needed reinforcements, and about 5,000 of the approximately 13,000 troops stationed in the Savannah area were readied for the trip north in early June.

Hurt by local criticism of inaction and improper preparation at Savannah, General Lawton received permission to accompany these units to Virginia.

Lawton redeemed himself on the battlefield. He fought well during the Peninsula campaign and assumed command of Major General Richard Ewell's division after Ewell lost a leg at the battle of Second Bull Run in August.

As part of "Stonewall" Jackson's corps, Lawton and his division distinguished themselves in the Maryland campaign before Lawton was badly wounded at Sharpsburg on September 17, 1862. His brief combat career was over.

"Six of our best regiments have been ordered to Virginia and one other is near Charleston," Mercer wrote on June 15. "We have now a very small force of effective men. A large number are miserably armed, and some without arms of any description. With the finest material that ever composed an army—the bravest, most cheerful and simple-hearted soldiery—our army is perhaps as ragged and soiled as any in existence. Poor soldiers, I see them every day marching from their camp for miles to labor there all day under the broiling sun, and then returning late in the evening, soiled, wet and weary. Little of the poetry and romance of war do they ever experience. Poorly armed, fed and clothed and hard worked, they are still cheerful and patriotic."[7]

A June 1 open letter from the Lowndes County Volunteers, stationed at Savannah, to their friends and loved ones back home is evidence of the concern and worry the average Johnny Reb felt for his family: "To the Citizens of Lowndes County: We have left our pleasant homes and families for protection, and we have left one certain James Howell that has raised and pitched and kicked up hell and got all of he could before the Conscription Act was passed. And when he found he had to go himself, he hired a substitute and is at home yet, and we fear from every circumstance that there is no good in his heart. And we further believe if the good men of Lowndes County don't watch him he will be a great injury to the desolate families left behind. You all well know that he deserted Captain Mosley's company and that goes to prove that he is not a friend to his country, for every man that is a friend to his country will never act as James Howell has. We do believe that he would steal from widows and orphans and soldiers' wives and therefore request of such men as Reuben Roberts and William Batz and Bryant Roberts, William McDaniel and M. S. Griffin and other citizens to watch him. It is the wish of the Lowndes Volunteers for this to be made public. We hope you will read [it] to every man and will oblige the friends of the South now in the field."

Langdon Cheves was told to bring his colorful balloon from Savannah to the Virginia front and aid in Lee's reconnaissance efforts. But Cheves' aerial adventure was doomed to an ignoble end. The balloon was being hauled down the James River aboard the CSS *Teaser* when the vessel was captured by the USS *Monitor* on July 4, 1862.

Through newspapers and letters from the front, Savannahians followed the campaigns to the north and also learned of the fall of Memphis to Union forces in June 1862.

Closer to home, they worried about loved ones involved in fighting near Charleston, where a Union attack at Secessionville, South Carolina, was repulsed on June 16. For at least one Savannahian, this was his first time under fire.

"Mamma, it was terrible to look at," Lieutenant Joseph Habersham of the Seventeenth Georgia wrote home the day after the battle. "I was under severe fire myself, and narrowly escaped a rifle cannon ball which passed over my saddle as I was mounting my horse! The wind of it almost knocked me down as it whistled by."[8]

Undismayed by the loss of his balloon, Langdon Cheves joined his younger brother, Dr. John Richardson Cheves, in Charleston. Dr. Cheves was even more of an inventor than his brother, experimenting with electrically detonated underwater mines and other high-powered explosives. On orders from Pemberton, Dr. Cheves was put in charge of Charleston defenses pertaining to chain and boom obstructions and harbor mines that could be detonated from shore. The Savannah brothers would later have the chance to destroy one of the Union navy's strongest monitors.

Alexander Lawton had been succeeded in command of the Georgia District by Brigadier General Hugh W. Mercer, whose grandfather was a patriot general killed at the Revolutionary War battle of Princeton. His son, George, already was a veteran of army life in Savannah's defenses and would serve as a staff officer to his father.

A native Virginian, Hugh Mercer would be the great grandfather of Johnny Mercer, the renowned Savannah songwriter and composer who wrote "Moon River." An 1828 graduate of West Point, General Mercer was stationed in Savannah early in his military career and married into a local family. He resigned his army commission in 1835 and stayed in Savannah. From 1841 until the war began, he was cashier of the Planter's Bank. When Georgia seceded, Mercer was appointed an officer of state volunteers.

On July 29 four Union gunboats attacked Fort McAllister, the Confederate stronghold on the Ogeechee River about twelve miles south of Savannah. Du Pont had ordered a reconnaissance in force up the Ogeechee and sent Commander Charles Steedman to lead the attack. Steedman's gunboats, the *Paul Jones*, *Unadilla*, *Huron*, and *Madgie*, engaged the fort for about ninety minutes, with little damage done to either side.

Captain Alfred L. Hartridge of the De Kalb Rifles commanded the battery and reported that although the Union shells made holes "large enough to bury a horse," he suffered only two wounded.

Although the ironclad CSS *Atlanta* was not yet ready for battle, her first trial run down the Savannah River caused quite a stir among the Federal forces two days later. The ironclad had been constructed from the steamer *Fingal*, which had been trapped in Savannah since her arrival the previous November.

Most of the conversion was done by shipbuilders Asa and Nelson Tift, who were considered Confederate naval pioneers for their design and work on the early ironclads. The Tifts had relocated to Savannah from New Orleans, where they had built the CSS *Mississippi*. That ironclad was not fully completed when Union forces captured the Louisiana city in April 1862.

The *Atlanta* still was being fitted for sea duty when she cruised toward Union-held Fort Pulaski on July 31. The Federals knew that at least one ironclad was being built at Savannah, but the sight of this leviathan made them even more nervous. The clamor intensified for the U.S. Navy to take measures to stop this threat.

"Unless some monitor comes to our succor, the fair weather yachts [Union blockaders] now reposing on the placid bosom of the Savannah River, have before them an excellent opportunity of learning what it is to be blown out of the water," wrote a New York *Herald* correspondent.[9]

At Venus Point soldiers of the Forty-eighth New York devised a plan to capture the *Atlanta*. They determined to fire "shot connected with chains, and so tangle her up and haul her ashore." The question soon arose how the Yanks would "get into their ironbound prize."

An officer posed the problem to his men. "'Now,' said he, 'you've been in this cursed swamp for two weeks, up to your ears in mud—no fun, no glory, and blessed poor pay. Here's a chance. Let every one of you who has had experience as a cracksman or a safe-blower step to the front.' It is said that the whole detachment stepped off its two paces with perfect unanimity," General Gillmore reported.[10]

Savannah's war turmoil was aggravated by a controversy in September involving the Jewish community. A number of Jewish families moved to Savannah from Thomasville, Georgia, after a band of hot-headed residents there literally forced them to flee. Jews in Thomas County were accused of passing counterfeit money, overpricing their goods, and, generally of not being patriotic Confederates. An angry crowd on August 30 passed resolutions calling for expulsion of Jews from the county, among other measures.

The September 12 *Daily Morning News* ran a story about the Thomasville resolutions. Many Savannah Jews noted that Editor W. T. Thompson had written nothing to denounce what happened in Thomas County. [In fairness, he also wrote nothing to condone it.]

Savannah's Jewish residents held a meeting on September 13 and emerged with a document condemning the actions in Thomasville. It also attacked the *Daily Morning News* for "giving currency to this slander and intolerance" and urged a boycott of the newspaper. Thompson defended himself, saying that he ran the resolutions story simply as a news item and denying any pro-Thomasville sentiments.

Jewish Rebels stationed in and around Savannah joined the war of words. A group of Jews in the Tattnall Guards wrote a letter published in the *Republican* on September 17 defending their honor and patriotism. "Go review the mighty hosts who are struggling to achieve our independence" among "the noble armies of the South," the soldiers wrote. "There you will behold the representatives of our sect, standing side by side with the gallant sons of the soil."[11]

Amid the war's rapid developments, the Jewish issues soon were forgotten. The patriotism and bravery of Jewish men and women, North and South, would become an undisputed but seldom recognized aspect of the conflict.

While Rebel gallantry and determination generally remained strong, the Union blockade was choking the commercial life out of Savannah. Downtown stores remaining open had scant products and "many empty shelves."

Major General Ormsby M. Mitchel was assigned command of the Union Department of the South in mid-September. He did not live long enough to have much impact on military operations about Savannah. A Kentuckian nicknamed "Old Stars" by his soldiers because of his passion for astronomy, Mitchel was an 1829 classmate of Robert E. Lee at West Point. Mitchel was appointed a brigadier general of volunteers in August 1861 and given control of the Department of the Ohio. This post was soon absorbed into General Don Carlos Buell's Army of the Cumberland.

For successful raids on railroads in Alabama, Mitchel was promoted major general in April 1862. But a festering feud with Buell resulted in Mitchel deciding to quit the army.

Washington, however, did not accept the resignation, and Mitchel was ordered to report to the Savannah-Charleston area. Headquartered at Hilton Head, Mitchel inspected Union posts along the coast, including Fort Pulaski.

His only major action occurred in late October, when he led a thrust against the Charleston & Savannah Railroad near Pocotaligo, South Carolina. Embarrassingly, Mitchel's force of about 4,500 was turned back by some 500 Rebels.

The general's humiliation was short-lived. Stricken by yellow fever, he died at Beaufort, South Carolina, on October 30, 1862.

IX

Completion of the Ironclads

The Savannah shipyards of the Tift brothers, Henry Willink, and Krenson & Hawkes sizzled like hell's furnace in autumn 1862 as grimy, sweating carpenters and ironworkers created some of the Confederacy's most lethal dreadnoughts.

Construction on the CSS *Georgia*, Savannah's first ironclad, was finally completed in October, and she was ready for action—at least as much as she would ever be. This ironclad was originally called "The Ladies Gunboat" because it was built with more than $115,000 raised throughout the state by The Ladies' Gunboat Association.

Built at Willink's shipyard and launched on May 19, 1862, the *Georgia* was not put into service until her guns, machinery, and armor had been properly installed. The *Georgia* had armor plating four inches thick forged from 500 tons of railroad iron. Armed with ten heavy guns, she was 250 feet long.

A Northern correspondent described her as a "nondescript marine monster," but most Savannah Rebels knew she was far from being monarch of the seas. The *Georgia* leaked badly and had engines incapable of propelling her against any current. She also was plagued by the experimental construction that marked the Confederacy's first ironclads.

"A splendid failure," one Savannahian described her, while another called her a "mud tub." One of the *Georgia*'s officers depicted her as "an iron box (for she is not a vessel)," adding that "She is not a fit command for a sargant [*sic*] of marines."[1]

Her lack of propulsion fated her to duty as a "floating battery," and she was towed to a specially built crib near Elba Island in the Savannah River.

Henry Willink, whose shipyard produced the CSS *Georgia*, Savannah's first ironclad warship. (Courtesy of the Georgia Historical Society.)

The *Georgia*'s position allowed her to be turned to bring a broadside to bear on either channel of the river.

The Tift brothers put the finishing touches on the ironclad CSS *Atlanta*, which was commissioned on November 22, making the river squadron even more formidable. The *Atlanta* was "one of the most powerful ironclads afloat," according to U.S. Secretary of the Navy Gideon Welles.

Weighing more than a thousand tons and 204 feet in length, the *Atlanta* could reach a top speed of six knots, powered by English engines among the best to be found in the South. Her armor consisted of slabs of railroad iron four inches thick. The *Atlanta* bristled with a seven-inch Brooke rifle at her bow and stern and a six-inch Brooke on each broadside. She also had an iron ram attached to her prow and a spar torpedo.

While the Federals feared that she would sweep their fleet from the seas and ravage the Eastern seaboard, the *Atlanta* had problems similar to those of the *Georgia* and other ironclads—poor steering, a deep draft, and perpetual leakage.

The warships also oven-baked their crews in the Savannah summer heat. "There is no ventilation below at all," wrote crewman H. B. Littlepage. "I would defy anyone in the world to tell when it is day or when night if he is confined below without any way of marking time. . . . I would venture to say that if a person were blindfolded and carried below and turned loose he would imagine himself in a swamp, for the water is trickling in all the time and everything is so damp."[2]

This illustration of the CSS *Georgia* and obstructions in the Savannah River was published in *Harper's Weekly* based on a sketch from a Union scout. (Courtesy of the Georgia Historical Society.)

Work on a third ironclad, the CSS *Savannah*, was well underway at Willink's shipyard, adding to Savannah's undisputed reputation as the busiest ship-building city in the Confederacy. The *Savannah* would not be ready for service until the following summer.

Captain Josiah Tattnall returned to Savannah in late July 1862 to resume command of the naval force. He had endured a stormy trial since leaving Savannah in March to lead the Rebels' James River squadron in Virginia. As a young midshipman more than fifty years earlier, Tattnall had sailed those same waters, fighting the British in the battle of Craney's Island near Norfolk.

From late March until May, Tattnall sparred with the Federal blockaders, including the USS *Monitor*, off the Virginia coast with negligible results.

At the helm of the CSS *Virginia*, he was unable to strike a decisive blow against the Union fleet. When Confederate forces abandoned Norfolk, the *Virginia* could not escape to safety because of her deep draft and the shallowness of the accessible rivers.

At Tattnall's direction, the historic ironclad was blown up on May 11, 1862, to keep her from being captured. Tattnall came under severe criticism for this act, although he apparently had few options. He demanded a court-martial to clear his name and was acquitted in July.

If the Federals considered the *Atlanta* a terror for their blockade, Tattnall did not share this assessment of his best warship at Savannah. He felt she could not win a fight against the enemy monitors based on his experiences facing the original *Monitor* off Virginia.

Knowing the *Atlanta* was constructed in similar design to the *Virginia*, Tattnall would write: "I considered the *Atlanta* no match for the monitor class of vessel at close quarters and in shoal waters particularly." There would be no monitors off Savannah until the first weeks of 1863.

In spite of pleas for action from Savannah's populace, the *Atlanta*'s leakage and steering problems compelled Tattnall to keep her close to port. Her crew was augmented in early November by the arrival of twenty-four C.S.A. marines transferred to Savannah from Mobile.

Weeks dragged into months, and still the *Atlanta* did not venture from the protection of Savannah's defenses. The public's impatience, as well as that of Confederate officials in Richmond, swelled with Tattnall's idleness.

Tattnall wasn't oblivious to this unrest and finally was spurred to take the initiative. He would open the coming new year with an attack by the *Atlanta* on the Federal fleet.

John Pemberton was promoted to lieutenant general in October and transferred to department command in Mississippi and eastern Louisiana. He was replaced on the southeastern seaboard by General P. G. T. Beauregard, the hero of Fort Sumter and First Manassas who had fallen on hard times as commander of the Army of Tennessee.

Beauregard was headquartered in Charleston and supervised construction of coastline defenses at Savannah.

In spite of a five-hour naval bombardment of Fort McAllister on November 19, Union offensive efforts were clearly aimed at Charleston, and Beauregard, out of necessity, spent most of his time there.

A native Louisianan, Beauregard was an 1838 West Point graduate who had served on Winfield Scott's staff with R. E. Lee in the Mexican War. Appointed superintendent of the Military Academy in January 1861, Beauregard was relieved a few days later because of his pro-Southern sentiments. He resigned his commission in February and was named a Confederate brigadier by March.

Beauregard's fame reached its zenith with his victories in 1861. But after being given the reins of the Army of Tennessee after the death of General Albert Sidney Johnston, his performance was less than impressive, and he was relieved of army command in August 1862.

Known for military engineering as well as his vanity, the bayou general who studied Napoleonic strategy would prove to be a sturdy warrior in defending the Georgia-South Carolina coast.

The flamboyant General Pierre Gustave Toutant Beauregard assumed command of Confederate troops and defenses at Savannah and the rest of the southeastern seaboard in fall 1862.

November brought the promotion of Charles Jones to colonel and chief of light artillery for General Mercer. Jones threw himself into the task of putting his coastal batteries in "good fighting trim.... Our enemies are gathering their energies for some heavy demonstration somewhere along our lines. I trust in God that we may be able successfully to meet and repulse them."[3]

The drain of the war effort already was showing its effects on Savannah and the rest of the South. "The resources of the Confederacy are limited and taxed to the utmost," George Mercer wrote in November. "We have plenty of salt in the water, leather, cotton, and wool in the country and ore in the earth, but we are not now prepared to render them available. All the old lead is being collected by the ordnance department. It is furnished in small bits by patriotic donors and consists of lead roofs, weights, water pipes, &c. The same is true of the old brass and iron. Iron is particularly needed. Agents have been sent over the whole country to purchase or collect it in any form. The iron railing of our parade ground has been taken for bolts for the obstructions. The large cylinders intended for the Charleston and Savannah Railroad bridge have been melted into shot and shell. All the old coverlets, blankets and even carpets are being sent to the army for blankets. Whole railroads are being torn up, so that the iron may be used for gunboats. These facts are quoted by the Yankees as evidences of our weakness. Do they not rather indicate the most unconquerable strength, do they not exhibit a spirit of patriotism and self-sacrifice, a moral power that is impregnable?"[4]

The rival armies in Virginia could not let the year close without clawing at each other in one last bitter, bloody embrace. On December 13 the Union Army of the Potomac launched a series of grand and doomed assaults on Lee's army entrenched on hills just south of Fredericksburg. The Federal infantrymen fell in droves before the Rebels' intense musketry and massed artillery, suffering some 13,000 casualties. "It was a great slaughter pen . . . they might as well have tried to take Hell," a Union soldier recalled.

Lieutenant Joseph Habersham was returning to the army after leave in Richmond. Unable to reach his regiment, Habersham, who had originally enlisted in the Savannah Volunteer Guards, sought out some familiar faces.

He found Savannah's Pulaski Guards and served with a gun crew during the battle. "The Battery really did service—slaughtering the Yankees at every shot," he wrote home. "On Saturday [December 13] the ground in front of us was literally covered with the enemy's dead."[5]

X

Arrival of the Monitors—1863

The new year was only weeks old when a terrible new menace threatened Savannah's extended defense line. Rebel pickets gaped in horrid fascination when the monitor USS *Montauk* arrived off Fort McAllister on January 26. Relatively few fighting men on either side had seen one of the new monitors at this point in the war. Accompanied by the gunboats *Seneca*, *Wissahickon*, *Dawn*, and *Williams*, the monitor dropped anchor in Ossabaw Sound.

Oddly, this show of Union naval might was a direct result of a planned bombardment of Charleston.

Samuel Du Pont, who had been promoted to rear admiral the previous July, was organizing a naval squadron off the South Carolina coast for the reduction of the port city. A number of the revolutionary monitors were to be included in the attack force, but most of them still were being fitted and would not be available for several months.

With Commander John L. Worden at the helm, the *Montauk* was the first to arrive. Because Du Pont did not yet have his armada assembled, he sent the monitor south to test its efficiency against land artillery. The target was Fort McAllister, located on Genesis Point at the mouth of the Ogeechee River. The earthwork had been constructed on land owned by Confederate Lieutenant Colonel Joseph L. McAllister and bore the name of his father.

Worden already was a Union naval hero and pioneer. As a lieutenant, he commanded the original *Monitor* in its clash with the CSS *Virginia*.

A Columbiad at Fort McAllister
faces seaward.

He was wounded and temporarily blinded by a *Virginia* shot that
exploded on the *Monitor*'s pilothouse. His injuries forced him to be relieved
of command during the battle but his conduct did not go unrecognized.
Twice honored with a vote of thanks from Congress, the New Yorker was
promoted to commander in July 1862 and was named skipper of the
Montauk in December 1862. The *Montauk* was a sister vessel of the *Monitor*.

Sizing up McAllister's defenses, Worden soon learned that the Georgians had placed stakes and other obstructions, including primitive
torpedoes, in the channel near the Ogeechee's entrance.

In the fort the Confederates readied their batteries and watched the
movements of the enemy fleet. Major John B. Gallie of Savannah commanded the garrison, supported by troops under Colonel Robert H.
Anderson. McAllister's most potent weapons were a rifled thirty-two-
pounder and an eight-inch Columbiad.

Gallie, fifty-six, was a Scottish immigrant and a former captain of the
Chatham Artillery. Serving on the coast near Savannah, he had been
promoted to major of the Twenty-second Battalion of Georgia Heavy
Artillery in April 1862.[1]

A substantial prize awaited the victor of the coming duel. The blockade-
runner *Rattlesnake*, also known as the *Nashville* and the *Thomas L. Wragg*,
had been shut up in the Ogeechee since July 6, 1862, when she arrived with
a cargo of military supplies from England. The 1,200-ton paddlewheeler

The Confederate blockade-runner *Rattlesnake*, better known as the *Nashville*, lies at anchor near the Atlantic & Gulf Railroad bridge over the Ogeechee River. (Courtesy of the Georgia Historical Society.)

built in 1853 was notorious for her ability to evade the Union navy on previous occasions and for her raids on U.S. commercial shipping on the high seas.

As the passenger steamer *Nashville*, she had been seized by Southern authorities at Charleston in 1861 and put into Confederate service. She was converted into a sea raider and renamed the *Thomas L. Wragg*.[2]

In October 1861 she slipped past the Union blockade outside Charleston to open her saga. Taking on coal at Bermuda, her captain, R. B. Pelgram, set a course for England. On November 18, the *Wragg* captured and burned the clipper USS *Harvey Birch*. Two days later she jauntily sailed into Southampton, the first ship to fly the Confederacy's flag in European waters. The *Wragg* steamed for home on February 3, 1862, capturing and burning a schooner two days out of Bermuda on February 26. Again slipping through the Federal blockade, she cruised into Morehead City, North Carolina.

On the moonless night of St. Patrick's Day 1862, the *Wragg* moved out of Beaufort, North Carolina, again heading for the Atlantic. By this time she had been sold to a private owner in North Carolina and was considered a Confederate privateer. Off Beaufort, the Rebel vessel surprised and sped past two Federal vessels on blockade duty.

The *Wragg* was loose again, spreading fear among Yankee commerce vessels and forcing the Union navy to send ships flying after her in pursuit. For the second time she had embarrassed the Federal blockade, causing some Northern newspapers to run editorial cartoons criticizing U.S. Secretary of the Navy Welles.

With a cargo from England, the *Wragg* tried to slip into Charleston in June 1862, but alert blockaders forced her to seek another port. She headed south to Ossabaw Sound, where she found refuge in the Great Ogeechee River behind McAllister's guns.

Her cargo was unloaded onto smaller vessels and hauled to the nearby Atlantic & Gulf Railroad bridge, where trains carried it into Savannah.

A few weeks later a runaway slave told U.S. authorities at Port Royal about the sleek vessel in the Ogeechee.

McAllister's defenders fought off a July 29, 1862 attack by Union gunboats, who were to overwhelm the fort, "continue to the bridge and destroy or capture the steamer." The blockade-runner was sold in November and converted into a privateer. Renamed the CSS *Rattlesnake*, she remained snared in the river, waiting for a chance to knife through to the open sea.

When the *Montauk* appeared, the *Rattlesnake* was anchored near the railroad bridge a few miles upstream from the fort, and was readied to be sunk to avoid possible capture. Her cannon were brought ashore and mounted in shore batteries. The steam tug *Columbus* tendered the *Rattlesnake*.

The *Wissahickon* had already tasted the marksmanship of McAllister's gun crews. She was one of the gunboats that attacked the fort on November 19 in a vain effort to reach the *Rattlesnake*. A Union flotilla under Lieutenant Commander John Lee Davis shellacked the fort in a five-hour bombardment with minimal damage.

In that battle the *Wissahickon* was hit amidships below the water line by an enemy shell, forcing her out of the fight. With water pouring in, she was run aground at low tide. Repairs were made to keep her afloat.

Davis earlier had made another incursion into the Georgia interior through the coastal waters. On November 7 he had taken the gunboat *Dawn* up the Little Ogeechee River where he had shelled and set fire to a Rebel vessel at Coffee Bluff. Now the Yankees were poised for another shot at the *Rattlesnake*.

On the night of January 26–27, 1863, Worden sent reconnaissance parties in two small boats that inspected the fort's defenses at closer range and removed range markers the Rebel gunners had buoyed in the river.

About 7 A.M., on January 27, the Union vessels closed in, carefully avoiding any obstacles believed to be torpedoes, and opened fire on the fort.

Confident of her armor, the *Montauk* steamed to within 150 yards of McAllister and blazed away in a point-blank firefight. Screaming at the

Rebels were 450-pound shells from the *Montauk*'s fifteen-inch gun, at that time the largest rounds ever fired from a warship at a land fort.

The Confederate cannoneers quickly found the range and pummeled the ironclad, but with no result. The Rebels might as well have been "throwing beans against a brick wall," wrote *New York Herald* correspondent Bradley S. Osbon aboard the *Montauk*. Likewise, the monitor did little damage to the fort's sand and mud-encased batteries. Worden withdrew after a four-hour attack in which he exhausted most of his ammunition. Osbon praised McAllister's defenders, who "stand up to their guns in a manner worthy of a better cause."[3]

The *Montauk* resumed her assault just before 8 A.M. on Sunday, February 1. On account of tidal conditions, Worden was forced to begin his bombardment from a greater distance than the attack five days earlier.

Rebel sharpshooters under Captain Arthur Shaaff were posted in rifle pits along the riverbank to pick off exposed Yankee seamen, and two rifled guns of the Chatham Artillery were emplaced about a mile to the rear of the fort in case the monitor slipped by the garrison's defenders.

The *Montauk* took position eight hundred to a thousand yards from the fort while her gunboat escort lay about two miles to the east. Captain George W. Anderson, Jr., of the Chatham Artillery described the attack: "The enemy fired steadily and with remarkable precision; at times their fire was terrible. Their mortar firing was unusually fine, a large number of their shells bursting directly over the battery."

During a five-hour cannonade, the monitor took forty-six hits, but was not seriously damaged before she steamed out of range. Federal observers noted that the Confederates' ability to constantly move their guns kept the artillery from being hit by the naval fire.

Major Gallie, however, was killed about 8:30 A.M. by a Yankee cannonball that also disabled the thirty-two-pounder. Gallie was standing by the gun when the round struck it. He was decapitated either by a shell fragment or a shattered piece of the cannon itself. Earlier in the fight he had been wounded in the face, but had refused to be relieved.

"Thus perished nobly a brave, good and gallant soldier," Captain Anderson wrote. Despite the loss of Gallie, there had been much noise and dirt flying but little harm to the fort. Gallie's body was returned to Savannah and buried at Laurel Grove.

McAllister's defenders mourned Gallie's loss and took pride in withstanding the monitor's best efforts to destroy their fort.

Colonel Charles Jones inspected McAllister after the February 1 battle and found her preparing for the *Montauk*'s expected return. "An effort is being made to secure torpedoes in the stream below the fort so as to blow up the ironclad [*Montauk*] when next she takes her position to bombard," he wrote on February 14. The submerged explosives "will inspire the abolitionists with a most wholesome dread of our rivers. The memory of the Yazoo torpedo is still quite distinct in their cowardly recollections." [Jones was referring to the December 1862 sinking of the Union gunboat *Cairo*, which hit a torpedo in the Yazoo River near Vicksburg.][4]

For more than three weeks enemy lookouts eyed each other over the coastal waters and through the salt marshes and swamps without any significant engagements.

With the *Montauk* still a threat, the *Rattlesnake* steamed downriver at dusk on February 27, 1863, looking to make a break for the Atlantic. Finding no opportunity, she headed back up the winding Ogeechee, but ran aground on a mud bar near the fort.

The Rebels brought up the tug *Columbus* and desperately, vainly tried to dislodge the steamer. The Yankees quickly spotted the raider's predicament, and Worden ordered an attack set for the next morning.

At daybreak on February 28 the *Montauk* and two gunboats slowly moved toward the mouth of the Ogeechee. McAllister's gun crews frantically banged away to protect the beached steamer, but the *Montauk* took position within 1,200 yards of the Rebel ship and opened fire. A rain of fifteen- and eleven-inch shells quickly set the *Rattlesnake* ablaze, the Union gunners only able to see the ship's upper works over about a half-mile of sea marsh separating the vessels.

By the fifth hit the Federals realized that the privateer had been dealt a mortal blow as flames and a plume of black smoke stained the sky. A cloak of fog and smoke blanketed the *Rattlesnake*, but the *Montauk*'s bluecoats continued firing according to the previous range and elevation.

The *Rattlesnake* exploded about 9:30 A.M. when flames reached her magazine. Realizing the hopelessness of the situation, her crew had earlier abandoned ship.

The *Daily Morning News* provided a fitting requiem for the famed Rebel raider: "Thus terminated the career of the *Rattlesnake* whom we fondly hoped soon was to be converted into a sea-serpent to plague the Yankees on the ocean."

The *Montauk* did not escape unscathed. Steaming away in triumph, with other Union seamen cheering her success, she slid over a submerged mine

This March 28, 1863, *Harper's Weekly* sketch depicts the USS *Montauk*,
foreground, shelling the hapless Rebel privateer *Rattlesnake*.
(Courtesy of the Georgia Historical Society.)

that exploded, ripping a ten-foot gash in her side. Engineers advised
Worden that she could be kept afloat by using her pumps, but water gushed
in at such a rapid rate that they soon advised running her aground.

The monitor careened toward a beach out of range of the fort's guns. An
inspection at low tide revealed the damage's extent, and crewmen used a
spare section of boiler iron to patch the hull. With her pumps running, she
was towed to the Union base at Port Royal. Within days, repairs had been
made and she was ready for action, but her service against McAllister was
finished.

The battle stoked fears that an attack on Savannah was imminent.
"The city was full of rumors yesterday, but so far as we could learn there was
no foundation for any of them," the *Daily Morning News* reported on
February 11.[5]

"The prevailing impression is that an attack is to be made in some
quarter very soon. It is not probable that the immense fleet that is assembling in our waters will long remain idle." The paper concluded that if an
assault occurred, the Yankees would find "our preparations complete and
our people resolute and confident."

From the pulpit a minister exhorted the First Presbyterian Church congregation during a Wednesday night service to "Let the enemy be thoroughly whipped here, and much will be attained towards closing the war."[6]

Generals Beauregard and Mercer inspected the river batteries on February 14 and watched Union vessels lying near Fort Pulaski. Beauregard "possesses by his manners and deportment the agreeable art of attaching his soldiers to him," wrote Colonel Jones who was among the generals' party. "He is a man of great physical power, capable of uncommon endurance, plain in his habits and . . . has a rapid, quick eye to positions and possesses all the qualifications of a first-class engineer."[7]

Fort McAllister endured another naval assault when three monitors—the *Passaic*, *Patapsco*, and *Nahant*—appeared in Ossabaw Sound in early March. Commanded by Captain Percival Drayton, the Union ironclads blasted the fort for seven hours on March 3. Mortar boats kept up the firing through the night. But again the earthen fort withstood the barrage, with three men wounded. The only fatality was "Tom Cat," the garrison mascot, who was killed by an exploding shell.

Drayton's flagship, the *Passaic*, was hit thirty-four times by McAllister's gunners, yet her armor held firm for the most part.

From marshfront rifle pits, a squad of Confederate sharpshooters watched as a Union officer with field glasses emerged on the *Passaic*'s deck. The monitor was some distance away, but the Rebels opened fire. A "Maynard rifle slug" zipped past the officer's head moments before another bullet dropped him. Other bluejackets pulled the man back inside a hatch. The Southerners quickly took cover before the *Passaic* raked their positions with grapeshot.

Drayton's summation of the battle showed the ineffectiveness of the monitors' fire on the fort: "No injury was done which a good night's work would not repair." Drayton himself was slightly wounded in the face by shrapnel while directing fire from the *Passaic*'s deck.

The Yankees' attention on Fort McAllister convinced the Rebels that an offensive was likely against Savannah. The brigades of generals W. H. T. Walker and Thomas Clingman were rushed to the city as reinforcements.

With the failure of Drayton's attack, Du Pont decided to concentrate on Charleston, and the monitors headed north. The admiral was impressed with the ironclads' ability to withstand enemy shelling, but the operations on the Ogeechee were inconclusive as to the effectiveness of the monitors against land defenses.

Horace Greeley, in his *American Conflict*, wrote that the Union sailors "saved their ammunition by letting McAllister alone."

"Skunks and ground hogs are smoked out of hollow logs and holes. Is there no way to smoke the Yankees out of their iron safes?" the March 6 *Daily Morning News* mockingly asked of the Union armorclads.[8]

XI

Epitaph for an Ironclad

If the Federals were discouraged by the monitors' performance at Fort McAllister, the Confederates themselves were having no better luck with their naval squadron at Savannah. As he had earlier promised, Josiah Tattnall tried to strike at the Union fleet during the first week of 1863. He had been cheered not only by the chance for battle but by the arrival of his son, Captain John R. F. Tattnall, who was to command the Confederate marines at Savannah. The younger Tattnall had resigned as colonel of the Twenty-ninth Alabama Volunteers in December 1862 and joined the C.S. Marines.

The *Atlanta* grandly steamed downriver on January 5 to engage the enemy. But river obstructions emplaced to keep the Yankees from coming upstream could not be removed. An embarrassed and frustrated Tattnall returned to port. "All on board had the mortification to see the anchor again dropped in Savannah River," a despondent crewman wrote.

As Fort McAllister was being battered, the Rebel navy at Savannah did not attempt to come to its aid. Simply put, there was no water route that allowed Tattnall to reach Ossabaw Sound without a direct confrontation with the Union fleet or that was not blocked by defensive obstacles.

In late January, however, Tattnall hesitantly agreed to try to run the *Atlanta* past the *Montauk* and engage any wooden Union ships he could find. The plan was abandoned when the monitor *Passaic* arrived in Ossabaw Sound on January 30. Considering the *Atlanta* "no match" for one monitor, Tattnall was not about to tackle two of them.

An "angry and excited public" continued to pressure Tattnall to attack. Another attempt was thwarted on February 3 on account of bad weather.

"So we were again disappointed," Midshipman Dabney Scales of the *Atlanta* wrote in his diary. "Of course we will be branded as cowards by the unthinking portion of the citizens of Savannah. . . . These people never stop to enquire into the cause [of] these delays; but stigmatize the navy generally."[1]

The *Atlanta*'s curse surfaced again on February 16, when her skipper, Commander William McBlair, died unexpectedly. He was succeeded by Lieutenant George T. Sinclair, who was to have taken the helm of the ill-fated *Mississippi* at New Orleans.

Du Pont sent his monitors north to Charleston in mid-March, and Tattnall believed he finally had a chance to hit the Union blockade and perhaps attack Port Royal. A March 18 reconnaissance showed Wassaw Sound to be clear of monitors, and Tattnall steered the *Atlanta* down the Wilmington River the next day.

Unfortunately for the Rebels, a deserter informed the Federals of the *Atlanta*'s movements. Du Pont hastily recalled the *Passaic* to Wassaw Sound, and Tattnall again retreated.

By late March the Confederate brass ran out of patience with Tattnall, who was relegated to command of the Savannah naval station. A relative wrote of him during this period: "Poor cousin Josiah is very much depressed."

The Rebel naval squadron afloat was assigned to Commander Richard L. Page, a Virginian who was a first cousin of Robert E. Lee.

Nicknamed "Ramrod" and "Bombast Page," the commander had spent more than three decades in the U.S. Navy and had served tours around the world. When Virginia seceded, he resigned his commission and supervised the construction of defenses along the James and Nansemond rivers.

April found the troublesome monitors, including the *Passaic*, clustered off Charleston, readying for a massive naval assault. Again opportunity presented the *Atlanta* with a chance to sweep away the Union blockade. But Page was plagued by the same mechanical problems encountered by Tattnall. The steering gear was undergoing repairs, and the *Atlanta* could not put to sea. To the frustrated Confederate government, however, this apparently seemed to be a flimsy excuse.

"Can you not strike the enemy a blow in Ossabaw [Sound] while his ironclads are off Charleston?" Navy Secretary Mallory telegraphed Page on April 6.

While Page languished, Charleston was being blasted by the U.S. Navy. Two of the monitors that joined in the April 7 bombardment of that city would play starring roles in the *Atlanta*'s saga.

The USS *Weehawken*, commanded by Captain John Rodgers, was hit fifty-three times by return fire from Charleston's defenders and seriously damaged. The USS *Nahant*, skippered by Commander John Downes, was disabled by Rebel land batteries and had to leave the battle. Within weeks, however, both had been repaired and were back in action.

Page's performance did not satisfy Mallory, and he was replaced in early May by Lieutenant William A. Webb. Page later resigned his CSN commission, but in March 1864 was appointed a brigadier general in the Confederate army. Commanding the outer defenses of Mobile Bay, he fought bravely in the August land and sea battle for Fort Morgan before being compelled to surrender.[2]

Known as a bullish, impetuous fighter, Webb intended to take a bite out of the Union fleet almost as soon as he could fill his coal bunkers. The Virginian had commanded the *Atlanta* since May, replacing George Sinclair.

Webb distinguished himself as captain of the gunboat *Teaser* during the CSS *Virginia*'s March 8, 1862, attack on the Union fleet at Hampton Roads.

A comrade described Webb as "a very reckless young officer," who was "boastful and disinclined to listen to the counsel of older and wiser heads."[3]

With the potent *Atlanta* at his disposal, Webb notified his superiors within a week after taking command of the Savannah squadron that he intended to attack the Union blockade with the least possible delay.

Webb also had a new gunboat, the wooden screw steamer *Isondiga*, built at Krenson & Hawkes. This little vessel was only 112 feet in length and was designed to operate on narrow channels like those that dominated Savannah's approaches. Krenson & Hawkes had landed a Navy Department contract in 1862 for three armed steamers, but could only deliver one.

Webb tried to attack the enemy blockaders on May 30, having no better luck than Page or Tattnall. He was thwarted when the *Atlanta*'s forward engine failed, causing her to run aground.

Repairs were made, and the *Atlanta* sallied forth again in early June. Webb steamed down the Wilmington River to Thunderbolt in preparation to strike the Yankees as soon as the tides were favorable. Mallory suggested that Webb wait until he could be reinforced by the ironclad CSS *Savannah*, which was nearing completion in Henry Willink's shipyard. Under no direct orders, Webb decided to attack. He did not need the *Savannah*. "I assure you the whole abolition fleet has no terror for me, though the co-operation of the *Savannah* would be of great assistance," he replied to Mallory.

Webb formed a grandiose plan to "raise the blockade between here and Charleston, attack Port Royal, and then blockade Fort Pulaski."[4]

The *Atlanta's* movements were not unnoticed by the Federals, who had been keeping a close watch on the enemy ironclad. Anticipating that she would emerge in Wassaw Sound, the *Weehawken* and *Nahant* were sent there, arriving on June 15.

For Webb the monitors presented a chance to earn everlasting fame in splendid combat. The ironclad's coal bunkers were loaded on the night of June 16 and, on the incoming tide, the warship steamed downriver toward the sound, trailed by the *Isondiga*.

Gunports were closed to hide lantern light and all hands were ordered to keep as quiet as possible. Webb intended to wake the Yankees with solid shot and blood. Finally, the *Atlanta* was to be christened in battle in what surely would be her finest hour.

Before dawn on Wednesday, June 17, a drowsy lookout on the USS *Weehawken* was jolted awake by an ominous sight. For months Yankees in the blockading squadron off Savannah had anticipated an attack from the vaunted CSS *Atlanta*. At 4:10 A.M. this day, the threat became a reality.

Across the black waters of Wassaw Sound, the *Atlanta* was churning full steam toward the *Weehawken* and *Nahant*.

Webb knew he would be facing two monitors. He planned to destroy one with his spar torpedo before engaging the other with his guns. Within minutes of the lookout's alarm, the crews of both monitors had stumbled and scrambled to battle stations. Both vessels backed away from the *Atlanta* so that they would have time to regroup, build speed, and attack.

As the monitors retreated, their sailors saw that the *Atlanta*, curiously and suddenly, had stopped her advance less than a mile away from the *Weehawken*.

Cruising to the glory of her first battle, the *Atlanta* grounded on a sandbar just southeast of Cabbage Island. Frantically Webb's men reversed engines. The ironclad momentarily tore free, but the flood of the incoming tide drove her back against the bar.

The *Atlanta* hung fast and was listing to such a degree that most of her guns could not be brought to bear on the enemy.

The *Weehawken*, meanwhile, had raised full steam and turned toward the

Rebel ship. Captain Rodgers was unaware of the *Atlanta*'s problem and puzzled by her erratic maneuvers. He advanced cautiously.

Webb's gunners fired one shot that screeched over the *Weehawken* and sent up a geyser near the trailing *Nahant*. Rodgers, however, withheld fire and silently closed with the *Atlanta*.

The *Weehawken* steamed to within about three hundred yards of her and commenced firing, its two Dahlgren guns ripping the Rebel vessel. The first shot tore into the starboard casemate, sending fragments of the *Atlanta*'s armor and wood splinters flying through the ship. This shrapnel put forty to fifty men out of action on the gun deck, either suffering from wounds or stunned by the shell's impact. A second hit did minor damage, but another Yankee shot knocked out most of a gun crew on the *Atlanta*'s starboard side. A fourth round almost shattered the pilot house and wounded two of the pilots.

The *Atlanta* had fired seven shots, but none came close to the mark, because of her list. Fifteen minutes into the battle, with dozens of his crewmen down and his ship being hammered at close range by the enemy, Webb decided to surrender.

Confederate naval Commander James D. Bulloch later wrote: "It can hardly be said that he [Webb] was fighting his ship—he was simply enduring the fire of his adversary."

As Union boarding parties readied to come aboard the *Atlanta*, Webb briefly addressed his sullen men: "I have surrendered our vessel because circumstances over which I have no control have compelled me to do so. . . . I most earnestly wish that it had been otherwise, but Providence, for some reason, has interfered with our plans, and we have failed of success. . . . You all know that, if we had not run aground, the result would have been different. . . . I would advise you to submit quietly to the fate which has overtaken us. I hope we all may soon be returned to our homes and meet again in common brotherhood."[5]

U.S. marines and sailors soon clambered aboard the *Atlanta* and made prisoners of Webb and his officers and crew of about 160. None of the wounded Southerners was fatally injured.

In what must have been an exaggerated report, a *Philadelphia Inquirer* account said that a small boat from the *Weehawken*, under the command of Lieutenant Commander David B. Harmony, was the first to reach the *Atlanta*. According to the newspaper, Harmony met Webb to receive his sword, but the Confederate was more concerned with the boat's anchors being dropped and accidentally exploding the *Atlanta*'s torpedo: "With the utmost nonchalance, Harmony replied, 'I don't care anything about your torpedoes. I can stand them, if you can, and if you don't wish to be blown up with me, you had better tell me how to raise the torpedo,'" the *Inquirer* stated.

Commander Downes aboard the *Nahant* was irritated that he had not gotten off a shot before Webb capitulated. He anchored near the *Weehawken* and demanded to know why the enemy vessel had surrendered so quickly. Wanting credit for bringing the *Atlanta* to bay, Downes stirred the controversy of the *Nahant's* role in the battle for several years. Finally, in 1866, the U.S. Supreme Court ruled that the *Nahant* should be considered one of the capturing vessels. Webb and his crewmen were shipped north to a prison compound at Fort Lafayette in New York Harbor.

The *Atlanta* was towed to Port Royal as a Union war trophy and underwent repairs. Within months she was taken to the Philadelphia Navy Yard, where further work was done. By February 1864 the *Atlanta* was back in service—this time as a U.S. warship, the USS *Atlanta*. She participated in the unsuccessful James River campaign against Confederate forces in Virginia that spring. In May 1865 she was among ten Union ships to receive a citation for their actions in destroying Confederate rams in the James during the final campaign to capture Richmond.

Ironically, the *Atlanta* survived her captor, the *Weehawken*. This monitor continued in the blockade off Savannah and Charleston into the winter of 1863. Stationed near Morris Island off Charleston on December 6, 1863, the *Weehawken* was swamped by a heavy wave that flooded through an open hatch. She went to the bottom with about thirty seamen.

Disbelieving Savannahians were stunned and indignant over the *Atlanta's* demise. Many suspected the ironclad's crew had mutinied, which was untrue.

"Yesterday's papers confirm the report of the *Atlanta*," Savannahian Josephine Habersham wrote in her June 18 diary entry. "Oh! how provoking! In Ossabaw [actually Wassaw] Sound, not so very far from us, now!"[6]

Rumors of the *Atlanta's* capture reached Richmond before the actual news. Reacting to the unconfirmed reports, a Confederate official wrote, "If this be so, the people will wish that the Secretary [Mallory] had been on the boat that surrendered."[7]

With Webb a Union prisoner, command of Savannah's naval squadron went to Flag Officer William W. Hunter, a native Pennsylvanian. Hunter, sixty, had served some four decades in the U.S. Navy before resigning his commission to join the Confederacy. Prior to coming to Savannah, he had seen combat at New Orleans and commanded naval defenses along the Texas coast from 1861 to 1863. He had also overseen shore batteries along the Rappahannock River in Virginia.

If the loss of the *Atlanta* decimated Hunter's squadron, he received a boost in late June, when the ironclad CSS *Savannah* joined his forces. Launched in February, she underwent trial runs and fitting for several months before her commission.

With a full crew of twenty-seven officers and 154 men, the *Savannah* was 150-feet long and had a draft of about twenty-two feet. She was armed with four 6.4-inch Brooke guns, a spar torpedo, and a ram.

Forty of the *Savannah*'s sailors were from the gunboat *Chattahoochee*, whose boiler had exploded on May 27 at Columbus, Georgia. "The men were all nicely dressed when they left here, and on their arrival in Savannah, being all straight and in good condition, were the cause of many remarks," wrote their lieutenant in Columbus.[8]

In spite of her ominous appearance, the ironclad was corked up in the Savannah with the rest of Hunter's ships—a combination of her deep draft, the enemy blockade, and Confederate obstructions in the rivers confining her to the immediate vicinity of the city.

The wooden gunboat *Macon* was also launched in July from the Willink shipyard. Equipped with steam engines and sails, this vessel was 150 feet long and designed to carry six guns.

Work delays meant the *Macon* would not make her first trial run until February 1864 and not join the squadron until months later. The Confederate government had contracted with Willink in November 1861 for construction of three gunboats. The *Macon* was the only vessel completed.

XII

"A Great Calamity Has Befallen Our Arms"

Savannah and the rest of the Confederacy were intensely interested in the Federals' siege of Vicksburg, the most important Rebel strongpoint on the Mississippi River. The defender of the river city was John Pemberton, who once had commanded in Savannah.

Attention was also turned northward, where Lee's Army of Northern Virginia, after a brilliant victory at Chancellorsville, was on the offensive. Throughout the summer Savannah also followed with much interest the Union land and sea campaign to capture Charleston and the port's successful defense.

Almost ignored, at least in Savannah, was the fighting in middle Tennessee, where Braxton Bragg's western Confederates were trying to blunt the advance of Union forces under Major General William S. Rosecrans.

"The papers were filled today with gratifying news that Lee was taking his army into Yankeedoodledom!" Mrs. Habersham wrote on June 20. "God grant that we may be enabled to teach these wretches the bitter lesson of experience in warfare on their own soil!"[1]

Mrs. Habersham's husband, William Neyle Habersham, was a Savannah businessman known for his shipping ventures and dealings on the rice market. Three of their sons wore Rebel gray. After his baptism by fire near Charleston in June 1862, Joseph Clay Habersham had seen combat with the Army of Tennessee in the western campaigns. He would be transferred to the Army of Northern Virginia as a staff officer in time to fight at Fredericksburg.

Better known to Savannahians as "Willie," William N. Habersham, Jr., was three years younger than twenty-two-year-old Joseph. He served on the Rebel cruiser *Thomas L. Wragg* (better known as the *Nashville* or *Rattlesnake*) before joining the Savannah Cadets in August 1862. The unit was incorporated into the Fifty-fourth Georgia Infantry.

The Habershams' youngest son, Robert Beverly Habersham, turned seventeen in the summer of 1863, and was assigned to a signal corps unit near Fort McAllister.

The boom of enemy cannon on Saturday, July 4, 1863, annoyed Savannahians, who knew the Federals were celebrating Independence Day.

"The insolent Yankees in our neighborhood are firing their guns in honor of the day!" Mrs. Habersham wrote from the family's summer home on the Vernon River. "Little do they know or appreciate the precious boon of Liberty left us by our fathers on that glorious day, 1776."[2]

These bluejackets had even more to celebrate than they realized. News had not yet reached them or the Confederates around Savannah that Vicksburg had fallen after a six-week siege. They also didn't yet know that Lee's army was in full retreat from Pennsylvania after a three-day holocaust of battle at Gettysburg. These catastrophic defeats, coupled with Bragg's retreat in Tennessee, the loss of Port Hudson on the Mississippi, and the disaster of Brigadier General John Morgan's cavalry raid into Ohio, dulled Confederate optimism in Savannah and elsewhere.

The defiance, however, remained keen. "Reverses will but nerve to greater energy and self sacrifice the Southern arm and the Southern heart," Mrs. Habersham wrote on August 1.

"It is impossible to disguise the fact that a great calamity has befallen our arms," the *Savannah Republican* said on August 14. "Since the fall of Vicksburg and the battle of Gettysburg serious apprehensions are felt for our future destinies."[3]

Among the dead at Vicksburg was Major General John S. Bowen of Savannah. An 1853 West Point graduate, Bowen was an architect in St. Louis when the war began. He became a captain in the Missouri militia and served as chief of staff to militia General D. M. Frost. Both were captured when Frost surrendered a force of pro-South troops at Camp Jackson near St. Louis in May 1861.

After his parole Bowen organized and commanded the First Missouri Infantry. Promoted to brigadier general, he was attached to Brigadier General John C. Breckinridge's division and was wounded at Shiloh.

Bowen was commissioned a major general for his actions in opposing U.S. Grant's advance at Port Gibson, Mississippi, in 1863.

He fought in most of the battles of the Vicksburg campaign and was suffering badly from dysentery when the city was surrendered. Weakened by illness and war deprivations, Bowen died on July 13.

While the battle fates were shifting on other fronts, there had been little excitement for either side at Savannah for several months, other than the capture of the *Atlanta*.

Sailors in the Yankee blockading fleet were among the most bored of all, including Lieutenant Alfred Thayer Mahan, skipper of the USS *Cimarron* on station off Wassaw Sound.

"Blockading was desperately tedious work, [I] make the best one could of it. Day after day, roll, roll," he wrote in his 1907 book *From Sail to Steam*.[4]

Mahan would rise to greater heights. His teachings on naval warfare influenced the evolution of global sea power for decades to come, and he is widely considered the father of U.S. naval strategy in the late nineteenth and early twentieth centuries. Indeed, Akiyama Saneyuki, considered the "father of Japanese naval strategy," was a student of Mahan's theories, primarily through Mahan's book *The Influence of Sea Power Upon History*. Saneyuki and others molded Japan's naval operations in the Russo-Japanese War and in World War II.

There was a shakeup in the Union naval leadership off Savannah in late summer 1863. Admiral Du Pont was relieved of command on account, in large part, of his handling of the sea attack on Charleston in the spring. An assault including eight monitors was repulsed on April 7, 1863, with significant damage to the Federal squadron.

Du Pont decided not to renew the offensive after a conference with his captains. The decision, though probably correct, doomed his naval career. Intense criticism immediately came from the Navy Department and the Northern press. The crescendo of negativism did not abate until June 3, when Secretary Welles relieved Du Pont, replacing him with Commodore Andrew H. Foote. The commodore was en route to join the squadron when he was taken ill and died suddenly on June 26. When Welles's second choice, Rear Admiral John A. Dahlgren, arrived in July, Du Pont headed north. He served on several naval boards and commissions until his death in June 1865.

Best known as the inventor of the Dahlgren rifled gun, Dahlgren would command the blockading squadron off Savannah and Charleston until the war's end. Born in Pennsylvania in 1809, Dahlgren was a son of the Swedish consul at Philadelphia. He was appointed midshipman in the U.S. Navy in 1826 and served as an ordnance officer for sixteen years. During this time he invented what would become the "Dahlgren guns." There were several types of these rifled cannon, used primarily by the navy and known for their "soda-water bottle" design.

Dahlgren's son, Colonel Ulric Dahlgren, would be killed in a controversial Federal cavalry raid against Richmond in January 1864. Rebels alleged that papers found on Dahlgren's body contained instructions for the raiders to kill Jefferson Davis and his Cabinet members. The argument remains as to whether the documents were planted by Confederates.

Major General Quincy Gillmore, the conqueror of Fort Pulaski a year earlier, returned to the coast, replacing David Hunter as commander of the Union Department of the South. Gillmore concentrated on besieging Charleston, but couldn't puncture the Rebel defenses.

Du Pont's April 7 naval assault on Charleston nearly ended with one of the ocean war's most brilliant accomplishments for Savannah's Cheves brothers. They had helped develop a massive mine containing some three thousand pounds of black powder and designed to sink an enemy vessel. The mine was positioned off Charleston, and a cable was strung from it to a post ashore. Relying on direction from the Signal Corps, Assistant Engineer Langdon Cheves was set to electrically detonate the mine when alerted that a Union ship was in its proximity.

According to the Confederates, they got their chance when the USS *New Ironsides*, the hercules armorclad of the Union fleet, anchored almost directly over the mine. Aboard was Du Pont, who was supervising his attack.

Excited Rebels flagged the news to Cheves, who threw the switch. Nothing! The *New Ironsides* still rode calmly on the waves. Cheves desperately checked his connections and tried the detonator again and again—in vain.

The enemy ship steamed away leisurely, Du Pont and his crew unaware of the explosive fate they had avoided. Frustrated, the Confederates angrily blamed each other for this botched opportunity. Reasons varied from the cable being too long to detonate the mine to the line being severed when a wagon ran over it on the beach.

On August 1, 1863, General Mercer issued a call to area landowners to send slaves to strengthen Savannah's fortifications. "It is best to meet the enemy at the threshold and to hurl back the first wave of invasion," Mercer declared.[5]

"Once the breach is made, all the horrors of war must desolate your now peaceful and quiet homes. Let no man deceive himself. If Savannah falls, the fault will be yours, and your ... neglect will have brought the sword to your hearthstones." Mercer added that the government would be "responsible for the value of such negroes as may be killed by the enemy, or may in any manner fall into his hands."

August also saw the watery death of the old CSS *Savannah*, the first flagship of Josiah Tattnall's state navy in 1861. The Confederates had tried to convert her into a blockade-runner and renamed her the *Oconee* in April 1863. Rebel authorities questioned her seaworthiness, however, and sold her to private owners, who re-christened her the *Savannah* during the summer.

The *Savannah* ran aground near Fort Pulaski while trying to reach the Atlantic on an August night. Surprisingly she floated free and made it back to Savannah without alerting the Federals.

Two weeks later the paddle wheeler made it to sea. Bound for Nassau, she had a hold full of cotton to trade for iron to be used in the construction of a Rebel ironclad. Those who had declared her unfit for naval service were proven correct when the *Savannah* foundered and sank off St. Catherine's Island on August 18.

During the last week of the month, Colonel Charles Jones received orders from Beauregard to report to James Island near Charleston, where he would command the light artillery. "Do kiss my precious daughter for me," he wrote to his mother before departing.

On the South Carolina coast, Jones marveled at the spectacle of war and prayed for the Confederacy's deliverance. The enemy buildup on nearby Morris Island was in itself an awesome sight: "You can almost imagine that you are looking upon Staten Island; there is such an aggregation of shipping of every sort of description, and such a collection of tents, etc., that the island presents the appearance of a continuous village."[6]

From the north Georgia hills came the exhilarating news that Bragg's Army of Tennessee had crushed Rosecrans' forces at Chickamauga on September 20. The triumph was a much-needed elixir for Savannah's fading war hopes.

"This victory is a Godsend so far!" Mrs. Habersham penned in her diary. "Pray God we may follow it up."[7]

Chickamauga's hades earned one Savannahian a general's commission; he would not live to accept it. Colonel Claudius Charles Wilson led a brigade in the reserve corps of Major General W. H. T. Walker. Wilson was an Effingham County, Georgia, native who graduated from Emory College in 1851 and was practicing law in Savannah when the war started. He entered Confederate service as a captain in the Twenty-fifth Georgia and was commissioned colonel of the regiment in September 1861. Wilson served on the Georgia and South Carolina coasts through 1862 and served under General Johnston in the Vicksburg campaign.

Wilson fought so well at Chickamauga that he was recommended for promotion to brigadier general. The commission was approved but Wilson, by this time, was gravely ill. Stricken by fever, he died in camp at Ringgold, Georgia, on November 27, 1863. The Confederate Senate posthumously confirmed his appointment the following February.

"Dear wife children and father," South Carolina soldier S. M. Crawford wrote from the Savannah defenses on September 2, 1863. "I seet my self this evening to drop you a few lines to let you know that I am well though I am tired and worn out for sleep we reacht this place this morning I found the boys tolerable well I hope these lines may come safe to hand and find you all well I havent no nuse of interest to write at this time as I havent bin here long a nuf to here much. . . . I want you all to do the best you can and I will do the same Mahala I want you to kiss the children for me so nothing more but remaning your afectionate husband till death."

Another Carolinian, James Alexander, expressed the same sentiments to his "wife and childring" from a camp near Savannah on September 6: "I never shall be satisfied again till I see you all but God only knows when that will be. I wish this war was done with and that we could git to come home in peace and remain so. . . . Tell Susan she must be a smart little girl till I come home. I dreamed I seen her last night and she run to me for me to take her up in my lap. O, that it had a bin so."

Savannah was abuzz over the anticipated visit of President Jefferson Davis in late October. The chief executive arrived on a Halloween Saturday after a swing west to inspect Bragg's army. He also met with Bragg's generals, many of whom were near mutiny, feeling that Bragg was incompetent to command in not following up the Chickamauga victory.

Leaving Richmond on October 6 and traveling by train, Davis also made appearances in Augusta, Atlanta, Selma, Meridian, Mobile, Montgomery, Macon, and Charleston.

Confederate President Jefferson
Davis received an enthusiastic welcome
from hundreds of Savannahians when
he visited the city in October 1863.
(Courtesy of the Georgia Historical
Society.)

He emerged from a car in Savannah that morning and was welcomed by
an energetic crowd, including Mayor Richard Arnold, who delivered "an
eloquent and appropriate address," the *Daily Morning News* reported.

After being escorted to his suite at the Pulaski House hotel, the president
boarded the steamer *Beauregard* for a tour of the river forts and batteries.
He went ashore at Thunderbolt and inspected the Phoenix Regiment. Later
he addressed a large crowd from the Pulaski House portico.

That night, after a torchlit parade with bands playing patriotic tunes,
Davis attended a packed reception at the Masonic Hall, where Josephine
Habersham met him.

"He has a good, mild, pleasant face, not very remarkable," she wrote
of Davis, "but thoughtful and, altogether, looks as a President of our
struggling Country should look—care worn and thoughtful, and firm, and
quiet."[8]

"The President's visit here caused considerable stir," wrote C.S. sailor
Henry Graves to his mother in Social Circle, Georgia, on November 3. "It
was the first time I had ever seen him. . . . The [Masonic] hall was densely
crowded and an immense crowd filled the street on both sides of the door
for thirty yards trying to get in. I joined the crowd at first and thought I
would get in and see the sight, though not to shake hands with him, for I
detest this way of running after the big folks of the land."

Graves eventually wedged his way into the building, but closed his night on a more pleasurable note: "I wound up the evening by calling on a pretty sweetheart of mine here, which was far more to my taste, I assure you, than to form one of the crowd who with open mouths and strained eyeballs gape after the coattails of the President."

Among Davis' many worries were memories of his grand review of Bragg's army surrounding Chattanooga. As he rode past the gray formations, many of the ragged soldiers shouted, "Massa Jeff, give us something to eat," or "I'm hungry!" He also had to decide how to handle the open hostility between Bragg and his generals.

Davis attended Sunday services at Savannah's Christ Church on November 1 and spent much of the day weighing reports from Chattanooga. The news was not good. Union Major General U. S. Grant had succeeded in opening a new supply line to help relieve the Federals besieged in the city. Thus Davis was not in the best mood when his special train pulled out of Savannah headed to Charleston on Monday, November 2.

Less than a month later, Federal forces burst out of Chattanooga, sweeping Bragg from his mountain positions and sending the Rebel army reeling south into northern Georgia. Tennessee was forever lost to the Confederacy. This calamity would directly affect Savannah. A year later a Union army would bear down on the port city after using Chattanooga as a base to launch an offensive into Georgia in spring 1864.

XIII

Glory and Gloom—1864

On January 3, 1864, a Union major general stepped from a train into the brutally cold wind blasting off the Mississippi River at Cairo, Illinois. William T. Sherman had spent Christmas at home with his family in Lancaster, Ohio. Now he was returning to fight the war like an avenging devil intent on the Confederacy's demise. Savannah would feel his wrath before the year was out.

In early February, however, it was Mississippi that would be sliced by Sherman's saber. On February 3, five days before his forty-fourth birthday, he led an army out of Vicksburg intent on destroying railroads in the Confederate state and weakening Rebel forces still threatening Union naval traffic on the Mississippi.

Sherman's advance with some twenty-five thousand men was coordinated with a Federal expedition from Memphis. This offensive, led by Brigadier General William S. Smith, was intended to destroy the gray cavalry of Major General Bedford Forrest. Sherman succeeded in ripping up miles of valuable railroad and capturing Meridian, Mississippi, but Smith had little luck in cornering the elusive and dangerous Forrest. On the contrary, the outnumbered Forrest offered Smith more than he could handle, forcing him back to Memphis.

Sherman assumed command of the Military Division of the Mississippi in mid-March after spending several weeks involved in Union military operations at Vicksburg, New Orleans, and Memphis. In his new post Sherman would lead U.S. armies in the western theater. He replaced his close friend, Grant, who had been promoted to lieutenant general and given command of all U.S. armies.

Within days of his promotion, Sherman returned to the vast Union base at Nashville to begin planning and organizing an invasion of Georgia. The spring thrust would coincide with Grant's massive onslaught aimed at destroying Robert E. Lee's army in Virginia and capturing Richmond.

Sherman's career had been a wild ride of deep disappointment and stunning defeats and victories to reach this point.

One of eleven children, Sherman was born in Lancaster on February 8, 1820. His father was an Ohio supreme court justice who died suddenly in 1829, forcing the children to be split up among friends and relatives. Sherman was taken in by Senator Thomas Ewing, whose daughter he later married. The congressman obtained a West Point appointment for Sherman, who graduated sixth in the class of 1840.

Sherman fought in California during the Mexican War and resigned his army commission in 1853 to become a bank representative. When the company failed, he went into law practice in Leavenworth, Kansas, with two of his brothers-in-law.

In 1859 Sherman was named superintendent of the Louisiana State Seminary of Learning and Military Academy (which would later become Louisiana State University). He quit this post in January 1861 as the country moved closer to war.

Sherman ran a streetcar company in St. Louis until May 1861, when he accepted an army appointment as colonel of the Thirteenth U.S. Infantry. He was assigned to lead a brigade prior to the battle of First Bull Run and saw considerable action there.

Promoted to brigadier general of volunteers in August, Sherman was sent to Kentucky, where he did little to advance his military standing. In fact he was relieved of command by General Don Carlos Buell and reported to General Henry W. Halleck in St. Louis.

Sherman was soon given a division that was among Union forces surprised and overrun by the Confederates on the first day of fighting at Shiloh. Promoted major general of volunteers in May 1862, Sherman was at the center of action in the Union campaigns to reopen the Mississippi River. He commanded the Fifteenth Corps in the fighting at Vicksburg and was a key figure in the battles for Chattanooga.

"Sherman could be easily approached by any of his soldiers," wrote a Massachusetts captain, "but no one could venture to be familiar. His uniform coat, usually wide open at the throat, displayed a not very military black cravat and linen collar, and he generally wore low shoes and one spur."[1]

"General Sherman is the most American looking man I ever saw," Union Major John Chipman Gray wrote from the Savannah siege lines in December 1864, "tall and lank, not very erect, with hair like a thatch, which he rubs up with his hands, a rusty beard trimmed close, a wrinkled face, sharp prominent red nose, small bright eyes, coarse red hands; black felt hat slouched over the eyes.... He carries his hands in his pockets, is very awkward in his gait and motion, talks continually and with immense rapidity, and might sit to *Punch* for the portrait of an ideal Yankee."[2]

"His constitution is iron," wrote Major George Nichols of Sherman's staff. "In the field he retires early, but at midnight may be found pacing in front of his tent, or sitting by the camp-fire smoking a cigar.... He falls asleep as easily and quickly as a little child—by the roadside, upon the wet ground, on the hard floor, or when a battle rages near him."[3]

By May 5, 1864, Sherman had assembled about a hundred thousand men in and around Chattanooga and pushed them south into the north Georgia mountains. This invasion force included elements from the Union Army of the Cumberland, Army of the Tennessee, and Army of the Ohio.

Facing this host were Joseph E. Johnston and his Army of Tennessee, composed of some sixty thousand Confederates entrenched on rocky slopes and ridges around Dalton, Georgia. Johnston had replaced Bragg after the Southern debacle at Chattanooga.

During the months while Sherman was ravaging Meridian and gathering his forces for the strike into Georgia, Savannah's war zone remained relatively quiet—except for a brief episode of bloodshed and excitement in February. Early in the month the Rebels had gotten wind that a Union task force, including many assault troops, had left Port Royal heading south along the coast. Savannah went on alert, but the fleet plied past Tybee Island. It soon became apparent that the Federals were targeting Jacksonville.

The first squads of about seven thousand Union infantry went ashore on February 7, 1864, and occupied the north Florida town. In response to this threat, Beauregard ordered Major General Jeremy F. Gilmer at Savannah to ready the Sixty-fourth Georgia Volunteers, the First Florida Battalion, and a light infantry battery for quick deployment to Florida. Within days these units were ordered south to join Confederates massing against the Union threat. Other troops, including Savannah's Chatham Artillery posted in Charleston's defenses, also were sent to Florida as the Yankees marched inland from Jacksonville.

Beauregard now was facing an even more dire manpower dilemma in defending Savannah and Charleston. His already sparse lines were decimated by the reinforcements sent to Florida and by the loss of about five thousand Georgia and South Carolina troops whose enlistments had expired. Additionally he was beleaguered by requests to send men to bolster the Army of Tennessee.

Adding to his woes, after months of idleness the Federals finally stirred along the Savannah coast. On February 22 two forces of Union troops landed on Whitemarsh Island along the Savannah River.

This attack apparently was a diversion for the Yankees' thrust from Jacksonville across northern Florida. Neither blue nor gray at Savannah knew that this offensive had been stymied two days earlier in a major Confederate victory at Olustee, Florida.

Coming ashore at Gibson's Landing on Whitemarsh, one of the blue columns advanced toward Oatland Island. At a bridge between the islands, the Southerners frantically hauled up two cannon and blasted the bluecoats, causing them to retreat. Before reaching the landing, these Federals tangled with a small unit of the Fifty-seventh Georgia and routed it.

Yet other Confederates swarmed about the two columns, coming on "like bees," a New Hampshire soldier remembered. The Federals were driven back to their boats and the threat was ended.

The Chatham Artillery, meanwhile, had fought heroically at Olustee, and the Savannahians of Captain John Wheaton could rightly claim a huge share in the Southern victory. At times during the battle the cannoneers were alone at the front of the Confederate line, blasting away at oncoming blue infantry. After the fighting the unit was rewarded with at least one artillery piece captured from the Federals.

Also performing with outstanding bravery was Colonel George P. Harrison, Jr., whose brigade of Georgia and Florida troops was heavily engaged at Olustee. Harrison was born on Monteith Plantation near Savannah. His father, George P. Harrison, Sr., was a Georgia legislator and a brigadier general of state troops. The younger Harrison had held command positions at Fort Johnson, Morris Island, and John's Island earlier in the war. At Olustee he was wounded and earned a citation for his gallantry.

The enemy had been repulsed on Whitemarsh Island, but the minor victory's glow quickly dimmed in light of the hardships and war fatigue shrouding the Rebels at Savannah.

Writing to Beauregard from the city on February 27, General Mercer expressed concerns that the depletion of troops left him vulnerable to any serious attack. The same dispatch stated that the Twenty-sixth Virginia was being sent from Savannah to Florida that day. After the Olustee disaster, the Yankees had retreated to Jacksonville, where they could mount another operation at any time.

Mercer's report said that the Savannah defenders now consisted of four regiments, two battalions, two batteries, and assorted companies. Most of the men were assigned to the various forts.

If the mood of the military and citizenry was dark, the city itself still held charms for visitors, even in wartime. "It is a beautiful place, and, to quote an American guidebook, 'regularly built, with streets so wide and so unpaved, so densely shaded with trees, and so full of little parks,'" recalled FitzGerald Ross, an English cavalry captain serving in the Austrian Hussars. As a military observer, Ross visited Savannah briefly in the first weeks of 1864.

"The neighbourhood is exceedingly pretty, with drives on the banks of the river, and avenues of live oaks, bay-trees, magnolias, and orange-trees. A favourite drive is to the Cemetery of Bonaventure, which was originally a private estate, laid out in broad avenues; and these avenues of live oak, now grown to an immense size, with their huge branches sweeping the ground, and carrying heavy festoons of the hanging Spanish moss, are magnificent."

Ross and his companions stayed at the Pulaski House, "a capital hotel," where they briefly visited with General Beauregard.

St. Patrick's Day 1864 came and went with little or no notice, most of the city's Irishmen in Confederate service.

"Could you not draw a pair of grey pants & a dark jacket & let me have them?" a Rebel marine lieutenant wrote to a Maryland friend from Savannah in April. "If you can I will be much obliged to you. Have them as large as possible & I can have them altered."[4]

Historian A. A. Lawrence relates the story of a Union prisoner of war who was in Savannah and Macon during summer 1864. After he was exchanged in September, the soldier wrote that he found "a general-deep-felt weariness of war" and a "sort of expectation" that the conflict would soon end.[5]

The war and suffering were far from over. By May 12 Sherman had slipped past Johnston's positions at Dalton without a pitched battle, setting a precedent in his campaign to capture Atlanta. The Union commander would avoid an open fight if possible by wrapping his army around the flanks of Rebel strongholds in his path. The strategy proved successful as Johnston was grudgingly forced to retreat south, deeper into Georgia toward Atlanta.

Time after time the defensive-minded Virginian posted his men in formidable positions awaiting Sherman's attack. And time after time Sherman outflanked these potential deathtraps, sweeping around them and threatening to cut off Johnston from behind if he did not withdraw.

Within a few weeks of Sherman's advance, a brigade of three Georgia regiments under General Mercer was transferred from coastal service at Savannah to Johnston's army. George Mercer, now a captain on his father's staff, headed north with the Fifty-fourth Georgia, reaching Dalton on May 2.

Also joining Mercer's brigade was Colonel Charles Olmstead, who had surrendered Fort Pulaski to the Federals in 1862. Olmstead had spent time in Union prisoner of war camps before he was exchanged and rejoined the Confederates.

With the loss of Mercer's men, Savannah's defense force was even further weakened. "The reserve troops in the condition they are now will answer for provost guards, and for the city lines, but would not be reliable otherwise," Confederate Major General Lafayette McLaws wrote from Savannah in May.

Willie Habersham was among Mercer's Savannahians who joined Major General W. H. T. Walker's division in the Georgia mountains. His older brother Joseph was now a staff officer for Brigadier General States Rights Gist in Johnston's army. Joe Johnston was very secretive of his plans for dealing with Sherman, prompting Willie to write his mother: "If his [Johnston's] coat knew his plans he would throw it away!"

These Habersham brothers would never see Savannah again.

"I still keep in the very best of health, dear Wife, thanks to a merciful Providence and my men, too, are just as well as I could hope for," Olmstead wrote from north Georgia on June 8. "Please have the [Savannah] *Republican* sent to me regularly. I need a paper to keep me posted up on what is going on in the world. We are completely out of it here.... Do write me as often as you can, darling. I have only two of your letters as yet. How is

Charlie May? I am uneasy about him. Love to Mother, a sweet kiss for baby. God bless you, my own true wife."

Hamilton Branch of Savannah was barefooted in leading a company of Georgians in Mercer's Brigade digging in on Kennesaw Mountain, Johnston's latest rocky citadel: "I have been barefooted for two days, and it is pretty hard, although by the time you read this I will have received a pair [of shoes]. If it were not for the rocks, I would get along better."

Sherman's worst mistake of the Atlanta campaign was a head-long assault against Johnston at Kennesaw, a bloody blunder on June 27, which resulted in some 2,500 Union casualties in less than an hour.

Undismayed by his repulse on the mountain slopes, Sherman resumed his flanking tactics. Within a week, he had outflanked the Rebels on Kennesaw and taken aim at Atlanta.

The enemy's prowess was not lost on the Southerners. One doughty Confederate was heard to remark: "Sherman'll never go to hell. He'll outflank the devil and make heaven despite the guards."

Savannahians watching the developments in north Georgia were cheered by a rare naval victory in June. Frustrated by the clamp of the Union blockade, civilian criticism, their own inaction, and boredom, the Savannah squadron finally went on the offensive.

A plan to seize a Federal vessel by a surprise boarding had been hatched that spring by Confederate Lieutenant Thomas P. Pelot, former executive officer of the CSS *Georgia*. A U.S. Navy lieutenant who resigned his commission in 1861, Pelot was promoted to CSN lieutenant in October 1862. He had also served as skipper of the flagship CSS *Savannah* and the *Resolute*. Pelot, a South Carolinian, received permission to proceed and by late May had assembled a picked force of 102 officers and crewmen from the *Georgia*, CSS *Sampson*, and CSS *Savannah*.

The raiders gathered at Fort Jackson on the morning of May 31, and the steamer *Firefly* towed their boats through Augustine Creek to the Isle of Hope. From there the Rebels rowed in two columns to Battery Beaulieu on the Vernon River several miles below Savannah. The Vernon and the Little Ogeechee River intersected at Rose Dhu Island before emptying into Ossabaw Sound. Pelot had received word that a Union warship was anchored near the mouth of the Ogeechee. He and his force embarked from Beaulieu on the night of June 1, but found no sign of the vessel.

Prior to setting out that evening, Pelot gathered his men for a brief speech. "He said that they had discovered a vessel & would board her that night & that he expected every man to do his duty & felt confident that they would do so," recalled Midshipman Hubbard T. Minor, Jr., of the *Savannah*. "[H]e also called their attention to the low muttering of the thunder that could be plainly heard & told them that it was an indication that God was with them for the thunder indicated a dark night which could be nothing but favorable to their enterprise."[6]

Their hunt was unsuccessful, however, and the weary sailors returned to camp early on June 2 to eat and rest most of the day. Pelot would try again that night.

"When supper again was over all were called to muster & Mr. Pelot told the men that he did not think it necessary to say anything more to them," Minor wrote. "The men responded with cheers & said that 'they were in for it.'"[7]

In spite of continued stormy weather, the Rebels again climbed into their boats at Beaulieu and rowed into the darkness, their oars muffled. Pelot knew his mission was a fishing expedition at best, but an enemy vessel had been seen from the battery earlier in the day.

The Southerners reached Raccoon Key at the mouth of Ossabaw Sound about midnight. There Pelot received exciting news from scouts posted on the island. A Yankee gunboat was anchored for the night in the sound a half-mile north of nearby Bradley Creek.

Lightning streaked the sky as the seven barges of drenched Confederates silently rowed toward their prey after midnight on Friday, June 4, 1864.

Their unknowing target was the USS *Water Witch*, a 378-ton sidewheel gunboat armed with four cannon that had been on blockade duty off Savannah for several months. She was skippered by Lieutenant Commander Austin Pendergrast.

"[A]s closer we came the lightning discovered her plainly to us while our boats being white washed were not so easily discovered," Minor remembered. "When with in Three hundred yards all seemed to be asking god as I know I was to prosper our undertaking to shield us from harm & to make us do our duty."

About 2 A.M. a Yankee seaman on deck watch squinted to see one of Pelot's craft about forty yards away. Calling for the phantom boat to identify itself, the guard received the reply, "Runaway negroes," from Moses Dallas, a black pilot in Pelot's party. By now the barges had closed alongside the gunboat.

"We are rebels! Give way boys! Three cheers and board her!" Pelot cried.

A quick burst of fire from the deck wounded several Confederates in one of the boats and its crew rowed away, returning to Beaulieu with news that the expedition had failed.

In seconds, however, other yelling grey pirates struggled up the sides of the *Water Witch* and were on deck brandishing revolvers, cutlasses, and sabers.

Although few of the surprised Federals resisted, those that did put up a desperate fight. Pendergrast stumbled on deck and was knocked unconscious by a sword blow, which likely would have killed him if the blade had been sharper. Some accounts state that Pendergrast was struck by Pelot himself.

Another Union officer, seeing Pelot's silhouette in a lightning flash, killed the Rebel lieutenant with a shot to the chest.

The most courageous Yank was a black hand named Jeremiah Sills, who was in charge of the small arms rack. Sills was a stalwart, firing revolvers at the Rebels until he went down, riddled by bullets. Most of the Union crewmen cowered below decks—some, no doubt, because one attacker growled to them "Stay down there or I'll cut your damned noses off."

Within twenty minutes the fighting was over and the *Water Witch* was a Confederate prize. Shot through the heart, Pelot had been among the first to fall on deck. Dallas also was among the nineteen Rebel casualties. Federal losses were two killed, fifteen wounded (including six officers), and seventy-seven captured.

"Mr. Pelot was said to be the first man on board & did not live long after getting there for he was shot directly thro the heart," wrote Minor, who was among the wounded.

With Pelot down, command went to Lieutenant Joseph Price, who was stunned by "several Cutlass cuts" across his head.[8]

Without Dallas to guide them, the victorious Rebels had some difficulty in escaping with their conquest. The gunboat ran aground three times before she reached the safety of Battery Beaulieu that night. The last grounding forced the crew to toss provisions overboard to lighten her.

"When we came up we had a boat penant [sic] flying above the stars & stripes & we met with hearty cheers from all the assembled spectators," Minor wrote. He received a "little mule skin tobacco pouch" from one admiring belle and a bouquet from another.[9]

Pelot was hailed as a hero in Savannah and buried in Laurel Grove Cemetery. At his funeral service in Christ Church, his cap, uniform jacket, sword, and the *Water Witch*'s signal book were placed on the lid of his coffin.

According to some reports, Pelot was trying to shield John Deveaux, another black man in the attack force, when he was shot on the *Water Witch*'s deck. Deveaux, who evidently saw service for the Confederates aboard the *Georgia*, survived the war. He later was editor and business manager of the *Savannah Tribune* and a U.S. Customs official appointed by President William McKinley. Deveaux was eternally grateful to Pelot for saving his life and tended the officer's grave until his own death. He was buried in the black section of Laurel Grove not far from Pelot's resting place.

In death Jeremiah Sills earned praise for his courageousness from an unlikely source, the *Savannah Republican*: "The bravest man ... is said to have been a negro who had charge of the small arms and stood his ground, firing revolver after revolver until he finally fell under a concentrated fire, six or eight balls having penetrated his body."[10]

Although he had lost his ship and was now a prisoner, Pendergrast had earlier had another brush with Civil War naval history.

On March 8, 1862, he was a lieutenant aboard the USS *Congress* when the steam frigate was attacked by the CSS *Virginia* off Hampton Roads, Virginia. When the warship's captain, Lieutenant Joseph B. Smith, Jr., was decapitated by a Rebel shell fragment, command devolved upon Pendergrast. Seriously damaged by the *Virginia*'s fire, the *Congress* soon came under shelling from other Confederate vessels and ran aground.

Pendergrast hoisted a white flag and officially surrendered the ship. While officers from both sides discussed terms and care for the *Congress*' casualties, Union infantry and artillery ashore opened fire on the Southern seamen, killing and wounding several. Some Federal prisoners also died from the "friendly" fire. The shelling forced the Confederates to back off, and the *Virginia* returned to rake the *Congress* with her heavy guns, setting the frigate aflame. Hours later the dying warship exploded.

While he apparently had nothing to do with what a Rebel officer described as the "unparalleled treachery" of the *Congress*' botched surrender, Pendergrast drew the ire of some Southerners who blamed him for this breach of war etiquette.

He escaped from the burning hulk of the *Congress* to find even greater ignominy as captain of the *Water Witch*.

Under armed guard, the *Water Witch* prisoners arrived in Savannah on the night of June 4. "Of the number, fifteen were wounded, with a few exceptions, in the head, with sabres," the *Republican* said. "The night was very stormy, and the revolvers of our men had become so thoroughly saturated that they refused to fire, and consequently their sabres were almost the only weapons used."

Pendergrast and the other wounded were taken to the Naval Hospital, where they were allowed treatment by the ship's surgeon, W. H. Pearson. The other crewmen were sent by train to Camp Sumter, the prisoner of war compound at Andersonville, Georgia, on June 5. Accompanying them were three Union officers who had escaped from a Rebel stockade in the city, but had been recaptured on Hutchinson Island. The Southerners spent most of the day unloading stores and ammunition from the gunboat.

The Confederate Congress issued an address of praise for the capture, and Price was promoted to commander. The *Water Witch*'s battle flag was presented to Secretary Mallory as a war trophy.

The raid on the *Water Witch* was indeed a daring exploit, but it did nothing to ease the Union blockade pressure. The gunboat, now commanded by Confederate Lieutenant W. W. Carnes, was moved up the Vernon River to White Bluff to avoid anticipated attempts to recapture her.

Among her gray sailors was John Thomas Scharf, a CSN midshipman from Baltimore. At the time Scharf was courting Anna Wylly Habersham, the pretty fifteen-year-old daughter of William and Josephine Habersham. The love never flowered, however, and Anna spurned her young suitor while he was stationed aboard the *Water Witch*. Scharf, originally assigned to the CSS *Sampson*, would later write the renowned *History of the Confederate States Navy*.

Trapped in the river, the *Water Witch* would be of no use to the Rebs. She was burned on June 19 to keep her out of Union hands.

"We have a reported landing of the Yankees on Wilmington and White-marsh," Mary Jones wrote to her daughter, Mrs. Mary Mallard, on June 7. "No doubt they are enraged at the recent capture of the *Water Witch*. The troops are all withdrawn and the defense of Savannah would devolve upon the light artillery. We are having most solemn and interesting prayer meetings every afternoon at five o'clock. Churches are crowded. Will not our Almighty Father, our Judge and Deliverer, hear and answer our cries for mercy?"

About the time of the *Water Witch* episode, Savannah received word that one of the city's romances was tragically over with the death of a young lover on the battlefield.

Confederate Brigadier General Gilbert
Moxley Sorrel of Savannah. (Courtesy of
the Georgia Historical Society.)

Colonel Edward S. Willis of the Twelfth Georgia Infantry was fatally
wounded in a blast of grapeshot while leading a charge at Bethesda Church,
Virginia, on May 30. He died the next day, hours before papers arrived
commissioning him a brigadier general, according to some accounts.

The twenty-three-year-old officer was engaged to the sister of future
Confederate Brigadier General G. Moxley Sorrel of Savannah. After
suffering his death wound, Willis gasped to officers trying to comfort him,
"Tell her not to be distressed. I die in the best cause a man could fall in."

He would be buried in the Sorrel family vault at Laurel Grove where his
sweetheart, Annie, eventually would join him.

Sorrel was also making a name for himself in the desperate fighting in
northern Virginia. He had risen through the ranks since his days as a bank
clerk and militiaman who joined in Fort Pulaski's seizure. He watched the
war-opening bombardment of Fort Sumter and served through the early
summer of 1861 with the Georgia Hussars on Skidaway Island. Like most
Southerners, he yearned for combat and decided to break with his comrades
on the coast. "Becoming impatient of inaction at Savannah . . . I decided to
go to Virginia and seek employment there."[11]

Sorrel found "employment" on Lieutenant General James Longstreet's
staff as captain and volunteer aide-de-camp. As a staff officer, Sorrel was at
First Bull Run and with Longstreet through the Army of Northern

Virginia's many campaigns. He had been promoted to colonel when his brightest moment occurred in the slaughter at the Wilderness in May 1864. There Sorrel displayed his combat leadership in rallying Rebel units for a successful attack on the left flank of Union Major General W. S. Hancock's II Corps, the veterans who had blunted Pickett's Charge at Gettysburg.

Sorrel's efforts resulted in his promotion to brigadier general in October and to command of a Georgia brigade in Major General William Mahone's division.

The June 21 sinking of the famed Rebel cruiser CSS *Alabama* off Cherbourg, France, was a depressing jolt to the entire South and for a Savannah family in particular.

Colonel Edward Anderson's son, Edward Maffitt Anderson, was a midshipman on the *Alabama* when the USS *Kearsarge* sent her to the bottom after a brief sea battle. Young Anderson was not among the listed survivors. "My worst fears are realised [sp] and my noble boy is no more," his father wrote. In spite of gruesome reports that young Edward had been hurled overboard, leaving a mangled leg on the deck, the family received better news two weeks later. Edward was alive. He had been slightly wounded, but managed to stay afloat until rescuers pulled him from the sea.

During the summer Father Peter Whelan volunteered to go to Andersonville and do what he could for the thousands of Yankees imprisoned there. He was recovered from his incarceration after Fort Pulaski's fall and often traveled to military posts in the state to oversee the soldiers' spiritual needs.

Arriving at Camp Sumter on June 16, Whelan spent four months in the hellhole at a time when the death rate among the prisoners was at its highest. Whelan spent his days visiting with the filthy, half-naked men, trying to cheer and comfort them. He also spent much time administering the last rites.

In north Georgia the war ground on, the armies of Johnston and Sherman edging ever closer to Atlanta in a lethal minuet of marches and countermarches.

Johnston's series of parries and inability to at least pick a fight quickly wore thin with the Southern public as well as with Jefferson Davis. A commander of action was needed, and Davis ordered Lieutenant General John Bell Hood to relieve Johnston on July 17.

Hood was a totally different breed from Johnston, preferring attack to any form of defense. He wrote of the "ruinous policy" pursued by Johnston in the retreat to Atlanta and said the soldiers of this army had "been so long habituated to security behind breastworks that they had become wedded to the 'timid defensive' policy, and naturally regarded with distrust a commander likely to initiate offensive operations."[12]

There were few timid souls in the Army of Tennessee. Hood immediately went on the assault, bludgeoning the enemy in a series of sledgehammer blows that did little but add to the body count on both sides. The fighting was horrific along Peachtree Creek and the Chattahoochee River.

Battle-savvy Rebels had referred to Mercer's brigade from Savannah as "New Issue" and the "Silver Fork Brigade" when they first reached the front. In the fighting before Atlanta, however, the brigade sustained about 170 casualties, earning respect with their blood.

Among the Savannahians lost defending Atlanta were the Habersham brothers.

"Willie and I are well," Lieutenant Joseph Habersham wrote his mother from Atlanta on the morning of July 21, 1864. He and his brother were among the thousands of Confederates preparing for Hood's massive assault that day. The lieutenant had written his mother a letter the previous night and added his postscript on the outside of the envelope.

The Habershams were in different units, but would be in the thickest of the fighting at Peachtree Creek. Tragically, they were slain within an hour of each other.[13]

Joseph Habersham fell mortally wounded, gasping, "Tell my Mother I die happy. I died at my post fighting for my country."[14]

Told of his brother's death, Willie fought with a vengeance, prompting comrades to caution him about needlessly exposing himself to enemy fire. He replied, "When I shoot these last ten cartridges I will take care, not before!" He was killed moments later.

A Georgian wrote to Mrs. Habersham from the battlefield the next day: "God only knows how you will bear this terrible affliction—this double affliction!"

Colonel Olmstead, also in the midst of the battle, described the double slayings as "a pathetic incident."

The brothers were returned to Savannah and buried at Laurel Grove, their graves marked by a marble obelisk inscribed "In Their Death They Were Not Divided."

Hood's fierceness could not override Sherman's superior numbers, and the Federals knotted their hold on Atlanta through the late, violent

Savannah brothers Joseph Clay Habersham and William Neyle
Habersham were killed in the same hour during heavy fighting along
Peachtree Creek near Atlanta. (Courtesy of the
Georgia Historical Society.)

summer. Hood evacuated Atlanta on September 1, taking his outnumbered
and demoralized army north and west of the city. He hoped to draw the
Federals out and perhaps crush them in the wilds of north Georgia, a
desperate hope at best.

Within two weeks of Atlanta's capture, trains carrying hundreds of Union
prisoners rumbled into Savannah. These Yankees were from Camp Sumter.
The Confederates had been forced to relocate hundreds of "healthy"
prisoners from the Andersonville site to Savannah, Charleston, and other
camps on account of the threat of Union raiding parties.

Father Whelan prepared to leave Camp Sumter to return to Savannah.
One of his last acts there probably saved a great number of the Federals'
lives. Whelan arranged to buy ten thousand pounds of wheat flour and had
it baked into bread for the prisoners. The grateful Yanks called it "Whelan's
bread."[15]

In Savannah the prisoners were herded from their cars and marched to several hastily erected stockades in and around the city. One of these makeshift prison camps was on the grounds of the Savannah Poor House and Hospital Society; another was near the city jail.

Confederate marines and sailors from the gunboats were among troops detailed to guard the camps, which may have contained as many as four thousand Federals for about five weeks.

The prisoners "were the most miserable, degraded, ragged, filthy wretches your eyes ever beheld," an officer wrote. Another Rebel wrote of seeing many of Savannah's "respectably dressed women" throwing bread to the captive Yankees.

Prisoner John Ransom of the Ninth Michigan Cavalry confided in his diary: "Rebel guards that I sometimes come in contact with are marines, who belong to rebel gunboats stationed in the mouth of the Savannah River. . . . They seem a kindly set, and I don't believe they would shoot a prisoner if they saw him trying to get away."[16]

Yankees in the poor house stockade were active in their escape schemes, especially tunneling. "On one occasion a cow caved in the hole they had dug, giving them away," a Confederate recalled. "They have to be watched very close to keep them from getting out. I don't blame them, would get out too if I was in the same condition and could get out."[17]

Some of Savannah's ladies presented a new battle flag to the First Georgia Regulars on September 29. The Regulars had been assigned to defenses on Whitemarsh Island, including the Turner's Rock battery.

The belles, no doubt, did not stay for dinner. These Rebs were in dire need of provisions, often feasting on rats and parched acorns. "I have tried the acorns but am not quite hungry enough to go the rats," wrote Sergeant W. H. Andrews of Company M.

"Rat details" were turned out each morning to dig up rodents burrowed near the camps. "The boys say they eat as well as a cat squirrel, but I am willing to take their words for it," Andrews recalled. The Confederates also survived on oysters and crabs.[18]

On October 5, a week before his forty-ninth birthday, Confederate Lieutenant General William J. Hardee assumed command of the Department of South Carolina, Georgia, and Florida. He succeeded Major General Samuel Jones, who was to head the Department of South Georgia and Florida. Hardee's appointment to the post came on September 28, but it took him several days to make the trip and join his troops.

"Old Reliable" Lieutenant General
William J. Hardee, Confederate
defender of Savannah

A Georgian nicknamed "Old Reliable" by his soldiers, Hardee was a veteran of most of the western campaigns and considered by many to be one of the Confederacy's best corps commanders. Born in Camden County in 1815, Hardee graduated from West Point in 1838. Among his classmates were future Confederate generals P. G. T. Beauregard and Henry C. Wayne.

Hardee served in Florida during the Second Seminole War and was twice breveted for gallantry in the Mexican War. From June 1856 until September 1860 he was commandant of cadets at West Point. During the pre–Civil War years, he also wrote *Rifle and Light Infantry Tactics*, a military manual published in 1861 and studied by officers on both sides. After Georgia's secession Hardee resigned his lieutenant colonelcy and by October was a Confederate major general.

Hardee spent the war's early months in Arkansas organizing troops before being called to join General A. S. Johnston's army in Mississippi prior to the battle of Shiloh. He led a wing of the Army of Tennessee in Bragg's blunderous Kentucky campaign in 1862. Promoted lieutenant general in October of that year, Hardee fought at Stones River and commanded a corps at Chattanooga. He was so well respected that he was offered command of the Army of Tennessee when Bragg was ousted during

Ill-starred Lieutenant General John Bell Hood, commander of the Confederate Army of Tennessee, criticized General Hardee for alleged shortcomings in the battles for Atlanta.

the winter of 1863. Hardee led the army on an interim basis, but refused the permanent command that then went to Joseph Johnston.

Hardee was rankled, however, when Hood was chosen to replace Johnston at Atlanta in July 1864. Hood was his junior in rank and Hardee felt he had been overlooked. Hardee also believed Hood was unequal in "both experience and natural ability to so important a command."

The hard feelings boiled over in the summer's ferocious battles for Atlanta. Hood blamed Hardee for the repulse of an assault at Peachtree Creek, stating "we failed on account of General Hardee." Hood went on to criticize Hardee for his handling of other actions, including the battle of Jonesboro.

Hardee biographer N. C. Hughes, Jr., wrote, "Certainly at Atlanta neither Hardee nor the Army of Tennessee seemed as effective as in the past. Too many factors enter into an explanation—lack of morale, difficulties of trench warfare, and others—to enable one to isolate a single cause.... As an aggressive optimist, Hood could hardly admit to himself or to others that perhaps his army lacked the capability to carry out its assignment or that he himself was deficient."[19]

With Hood calling for Hardee's relief from command and Hardee requesting reassignment, President Davis sent Hardee to the South Atlantic seaboard in late September.

Hardee arrived in Charleston by train from Augusta on October 5. He had only about 12,500 scattered troops to defend his vast domain, most of them stationed around Savannah and Charleston. He spent several weeks trying to bolster defenses guarding the two seaports and making inspection tours.

"We have seen a great deal of service with him & the men all admire him," a Kentucky Confederate wrote from Savannah.

By mid-October another well-known Confederate, Beauregard, had assumed command of the newly formed Military Division of the West, which included Georgia. The position was primarily that of an adviser, although Beauregard held authority over Hardee and Hood.

"The army of Sherman still defiantly holds the City of Atlanta," Beauregard decreed from his headquarters on October 17. "He can and must be driven from it. It is only for the good people of Georgia and surrounding States to speak the word and the work will be done."[20]

Beauregard could not know that Sherman was perfectly willing to leave Atlanta on his own. The problem was that his departure would herald a devastation that would virtually gut Confederate Georgia.

XIV

"Give Sherman
Hail Columbia"

While Beauregard and Hardee sized up their isolated and sparse forces, Sherman was doing his homework in camp near Atlanta. Poring over prewar documents and reports, he studied census figures from Georgia counties and devoured data about crop types, patterns, and yields. This same type of research had served him well in the march from Chattanooga to Atlanta.

Sherman had no innate interest in geography. He wanted to know about how many people might possibly oppose him on a march of hundreds of miles through hostile country. He also wanted to know if the enemy's farmlands could sustain his army.

On October 9 Sherman wired Grant proposing "that we strike out with our wagons for Milledgeville, Millen, and Savannah. Until we can repopulate Georgia, it is useless for us to occupy it; but the utter destruction of its roads, houses, and people, will cripple their military resources.... I can make this march and make Georgia howl!"[1]

Late October found Hood's army in northern Alabama, preparing for an offensive into Tennessee that the Rebels forlornly hoped might penetrate as far as Ohio.

Sherman had spent several weeks in futile maneuvering to close with Hood, but when the Confederate moved his army away from Atlanta, Sherman gave up the chase. He decided to let Major General George H. Thomas in Nashville deal with Hood while he concentrated on carving his name somewhere in the Confederacy's hollow interior.

Union Major General
William T. Sherman in an 1864 portrait

"This army is ready to march to Mobile, Savannah or Charleston," Sherman wrote his wife, Ellen, on October 21, "and I am practising them in the art of foraging and they take to it like ducks to water. . . . We won't starve in Georgia."[2]

After some initial reservations, Grant agreed to Sherman's plan, provided that he did not start before the presidential election on November 8. Both generals supported Abraham Lincoln and wanted him safely reelected before embarking on such a daring scheme. Lincoln easily defeated Democratic opponent George B. McClellan, and Sherman prepared to cut loose from Atlanta.

Grant favored Sherman's idea to march to the Georgia coast, putting the army in a position to be shipped north to reinforce Grant's armies in Virginia. There were other options. In addition to Mobile, Sherman also considered a thrust from Atlanta toward Pensacola.

Grant and Sherman decided on the "march to the sea" through Georgia, but Savannah was not a set target from the start. "I had no purpose to march direct for Richmond by way of Augusta and Charlotte, but always designed to reach the sea-coast first at Savannah or Port Royal, South Carolina, and even kept in mind the alternative of Pensacola," Sherman recalled.

Beauregard and Hood, meanwhile, believed Sherman was on the march—but still chasing Hood's army into Tennessee.

By November 14 Sherman had reassembled his forces in and around Atlanta after their pursuit of Hood. He sent his wounded and sick back to Chattanooga, trimming his army for the campaign.

He grouped his troops into two strike columns: the right wing, consisting of the Fifteenth and Seventeenth Corps, would be led by Major General Oliver O. Howard; while the left wing, composed of the Fourteenth and Twentieth Corps, would be commanded by Major General Henry W. Slocum.

The army was about sixty-two thousand strong, including more than fifty-five thousand infantry, 5,500 cavalry under Brigadier General Judson Kilpatrick, and 1,800 artillerymen with sixty-five guns. Three thousand supply wagons would accompany them loaded with ammunition, a twenty-day supply of hardtack, forty days' rations of sugar, and coffee and salt.

Sherman wrote that the army "stood detached from all friends, dependent on its own resources and supplies." Each of the corps had 150 ambulances and pontoons for river crossings. Herds of cattle, enough for forty days of beef, followed the army.

Opposing this blue horde were some thirteen thousand Rebels, including scattered units of state militia, local defense troops composed of convalescents, boys and old men, and the cavalry of Major General Joseph Wheeler. They would prove to be little more than an annoyance to the superior enemy they faced.

Sherman had great confidence in both his wing commanders. Nicknamed the "Christian General" and "Old Prayer Book," on account of his deep religious ties, Oliver Howard was a career soldier from Maine who was just short of his thirty-fourth birthday. He graduated fourth in the West Point class of 1854, which included J. E. B. Stuart, Custis Lee, John Pegram, and others whose fates converged in the war.

Howard was a West Point instructor when the conflict began. Elected colonel of the Third Maine volunteers, he led a brigade at First Bull Run that was among many Federal units driven from the field in disorder. Nevertheless, he was promoted to brigadier general of volunteers in September.

Howard lost his right arm at the battle of Seven Pines, but fought at Second Manassas. He also commanded a division in the Union Eleventh Corps at Antietam (after John Sedgwick was wounded). Promoted to major general in November 1862, Howard was at Fredericksburg in December and

Union Major General W. T. Sherman (*seated center*) and some of his
principal commanders in the Georgia Campaign. *From left:* generals
O. O. Howard, John A. Logan, William B. Hazen, Sherman, Jefferson
C. Davis, Henry W. Slocum, and J. A. Mower. Logan led the Union
Fifteenth Corps until he was wounded in combat before the fall of
Atlanta. After the capture of Savannah, he returned to active duty.

assumed command of the Union Eleventh Corps in March 1863. At
Chancellorsville in May 1863 Howard's corps bore the full brunt of
"Stonewall" Jackson's flank attack and was routed.

On the first day at Gettysburg, Howard assumed overall command of
Union forces after the death of Major General John Reynolds and before
the arrival of Major General W. S. Hancock. He received a vote of thanks
from Congress for his actions at Gettysburg, but is often criticized for his
indecisiveness there.

The Eleventh Corps was transferred to Chattanooga in fall 1863, and
Howard led it in the Atlanta campaign. When Major General James B.
McPherson was killed, Sherman assigned Howard to command the Army
of the Tennessee, which became a wing in Sherman's march to the Atlantic.

A New Yorker, Slocum was an 1852 West Point graduate and a veteran
of the Seminole wars. He resigned from the service to practice law in 1856,
but remained active in the state militia. As colonel of the Twenty-seventh
New York, Slocum was wounded in the thigh at First Bull Run. Promoted
to brigadier general in August 1861, Slocum was appointed major general in

July 1862. He fought in the Peninsula campaign at Second Manassas, and was given command of the Twelfth Corps after the battle of Antietam. Slocum also performed admirably at Chancellorsville, Gettysburg, and Chattanooga. He assumed command of the Twentieth Corps during the Atlanta campaign.

Sherman torched much of Atlanta before the first units of his army set out for the sea on November 15. The general himself left the next morning, riding out the Decatur Road and listening as thousands of bluecoats on the march belted out the words to "John Brown's Body."

"Behind us lay Atlanta, smouldering and in ruins, the black smoke rising high in the air, and hanging like a pall over the ruined city," Sherman remembered.[3]

Splitting his wings, Sherman moved east, Howard's columns and the cavalry headed toward Macon, and Slocum marched in the direction of Augusta. These movements kept the Confederates guessing as to his true destination and did not allow them to concentrate their meager forces.

Among the general orders issued by Sherman on November 9 was this: "The army will forage liberally on the country during the march." He added that each brigade would organize a foraging party to sustain the commands and that the destruction of houses, mills, cotton gins and other buildings was left to the discretion of the corps commanders.[4]

"No doubt, many acts of pillage, robbery, and violence were committed by these parties of foragers, usually called 'bummers,'" Sherman wrote in his memoirs. He defended the army, however, adding that such occurrences were "exceptional and incidental" and that he knew of no cases of murder or rape. Undoubtedly some assaults on women occurred during the march.

The army's three-hundred-mile trek from Atlanta to the sea was marked by the destruction of hundreds of buildings, looting, and pillaging along a sixty-mile-wide swath. Sherman's troops also wrecked hundreds of miles of railroad so crucial to the Confederacy.

Still thinking Sherman had marched into Tennessee, Beauregard did not learn of the enemy's real location until November 17. By this time Hood's army was some three hundred miles to the west and would be of no help against Sherman.[5]

Hood also refused Beauregard's order to send a cavalry division to reinforce Wheeler's troopers, who were already engaging Sherman's columns spilling out of Atlanta to the east.

Beauregard had received some early warning of Sherman's threat on

November 15, when a dispatch from Rebels outside Atlanta was forwarded to him from Lieutenant General Richard Taylor, commander of the Department of Alabama and Mississippi headquartered in Selma. Taylor's report stated, "Scouts and prisoners report enemy destroying railroad between Atlanta and Marietta. Prisoners report Sherman in Atlanta, and that camp rumor says he will move towards Mobile or Savannah. Prisoners also report 15th and 20th Corps at Atlanta. Large fires observed in Atlanta for last three days."

In desperation, the Confederate government ordered Hardee to consolidate his forces under General Bragg, now commanding at Augusta with about ten thousand troops. These blue vandals had to be stopped!

Believing that Sherman intended to attack Augusta, Bragg and his garrison watched in vigilant idleness as the Yankee columns plundered their way well south of them to the coast.

The only notable battle before Sherman reached Savannah's defenses occurred on November 22 near the village of Griswoldville. There Georgia militia clashed with the rearguard of the Union Fifteenth Corps. The Rebel attack was beaten off with the militia suffering some five hundred casualties, many of them young boys and gray-haired men. "I hope we will never have to shoot at such men again," a shaken Union captain wrote after inspecting the battle carnage. "They knew nothing at all about fighting, and I think their officers knew as little."[6]

Units of Slocum's wing captured Milledgeville, the Georgia capital, on November 23 while the right wing was temporarily delayed at the Oconee River by Confederates dug in on the opposite bank. Among Rebels captured when U.S. troops crossed the Oconee were a number of convicts released from the state prison on condition that they fight for the Confederacy.

Beauregard was in close communication with Jefferson Davis during this time and received these instructions from the president on November 30: "It is probable that the enemy, if short of supplies, may move directly for the coast. When that is made manifest you will be able to concentrate your forces upon the one object, and I hope, if you cannot defeat his attempt, that you may reduce his army to such a condition as to be ineffective for further operations."

Sherman's troops reached Millen, about seventy-five miles northwest of Savannah, on December 3, shortly after the Rebels abandoned Camp Lawton, a prisoner of war complex at nearby Magnolia Springs. The prisoners had been hastily sent off by train.

At Millen, Sherman's forces shifted direction from east to a more southerly course. The Union wings continued their advance along routes roughly parallel to the Savannah and Ogeechee rivers, meeting weak resistance.

Wheeler's three thousand gray cavalry were outnumbered by Kilpatrick's troopers, but kept up a running fight throughout the march. There was sharp combat between the mounted squadrons in the Waynesboro vicinity on November 27 and again on December 4. At the time, Kilpatrick was raiding in the direction of Augusta to keep the Confederate brass guessing as to the army's objective. He also had been ordered by Sherman to fight Wheeler at every opportunity.

Wheeler was arguably one of the South's finest cavalry generals. Born in Augusta in September 1836, he graduated from West Point in 1859, with some of his worst grades coming in cavalry tactics. A second lieutenant in the U.S. Mounted Rifles, he resigned his commission in April 1861 to join the South. First assigned as an artillery lieutenant, Wheeler was appointed colonel of the Nineteenth Alabama Infantry in September and led the regiment at Shiloh. Shortly afterward he transferred to the cavalry and was promoted to brigadier general in October 1862. At age twenty-six, his leadership resulted in a major generalcy in January 1863, and Wheeler was given command of cavalry in the Army of Mississippi the following July.

Nicknamed the "War Child" and "Fighting Joe," Wheeler was a daring combat officer who suffered three battle wounds and had some sixteen horses shot from under him. He headed the Rebel cavalry in Bragg's ill-fated Kentucky invasion and fought at Stones River and Chattanooga.

In the battles before Atlanta, Wheeler was extremely active, hitting Sherman's communications and supply lines. His fortunes waned, however, when Sherman opened his "March to the Sea."

"I know he's a hell of a damned fool, but I want just that sort of man to command my cavalry on this expedition," Sherman is said to have remarked about Kilpatrick before embarking on the march.

A veteran and tough fighter, Kilpatrick was also known as a swaggering womanizer notorious for his exaggeration of combat action. He and Joe Wheeler had been cadets together at West Point. Kilpatrick was still recovering from a severe wound sustained at Resaca, Georgia, in May when he was given command of Sherman's cavalry for the drive toward Savannah.

Born in rural New Jersey in January 1836, Kilpatrick graduated from

West Point in 1861, and became a captain of the Fifth New York Infantry. Wounded in a skirmish at Big Bethel weeks later, Kilpatrick recovered to rise through the ranks to brigadier general of volunteers by June 1863. During this time he saw battle in the Army of the Potomac's campaigns in Virginia, including Brandy Station and Stoneman's raid in 1863. Kilpatrick served admirably during this time and deserved his promotions. But leading a cavalry division at Gettysburg, he ordered the ill-fated charge that resulted in the controversial death of Union Brigadier General Elon Farnsworth.

His reputation was further sullied in February 1864 when his cavalry raid to free Union prisoners in Richmond was repulsed. Sent to the Tennessee-Georgia front in April, Kilpatrick commanded a cavalry division under Sherman until wounded at Resaca. He returned to duty in July and served with Sherman throughout the rest of the war.

While the Confederate horse generally held its own against Kilpatrick, the Rebels could do little to hinder Sherman's advance. Indeed, Wheeler and his men came under severe criticism for their conduct in the campaign. One Confederate described Wheeler's troopers as "the meanest set of men that ever lived," adding that they had "stolen and destroyed more than the enemy."

"They are doing us little good and an immense amount of harm," the *Daily Morning News* said of Wheeler's boys on December 1.[7]

Even one of Beauregard's staff officers condemned the conduct of the mounted Confederates. Colonel Alfred Roman reported that the troopers' "alleged depredations and straggling propensities and reported brutal interference with private property have been common by-words in every country where it has been their misfortune to pass. Public rumor condemns them everywhere."

The Rebel cavalry probably did forage as liberally as the enemy while falling back toward Savannah in 1864. Their bony horses were exhausted and provisions were scarce. In spite of the criticism, Wheeler's horsemen would play a crucial role in the struggle for Savannah.

Kilpatrick's troopers were hated by the unlucky Georgians they encountered on their ride and also weathered criticism and derision from within Sherman's marching columns. Infantry and cavalry have routinely clashed in every army in history, but the venom directed at these blue horse soldiers was especially bitter.

Infantry Major James A. Connolly of the Union Fourteenth Corps described Kilpatrick as "the most vain, conceited, egotistical little popinjay I ever saw." The major also wrote that Kilpatrick's men were "a positive nuisance; they won't fight, and whenever they are around they are always in the way of those who will fight."

Connolly continued his tirade the next day: "Confound the cavalry. They're good for nothing but to run down horses and steal chickens. I'd rather have one good regiment of infantry than the whole of Kilpatrick's cavalry."

To the Confederates the weeks of November and December were a daily calendar of defeat, not only in the Savannah campaign but elsewhere. Lee's army was pinned in the miles of trenches surrounding Petersburg, Virginia, slowly being bled to death by besieging Federal armies under U. S. Grant. And the reelection of Lincoln was salt in the wounds of all true Rebels.

Disaster also dogged Southern forces west of the Mississippi. Major General Sterling Price's October offensive into Missouri was blunted, and the war effort there had been relegated to scattered guerrilla raids.

Desertions plagued the Confederates on all fronts, including Savannah. W. H. Andrews of the First Georgia recalled how some comrades gathering oysters in a boat surrendered to the Yankees at Fort Pulaski. "Well it will be a cold day in August when I go to the enemy," he wrote. "I would as soon go to the devil and be done with it, for I have about as much love for one as the other."[8]

Hood, having failed to draw Sherman into a knock-down fight or to significantly damage the enemy's supply line between Chattanooga and Atlanta by mid-November, marched north to threaten Nashville. The battle flags of the Army of Tennessee were headed north again. In this choice, however, Hood had left the heart of the Confederacy virtually defenseless before Sherman, whatever direction his blue adversary chose to take from Atlanta.

Hood dashed his brigades to pieces at Franklin, Tennessee, on November 30, making a spectacular but tragic assault with some eighteen thousand men, more Rebels than took part in Pickett's Charge at Gettysburg. Never in the war would another one-day battle end with so many Southerners being killed, including six generals. Bloodied but unbowed, Hood's army staggered on toward Nashville, enduring one of the worst winters on record.

"We know but little of Sherman's army," Baz Peterson, of the Nineteenth South Carolina, wrote his parents on December 6 from Hood's lines. "We have a report that he is trying to make his way out of Georgia via

Savannah. I am very much in hopes his army will be gobbled up and destroyed. I am very hopeful."

The flickering hope of the Tennessee campaign's climax came on December 15–16, when General Thomas' forces overwhelmed Hood on the icy hills south of Nashville. Among the hundreds of Southerners taken prisoner was Brigadier General Henry R. Jackson of Savannah. Jackson had returned to national service after the Georgia troops he commanded were conscripted into the Confederate military. Leading a brigade in Cheatham's Corps, Jackson had fought in the Atlanta campaign and shared in the gray nightmare of Hood's Tennessee offensive.

As Sherman tightened a mailed fist on Savannah, Hood and the pitiful remnants of his army were plodding south in demoralized retreat, many of the shoeless Rebels leaving bloody footprints in the snow.

"I am more than ever convinced that Sherman is moving by the most direct routes to the Atlantic coast, as a base whence to attack Charleston or Savannah, or to reinforce Grant in Virginia," Beauregard wired Hardee on November 27.[9]

With Sherman's blue tide washing ever closer to the city, many Savannahians became increasingly jittery. Savannah was in turmoil. Artillery caissons trundled through the streets amid the yells and curses of teamsters. Ragged Confederate soldiers and sailors mingled with civilians on the boardwalks. Within days the distant sound of gunfire, coming ever closer, would be heard from "the Bay," as Bay Street was called.

Along the waterfront sagged tons of bales of wet, rotting cotton, white gold that could not be cashed in because of the Union blockade.

A Southern woman who had fled with her family before Sherman's advance had a less than appetizing meal at the Pulaski House: "I had for supper in the famous hotel a half biscuit and a cup of tea made from already used leaves," wrote Mrs. T. W. Lott.

On November 28 Mayor Arnold issued a desperate plea for able-bodied men to take up arms: "Fellow Citizens—The time has come when every male who can shoulder a musket can make himself useful in defending our hearths and homes. Our city is well fortified, and the old ones can fight in the trenches as well as the young, and a determined and brave force can, behind entrenchment, successfully repel the assaults of treble their number."[10]

"No man who is a friend to his country will stand back a moment," the *Daily Morning News* said the next day. "Let the old men come forward.

... If all ... will come up to the scratch they will give Sherman Hail Columbia with a vengeance." The only problem was that almost all of Savannah's men were with Hood's army, with Lee in Virginia, or on some other front.

November 29 also saw Captain Tattnall and Flag Officer Hunter of the naval squadron begin preparations to remove supplies and vessels under construction. They also made plans to destroy the shipyards, and Hunter sent a requisition for haversacks and canteens—his seamen would be ready to fight in the trenches or march if the squadron was lost.[11]

If these measures increased anxieties in the city, the *Daily Morning News* on the same day gave an account of Sherman's advance that, far from factual, should have boosted Rebel confidence: "Sherman seems to be making no progress in his invasion of the State. He is no nearer the coast than he was several days ago.... Afraid to go forward, and cannot go back, his men and animals tired and hungry, with our forces rapidly closing in around him—all these things excite the liveliest hopes of his utter destruction."[12]

After falling back from Millen, General Harry Wayne and a small force entrenched along the Little Ogeechee River to impede the Federal tide on November 28. His men included the corps of cadets from the Georgia Military Institute, a militia company from Washington County, and some artillery. The position was on high ground overlooking the river and offered an ideal chance to contest Howard's march. But the stream of Union troops flooding in on other roads forced Wayne to abandon his earthworks without a fight.

Savannah put up a brave front, but it daily became clearer that the Yankees were bearing down on her. In spite of Sherman's known aggressiveness, the Confederates believed almost until the last moment that his destination might be the Union base at Port Royal, avoiding direct battle or a siege of Savannah.

Still, the city was bracing for a Yankee hurricane. Hardee was moving heavy guns to the westside. Every available man was expected to aid in the defense, including Chatham County's reserve militia, who were organized and armed within hours of Arnold's appeal.

"They are nearly all old men, between 50 and 65, but all looked like they would be able to give a good account of themselves when the time for action arrives," an observer wrote.

"If all will come, we can close out Sherman's big job for him a little different from what he calculated on," the *Daily Morning News* added.

Union troops entered Statesboro, about sixty miles west of Savannah, after a skirmish on December 4. Confederates drove off a party of mounted foragers, but a volley and bayonet charge by the Seventieth Ohio Infantry scattered the Rebels defending the town.

Other enemy columns were pressing in toward the coast from the southwest. By December 5 the Rebel high command was at last convinced as to Sherman's target.

"Everything now appears to be moving toward Savannah," Beauregard wrote Hardee that day.

"With the limited reliable means at our command I believe that all that could be has been done, under existing circumstances, to oppose the advance of Sherman's forces towards the Atlantic coast," Beauregard said in a December 6 letter to Jefferson Davis. "That we have not, thus far, been more successful, none can regret more than myself, but he will doubtless be prevented from capturing Augusta, Charleston, and Savannah, and he may yet be made to experience serious loss."[13]

The Confederate frenzy increased to assemble troops to defend Savannah. One major step had been taken a few days earlier. When Sherman no longer appeared to threaten Augusta, Bragg sent three thousand troops to Savannah by railroad on November 29. Other reinforcements were rushed south from Charleston and Wilmington, not all reaching Hardee in time to face Sherman.

"Not many days will elapse before the time to do our work," the *Daily Morning News* said on December 7. "Let every man set his house in order, and be on hand at the tap of a drum."

About the time that Savannahians were reading this call to action, Federal columns of Howard's wing were crossing the Ogeechee River on a pontoon bridge about twenty miles west of Savannah. The site was at Jenck's Bridge on present-day U.S. Highway 80, where the original wooden span had been burned by retreating Rebels. Union Brigadier General Elliott W. Rice sent his men over the swampy river amid sporadic fighting.

The Union brigade of Colonel John M. Oliver was sent to seize a bridge over the Canoochee River in Bryan County southwest of Savannah. Oliver's squads encountered resistance from gray cavalry, but reached the river, only to find the bridge going up in flames. The opposite bank appeared to be thick with Confederates well dug in. Oliver retreated to Bryan Court House and waited for the arrival of the rest of his division commanded by Major General William B. Hazen. These westerners marched into the village on December 8, and Hazen's scouts found an abandoned ferry site downstream from the bridge. After dark Hazen sent a force across the Canoochee at this point and outflanked the Rebels defending the span. The graybacks retreated and the Federals resumed their advance.

Sherman remained in fine spirits during the march: "The weather was fine, the roads good, and every thing seemed to favor us," he remembered. "Never do I recall a more agreeable sensation than the sight of our camps by night, lit up by the fires of fragrant pine-knots."

The Rebels had offered little opposition to this point, other than trying to impede some enemy river crossings and sniping in the woods. Resistance increased as the Yankees neared Savannah, and Sherman encountered what he considered the most despicable weapon of the war—buried torpedoes. The Confederates used artillery shells with primitive detonators that exploded when trod upon. They would be used with some success in the December 13 battle for Fort McAllister. On Sherman's advance, however, the primary effect was to infuriate the Union commander, although some casualties were inflicted.

"This was not war, but murder, and it made me very angry," Sherman wrote after seeing a "handsome young officer whose foot had been blown to pieces" by one of the mines. Sherman used squads of Confederate prisoners to clear the roads.[14]

By December 8 elements of Slocum's wing moved through Springfield and Ebenezer in Effingham County, while some of Howard's regiments advanced to Pooler's Station, a stop on the Central of Georgia Railroad. Other Federal units were ripping up miles of track on the Atlantic & Gulf Railroad at Cross Roads (present-day Richmond Hill), south of Savannah, and the Central of Georgia near Eden.

Some of these Yankees at Cross Roads were busy working on the rails with picks and axes when a southbound train carrying a number of important Savannahians chugged into view. Spotting the multitude of bluecoats ahead, the engineer halted and put his locomotive into reverse, hoping to escape.

As the train sluggishly moved backwards, Captain William Duncan of Howard's headquarters scouts acted quickly. Duncan led a mule onto the track behind the train and shot it. The mule dropped dead on the rails and derailed the last car when it backed into the carcass. The train was now helpless, and Union soldiers clambered aboard. Among the Savannah passengers briefly detained for questioning was Richard R. Cuyler, president of the Central of Georgia.

Hardee wired several messages to Beauregard on December 8. One of his first called for reinforcements of a thousand men plus artillerists. In all likelihood he would have asked for more men, but he knew the pitiful state of Confederate affairs.

Later that Thursday he received a request that he and Major General Samuel Jones, whose troops were defending the Charleston & Savannah Railroad at Pocotaligo, South Carolina, join Beauregard for a war conference in Charleston. Hardee realized the crisis he was facing and fired off a telegram to Beauregard: "I cannot leave Savannah for the conference you desire without injury to the service." Hardee added that he "deemed it also important" that Jones remain at his post and that possibly Beauregard could journey to confer with both of them. Diplomatically, he closed by stating, "I am, however, ready to conform to your wishes if you think otherwise."

While Savannah's garrison remained combative, the enemy was methodically beginning to encircle it. "During the next two days, December 9th and 10th, the several corps reached the defenses of Savannah," wrote Sherman.

On December 10 General Howard sent a message to Washington stating that the march was a success. Scouts carried the dispatch overland to Port Royal, where it was telegraphed north and reached the capital on the night of December 14. The next day army Chief of Staff Major General Henry W. Halleck relayed Howard's note to President Lincoln: "We have met with perfect success thus far, troops in fine spirit and General Sherman nearby."

Howard also sent Duncan and two men in a canoe to drift past Fort McAllister out to the Union naval squadron and inform the navy of Sherman's approach.

"These brave men of ours have seen too many wounds and death has passed too near them to suggest any terrors now," wrote a Union officer contemplating the coming attack on Fort McAllister. "The glory of the flag and victory is the noble thought which animates and stimulates."[15]

XV

Besiegers and Besieged— December 1864

> I think Hardee, in Savannah, has good artillerists, some five or six thousand good infantry, and, it may be, a mongrel mass of eight to ten thousand militia.—Union Major General W. T. Sherman to Lieutenant General U. S. Grant, Commander in Chief of the U.S. Armies on December 16, 1864.[1]

Savannah boasted a formidable system of defenses—but few men in the trenches—as Sherman's army closed in. Facing the blue legions, Hardee had between nine and ten thousand men, including militia, to defend the city from attack in any direction. If besieged, he had provisions to feed them for about a month.

The chess game to decide Savannah's fate had opened in bloody fashion on November 29 about thirty miles to the north in South Carolina. A Union force of about five thousand infantry, sailors, and marines advanced up the Broad River from Port Royal and threatened to cut the Charleston & Savannah Railroad near the village of Grahamville, South Carolina.

Called the "Coast Division," the Federals were led by Brigadier General John P. Hatch of New York. A break in the railroad would slice Hardee's only supply and communications line with Charleston and possibly force him to evacuate Savannah immediately.

For Hardee, the cavalry coming over the hill was two trains carrying some one thousand Georgia militia and State Line troops commanded by Major General Gustavus W. Smith. More of Smith's men might have

Major General Gustavus W. Smith commanded Georgia militia who helped defend Savannah in 1864.

reached Savannah, but no other locomotives and cars were available on account of the poor condition of the Confederacy's railroads.

Coming from Macon on a roundabout circuit through Albany and Thomasville, Smith and his men arrived in Savannah about 2 A.M. on November 30. They received immediate orders to proceed north to the danger zone.

Leaving his sleeping men on the trains, Smith awoke Hardee at his quarters in a private home. Smith told Hardee that without a special act of the legislature he could not take his troops out of the state based on a decree from Governor Brown. Smith added, however, that if Hardee could convince him that it was "absolutely necessary," he would take his force into South Carolina. Hardee persuaded Smith that the emergency was dire, and the Georgia militia trains headed over the river.

These Georgians provided the backbone for an outnumbered Confederate force that blunted Hatch's advance on the railroad at the battle of Honey Hill, South Carolina, a few hours after their all-night train ride.

Some of Smith's militia were boys not yet of conscription age and not even tall enough to fire their muskets over the parapets. The youngsters solved this problem by taking turns crouching on their hands and knees to provide a firing platform for their comrades. The Athens and Augusta battalions of reserves and the Forty-seventh Georgia were among units commended for their exceptional work at Honey Hill.

In triumph, Smith's exhausted boys returned to Savannah about 10 P.M.

that night and soon filtered in to Hardee's defenses facing Sherman. Other contingents of Smith's militia arrived from Macon by rail over the next few days.

With the Union army slowly tightening its coils about Savannah on December 8, Hardee urgently needed some advice. He again telegraphed Beauregard in Charleston: "I hope you will not fail to come here tonight. It is all important that I should confer with you."[2]

Knowing the tense situation at Savannah, Beauregard boarded a train for the city, but not before wiring a message to Hardee: "Having no army of relief to look to, and your forces being essential to the defense of Georgia and South Carolina, whenever you shall have to select between their safety and that of Savannah, sacrifice the latter."[3]

In other words Hardee's ragged soldiers were more important to the Southern war effort than the city of Savannah.

Beauregard received the backing of the Confederate government in this decision. "It is hoped Savannah may be successfully defended," Adjutant and Inspector General Samuel Cooper wrote to Beauregard. "But the defence should not be too protracted, to the sacrifice of the garrison. The same remarks are applicable to Charleston."[4]

Beauregard arrived in Savannah early on December 9, as troops of the Union Twentieth Corps crept closer to the Charleston & Savannah Railroad bridge about twelve miles up the Savannah River from the city. Hardee had sent the gunboat *Macon* to try to protect the bridge. Because of the enemy's proximity to the tracks, Beauregard was forced to travel by steamer and wagon to meet his train in areas safely within Confederate control.

Hardee met with Beauregard and was given written orders reiterating the instructions in the telegram. He also received instructions to "preserve the garrison for operations elsewhere" should evacuation become necessary.[5]

Before returning to Charleston, Beauregard also issued orders for the construction of a series of pontoon bridges over the river. Under the direction of Chief Engineer Colonel John G. Clarke, the work began immediately.

Even so, Hardee grew more anxious as the invaders slowly engulfed him, forcing him to extend his lines. The Charleston & Savannah had to be kept open if he was to hold Savannah.

Although the Yankees had been repulsed at Honey Hill, a Union force was threatening the railroad again near Pocotaligo, South Carolina, a few miles further north. Hardee also had to keep an eye on Major General John

G. Foster, Union commander of the Department of the South, operating from bases at Hilton Head Island and Port Royal. Those were Foster's troops at Pocataligo, but he had more men to play hell with Hardee if he so desired.

Ironically, the Charleston & Savannah proved too vulnerable on the Georgia side of the Savannah River. Because its bridge crossed the Savannah so far out of the city, the span could not be adequately guarded in Hardee's network of fortifications. With little choice, Hardee was forced to pull back scattered units defending his "outer" defenses there.

He decided to destroy the span and sent gunboats upriver to do the job. Sherman's boys saved him the trouble, torching the bridge on December 11 after brushing aside weak Rebel resistance.

In spite of this setback, Hardee could reach the railroad at a more northern point by taking a plank road running northward on the South Carolina shore across from the city. This route, the Union Causeway, would prove to be Hardee's lifeline.

Hardee tried to incorporate the naval squadron into his defenses, but with little success. Gunboat *Macon* had failed to keep the Union troops away from the railroad bridge.

Flag Officer Hunter was ordered to take the ironclads *Savannah* and *Georgia* as far upriver as possible to guard his right flank. But the *Savannah*'s deep draft kept her from proceeding too far above the city, and bad weather prevented the *Georgia* from being towed from her station at Elba Island.

The one bright spot was the gunboat *Isondiga*, which shelled the enemy positions on a daily basis. Although the *Isondiga* inflicted only minor damage, the threat it posed contributed to Sherman's decision not to send a major force to the South Carolina side of the river, where it might be isolated and cut off.

On December 10 some Union troops tested Savannah's main defensive line with musketry and cannon fire flaring at several points along the lines. Sherman's divisions began to dig in, sometimes only a few yards from the Rebel positions.

That same day the river steamer *Ida* was captured by Union troops. Apparently unaware that the enemy was so close, the *Ida* was waylaid by foragers from the 150th New York where the channel narrowed near Argyle Island, several miles upstream from the city.

Among the *Ida* prisoners was Duncan L. Clinch, an officer on Hardee's staff. Clinch also was a brother-in-law of retired Union Brigadier General Robert Anderson, who commanded Fort Sumter on April 12, 1861, the war's first day.

Sherman was almost killed by a Rebel artillery round on December 10. Riding with elements of the Union Seventeenth Corps advancing toward Savannah and continuing the destruction of the Central of Georgia line, Sherman reached the depot at Pooler's Station, about eight miles from Savannah, on December 8. He and corps commander Major General Francis P. Blair established headquarters about three hundred yards west of the depot.

Resistance was continuing to stiffen gradually as the Confederates tried to slow the Yankees' progress in reaching Savannah. Troops of Major General Joseph A. Mower's division of Blair's corps had suffered losses in reaching and taking the station. Also menacing the Northerners was a cannon mounted on a railroad car, which the Rebels used to significant effect.

Reconnoitering in person near the rail line, Sherman rode to the front and, leaving his horse, walked through the woods along the tracks. About eight hundred yards away, he saw a Rebel earthwork and battery. "I could see the cannoneers preparing to fire, and cautioned the officers near me to scatter, as we would likely attract a shot," Sherman wrote in his memoirs. "Very soon I saw the white puff of smoke, and, watching close, caught sight of the ball as it rose in its flight, and, finding it coming pretty straight, I stepped a short distance to one side."[6]

Another soldier recalled the shot did not miss Sherman by "over a foot." Nearby, another man was crossing the rails and was not so lucky. The cannonball struck the ground, ricocheted up, and decapitated him.

The First Georgia Regulars pulled out of their Whitemarsh Island defenses on December 9 and were put into line west of the Savannah. Their position was anchored by a huge coastal howitzer facing a thick swamp. The Regulars were assigned to Brigadier General Joseph H. Lewis' command, which included about 165 men from the famed "Orphan Brigade" of Kentucky. The Orphans had been riding with Wheeler's cavalry, but were now fighting as infantry.

"About 150 yards in front of our regiment, the yankees have two six-pound rifle pieces and when they open on our battery, they certainly make the wool fly," W. H. Andrews remembered.[7]

"Our 60-pound piece sends a shell through the gum swamp making noise enough to wake the dead. We can hear the yankees tell one another when they get to making too much noise, 'Better keep quiet or the Rebs will turn that wash tub loose on you again.'"[8]

The Confederate navy at Savannah suffered another embarrassing setback on December 12. Aboard the steamer *Sampson* and accompanied by gunboats *Macon* and *Resolute*, Flag Officer Hunter was returning downriver from his aborted mission to burn the railroad bridge. The Yankees had beaten him to the punch.

Suddenly the quiet woods on the south bank exploded in a roar of cannon fire as Hunter's little force came under attack from a hidden Union field battery. From a bluff overlooking the river near Argyle Island, Federal rifled guns slammed the Rebel ships from about 2,500 yards.

The *Sampson* was rocked three times by hits, while the *Macon* took two rounds and the *Resolute* one.

In the narrow channel the Rebels frantically tried to turn back, and the *Resolute* collided with the others. Damaged, she drifted onto the beach of Argyle Island, where she was boarded and taken by soldiers of the Third Wisconsin.

With the aid of "a barrel of bacon in the furnaces," the *Sampson* and *Macon* fled upriver to Augusta. According to Union accounts, some of the *Resolute* crewmen cursed their comrades for leaving them without putting up a fight. General Sherman mentioned the capture of the *Resolute*, "with seven naval officers and a crew of twenty-five seamen," in a December 16 dispatch to Grant.

The *Resolute* was burned within days of her capture in what one Union general described as "an unfortunate mistake." Sherman could have used the boat to ferry troops to the South Carolina side of the river.

Hunter's hasty retreat meant that he was cut off from rejoining the Savannah squadron, along with two vessels the Confederates desperately needed. With his escape, Hunter virtually sailed out of the war.

Commander Thomas W. Brent of the CSS *Savannah* assumed charge of the naval squadron. A veteran of the "old navy" who joined the Confederacy in January 1861, Brent saw duty at Pensacola and along the Red River defenses before joining the navy at Savannah.

Hardee's main defenses west of the city ran in an arc some fifteen miles long from the Williamson Plantation on the Savannah River near

Pipemaker's Creek to the Atlantic & Gulf Railroad bridge on the Little Ogeechee River and beyond to Coffee Bluff.

In distance from the city, the defensive line varied from about three to nine miles. The Southerners opened dams and dikes to flood many of the rice fields and other low-lying areas in their front. The Federals also were hampered by innumerable swamps and creeks. Five narrow causeways, which served as roads or railroad beds, led into the city, but were heavily defended by batteries and earthworks.

The Rebels had just over a hundred cannon, including fifty-four heavy guns, to guard Savannah's westward approaches. Hardee posted twenty-four- and thirty-two-pound cannon, some of the biggest he had, at points where the causeways entered his lines. Portions of the opposing trenches ran along Dean Forest Road, where Union forces faced Confederate batteries aligned behind Salt Creek.

Here is a disposition of Sherman's army:

Slocum's wing occupied a front of about six miles from the Savannah River to Lawton's plantation, west of the city. This wing was composed of the Fourteenth Corps of Major General Jefferson C. Davis and the Twentieth Corps under Brigadier General Alpheus S. Williams. The two corps commanders of Howard's right wing were Blair of the Seventeenth Corps and Major General Peter J. Osterhaus of the Fifteenth Corps. Blair's units stretched from the Lawton plantation to the Atlantic & Gulf bridge over the Little Ogeechee. Osterhaus' men occupied the far end of Sherman's line near the Ogeechee Canal.

Hardee's Confederates were divided into divisions under major generals Gustavus W. Smith, Lafayette McLaws, and Ambrose R. Wright. Hardee's artillery chief was Colonel Charles C. Jones, the former Savannah mayor.

Wright held the left of Hardee's works, his line running about seven miles from the Little Ogeechee River to Shaw's Dam. McLaws, with about four thousand of Hardee's best troops, anchored the middle, manning a four-mile stretch of the line from the dam to the Central of Georgia railroad crossing.

On Hardee's right, Smith had about two thousand, mostly militia, to guard a two-and-a-half-mile section from the railroad to the Savannah River. A few miles south of Savannah, Fort McAllister, one of the strongest works in the Rebel line, guarded the mouth of the Great Ogeechee River.

McLaws was the most battle-tested of Hardee's commanders and had organized a fighting retreat to hamper Sherman. The Georgian had seen considerable combat with the Army of Northern Virginia and in the west

Confederate Major General Lafayette McLaws was Hardee's most combat-tried commander in the Savannah defenses.

before coming to Savannah. A Mexican War veteran, McLaws resigned from the U.S. Army in March 1861 and was named colonel of the Tenth Georgia Infantry. By May 1862 he had been promoted to major general for his performance in the Peninsula campaign. McLaws ably served as a division commander under Lee in Longstreet's corps. Clashes with Longstreet, however, ended with his relief of command after an unsuccessful assault on Fort Sanders in the 1863 Knoxville campaign.

Supported by President Davis and Bragg, McLaws was restored to duty. Transferred to Savannah, he aided Hardee in selecting terrain on which the Rebels erected their defensive lines to oppose Sherman.

Gustavus Smith celebrated his forty-third birthday with his victory at Honey Hill. A Kentuckian, he was an 1842 West Point graduate who had a distinguished combat record during the Mexican War, and later he served as an instructor at the military academy. He resigned in 1854 to become a civil engineer and was street commissioner of New York City when the war began. Smith returned south and was appointed major general in the Confederate army in September 1861. He commanded a wing in what would later be known as the Army of Northern Virginia during the Peninsula campaign. When the army's commander, Joseph Johnston, was severely wounded on May 31, 1862, Smith led the Rebel forces for several hours before suffering some type of physical breakdown. Later describing his condition as paralysis, Smith was taken from the field. He was replaced by Robert E. Lee, who was to officially assume command of the army on June 1.

Smith recovered and served as interim CSA Secretary of War in

November 1862. Upset by the promotions over him of several junior officers, Smith resigned his commission in January 1863. Appointed a major general of Georgia militia, Smith organized the state force and fought well in the Atlanta and Savannah campaigns.

"Rans" Wright was new on the scene, having replaced Brigadier General Hugh Mercer on December 10 on account of Mercer's poor health. Mercer had returned to Savannah after the battle of Jonesboro but saw no further action of note.

President of the Georgia Senate, Wright had taken command of state troops east of the Oconee River after Sherman captured Milledgeville. A lawyer and politician before the war, Wright entered Southern service as colonel of the Third Georgia Infantry. Promoted to brigadier general in June 1862, Wright and his Georgia brigade joined the Army of Northern Virginia. He and his command fought from the Seven Days battles through the Petersburg campaign.

Badly wounded at Antietam, Wright recovered and was promoted to major general in November 1864. Wright was ordered to Georgia and soon joined Hardee's Savannah garrison.

McLaws retreated into Savannah's defenses after fighting a delaying action against Sherman's advance. Both sides suffered casualties during sharp little clashes in the swamps and pine barrens, but McLaws hardly slowed the enemy columns.

While the opposing siege deployments were being made, the weather turned ugly. Temperatures dropped and freezing rains soaked the soldiers huddled in the trenches or forced to wade through murky backwaters.

A Union regiment assigned to erect a bridge across a swamp encountered Rebels within twenty rods of its front. Through the undergrowth the Confederates "sometimes fired at us, sometimes talked to us," a Yankee private recalled.

"They cracked many a joke," wrote Robert H. Strong of the 105th Illinois. "They asked us why we were building a bridge, when the easiest way to get into the city would be to walk right in along the road and surrender. . . . They shouted, 'As soon as you get close enough for us to see you, our bullets will make sieves of your hides.'"

For the most part, however, the siege lines about Savannah offered a deadly invitation for any Yank or Reb who exposed himself.

W. H. Andrews remembered a careless Confederate who ventured into the open to retrieve a plank, probably to build a fire: "The yankees opened on him. He stopped and stood the plank up in front of him for protection. Two balls were put through the plank and the soldier too. A dear piece of plank to cost him his life."[9]

Front-line Yanks who built fires chanced drawing attention from Rebel artillery or sharpshooters scattered in the woods. Gray snipers in the trees also were prevalent. Wet and miserable bluecoats danced about to keep from freezing and made beds of pine needles, boughs, and Spanish moss.

"Our bones were fairly frozen and the marrow within them congealed," wrote an Illinois captain after sloshing across an icy canal.

The Northerners had an even more immediate problem. By no extreme was Sherman's army a fat and sassy bunch when it reached Savannah, in spite of Sherman's contention that they were "in better order when they reached here than when they started."

Like blue locust these soldiers savaged plantations and farms for more than two hundred miles before reaching Georgia's coastal plain. There the countryside was less populated and crops were scarce—other than the abundant rice that many of the Northerners had not before encountered. Some resourceful Yanks figured how to hull the rice by crushing it with their musket butts.

"We played cards, laid low and our diet was rice for breakfast, rice for dinner, rice for supper, and then more rice," Captain John Storrs of Connecticut remembered. Even the army's supply of hardtack had almost disappeared.

"We were as brown as Turks and ragged as beggars," wrote an Illinois infantryman. "Our hair and beards were long, and we looked about as much like proper soldiers as a long-eared mule looks like a race horse."

In probably no other campaign of the war were the opposing troops equally as destitute. Hardee's "Johnnies" had little more to eat than the bluebellies facing them, living on rice, sweet potatoes, and hard bread.

Most of the Rebels, like their enemies, lacked tents or good shelters to shield them from the frigid weather. And uniforms were uniformly bad on both sides. Months of campaigning without resupply left many of Sherman's veterans virtually barefoot and in rags, resembling tattered Confederates who had rarely known any better conditions. Here the troop comparisons ended.

The Union army arrayed before Savannah was a fighting machine sharpened in combat at Resaca, Peachtree Creek, and New Hope Church among many engagements. They had an advantage in numbers of about six to one over a Rebel garrison comprised of some veteran troops but also of state militia, walking wounded, youngsters, and elderly men along with "galvanized Rebels," foreigners captured while serving for the Union and impressed into Confederate service. In plotting their tactics Beauregard and Hardee were well aware of their deficiencies.

A New Jersey major wrote of how troops in his wing deployed and would have been chewed up if opposed by seasoned Rebels: "Twice the head of our column came within pistol range of the enemy's entrenched artillery and they did not fire. Veterans would not have been so considerate of our welfare."[10]

"The yankees always have the last shot," wrote W. H. Andrews. "If you were to shoot a month, it would be all the same." The sergeant noticed that Union artillery in his front fired over his head: "The boys say they are hunting for our commissaries in the rear. And sure enough they were."

Andrews also noted the suffering of Smith's young militiamen: "Can't help feeling sorry for the boys, as the hardships of camp life is new to them. . . . If they draw three days' rations at one time, will sit down and eat it all up and have to go hungry until they draw again. . . . Poor boys. . . . Home would be the proper place for them." Andrews added, however, that the teenagers were "hard fighters, don't seem to have any better sense than to go right into it."[11]

The "Foreign Battalion" of Major J. Hampden Brooks in Wright's division did not fit the same description. This unit was composed of about 450 immigrants captured while serving in the Union armies. Culled from men held in the prison stockade at Florence, South Carolina, these soldiers had taken an oath of allegiance to the Confederacy, but their reliability was questionable at best. They were led by South Carolina officers loyal to the Southern cause. General Smith was dubious of these soldiers as they occupied their rifle pits. "Because of suspicious circumstances reported to me, I had given orders to the troops in the line on the right and left of this battalion, to fire upon and destroy these renegades in case they committed any overt act of treachery to us," he later wrote.

Having been formed in October, the command was seeing its first action when it joined Hardee's force in December. "We were under fire in taking our position, and the men behaved very well," Brooks recalled. The coolness under fire was short-lived.

The battalion showed it was unreliable when seventeen soldiers deserted on the night of December 14. Brooks obtained permission to take the unit to the rear the next night, but the officers soon got wind that two of their companies planned to mutiny and make a run to the Union lines en masse.

Brigadier General Hugh W. Mercer of Savannah faced a court-martial in the execution of mutinous Rebel deserters. (Courtesy of the Georgia Historical Society.)

Brooks and members of his staff rode for help, leaving captains Vincent F. Martin and Lewis Wardlaw to face the mutineers. Backed against a tree, the two officers were soon surrounded by the hostile soldiers and appeared to be finished. Suddenly all were distracted by the approach of other Confederates coming from the rear. A force of Georgians arrived and quickly disarmed the rebellious troops.

A court-martial was held that evening and seven men, including five alleged conspirators and two deserters who had been caught, were shot. Unfortunately some of the executioners took bad aim and two of the convicted men were only wounded, raising "such wails and dismal cries as never were heard on the field of battle."[12]

Shooting at random, the shaken firing squad still could not finish the bloody job. Martin ended the nightmare with a bullet to the head of each man.

General Mercer later faced a military court for the deaths of the deserters and was acquitted.

The "Foreign Battalion" was quickly dissolved, most of the men being sent back to imprisonment at Florence. Some, however, were allowed to join Rebel infantry and artillery regiments.

Brooks wrote: "My appointment to its command was intended as a compliment to me, and I accepted it as such, but really, I was never sanguine of the success of the experiment. In a fortress, it might have succeeded, but in the open field it was a hazardous undertaking. If success had been possible, the officers I had were pre-eminently fitted to achieve it."

Hardee correctly guessed that Sherman would land troops on the north side of the Savannah to try to cut the plank road, his only escape route. He ordered some light artillery and units of Wheeler's cavalry, primarily the brigade of Brigadier General Samuel W. Ferguson, across the river to meet the threat.

The Federals established the first stage of this beachhead on December 11 when a regiment occupied Argyle Island. Sherman would use the island as a springboard to launch troops across the river and threaten Hardee's last open road to safety several days later.

Even while he was dealing with the question of putting units over the Savannah, Sherman had his eye on another prize—Fort McAllister.

The lines were drawn, and the final curtain was about to rise on Confederate Savannah.

XVI

Fort McAllister's Last Stand

The sporadic crackle of musketry echoed through the woods and marshes as Union patrols probed the defenses of Fort McAllister on Tuesday, December 13, 1864.

Hunched in the fort were about 230 Confederates commanded by Major George W. Anderson, Jr. All of them knew they faced a grim and probably hopeless task in repelling the expected attack.

The Yankees dodging through the trees were the advance elements of Brigadier General William B. Hazen's division. They were coming on through the woods and swamps toward the fort's rear, its weakest point.

Behind these skirmishers and shielded by forests, Hazen's four thousand Federals were deploying, intent on overrunning the fort at any cost. McAllister had a number of large-caliber guns, but most were aimed toward the sea.

As it had been throughout the war, Fort McAllister was the kingpin of the city's southside defenses. If Sherman could capture it, he could open communications and obtain supplies from the Union fleet waiting off the coast.

Under the direction of engineer Captain Thomas A. White, the Confederates had done everything possible to strengthen McAllister, especially the landward defenses, as Sherman's troops neared the sea. A camp outside the lines was abandoned and several buildings were torn down. The Rebels hastily cleared a field of fire, chopping down trees and removing brush. Carelessly they left many of the tree trunks where they fell, possibly to obstruct attacking infantry. These logs, however, would provide great cover for blue sharpshooters when Hazen's units invested the fort.

A deep ditch was dug just outside the earthworks, and a network of abatis, along with a palisade, were constructed by the Rebels. White's squads also seeded the open ground and approach causeways with land mines, mostly seven- and eight-inch shells buried just beneath the surface and three feet apart.

Bracing for a possible siege, Anderson stockpiled supplies. He had over a thousand pounds of bacon, two thousand pounds of bread, forty gallons of molasses, and an ample supply of salt stored within the fort.

The Savannahian had been a captain at the fort during the January-February 1863 naval bombardments and assumed command when Major John Gallie was killed on February 1, 1863.

Anderson realized it would be much more difficult to hold the fort against a land assault, but vowed a fight to the last. "I determined under the circumstances, and notwithstanding the great disparity of numbers, between the garrison and attacking forces, to defend the fort to the last extremity," he later recalled. Numbering his effectives as 150 men, Anderson added that "with no possible hope of reinforcement, from any quarter, ... holding the fort was simply a question of time. There was but one alternative—death or captivity."[1]

With his infantry settling into positions around Savannah, Sherman sent Kilpatrick cavalry to test Fort McAllister's strength and try to communicate with the Federal fleet.

The blue horsemen raided into Bryan County and moved down Bryan Neck, south of McAllister, on December 12. Kilpatrick skirmished with Rebel pickets, driving them back to the fort before his troopers withdrew. Kilpatrick offered to use his "old infantry regiments, with Spencer rifles" to work their way close to the defenses then rush the works, but Sherman had other plans.

Knowing that McAllister's big guns faced the ocean, Sherman decided to attack the fort from behind. He and Howard agreed that Hazen's division should make the effort.

At dawn on December 13, Hazen's men crossed to the south bank of the Ogeechee at King's Ferry. The Rebels had burned the one-thousand-foot bridge there, but Howard's engineers and pioneer troops under Captain Chauncy B. Reese worked for three days to rebuild the span, completing it the night before.

Brigadier General H. J. Kilpatrick
led Sherman's cavalry in the "March
to the Sea." (*Harper's Weekly*,
Mar. 19, 1864, courtesy of the Georgia
Historical Society.)

Sherman spent the night at the ferryman's home and gave Hazen personal orders on the attack, which was to be made without delay.

"I explained to General Hazen, fully, that on his action depended the safety of the whole army, and the success of the campaign," he later recalled. Sherman knew the men he was sending into the breach. He had recruited this command in Kentucky and led it at Shiloh. As part of the Fifteenth Corps, the division had served under him at Vicksburg and earned Sherman's "special pride and confidence." Hazen's division consisted of three brigades of about 4,300 Ohio, Missouri and Illinois troops.

Hazen was a thirty-four-year-old Vermonter who grew up in Ohio and was a childhood friend of future president James A. Garfield. Graduating from West Point in 1855, Hazen served in the Pacific Northwest and in Texas.

Severely wounded fighting Comanches, Hazen carried an Indian bullet in his back for the rest of his life. His injuries disabled him for almost two years, but he was recovered enough to be promoted to captain of the Eighth U.S. Infantry shortly after Fort Sumter. Appointed colonel of the Forty-first Ohio in October, Hazen led a brigade at Shiloh and was promoted to brigadier general in April 1863. He had a distinguished combat record at Perryville, Stones River, Chickamauga, Knoxville, Chattanooga, and Atlanta. In August 1864 Hazen was given command of the Second Division of the Fifteenth Corps, Army of the Tennessee.[2]

In the chilly darkness Hazen's units marched through Cross Roads and turned east onto Bryan Neck Road. The route put him south of McAllister and out of danger from the fort's coastal guns. By 8 A.M. Hazen was close enough to the fort to begin positioning his men for the assault.

While Hazen was on the move, Sherman, Howard, and their staff officers rode about ten miles to the Cheves plantation on the Ogeechee's north bank. A Union signal station had been set up atop a two-story rice mill there, and the generals climbed to the roof of an attached shed to watch the attack. Sherman wanted not only to keep track of Hazen's progress, but also to possibly contact the fleet. Through field glasses the officers could easily see the fort about two miles to the east, its Confederate flag snapping in the breeze.

Two twenty-pounder Parrott guns had been unlimbered at the mill and fired random shots at the fort, receiving an occasional reply from the enemy gunners.

Anderson's decision to make the Yankees take McAllister rather than surrender it had been made after he received no orders or telegraph communications from Hardee regarding how he should react to this threat. For his part Hazen did not send a surrender demand. Knowing the desperation of his situation, Anderson assembled the garrison and told the older soldiers and married men to leave the fighting to the younger troops in his command. He described some of his garrison as "mere boys" who had never before been under fire.

Hazen spent most of the day positioning his division for the assault. The terrain was difficult, composed of thick pine woods, swamps, and marshlands. He would use about three thousand men for the attack, with the others held in reserve.

In the early afternoon the clatter of gunfire diverted Sherman's attention from trying to signal the Union naval squadron. "About 2 P.M. we observed signs of commotion in the fort and noticed one or two guns fired inland, and some musket-skirmishing in the woods close by," he recalled.

Sherman signaled Hazen that he expected the fort to be taken by nightfall: "The sun was rapidly declining, and I was dreadfully impatient."

Minutes later the mill's lookouts spotted the smokestack of a vessel cresting the horizon and approaching the Ogeechee. They soon made out her Union flag. Sherman wrote: "Soon we made out a group of officers on the deck of this vessel signaling with a flag.

"'Who are you?'

"The answer went back promptly, 'General Sherman.'

"Then followed the question, 'Is Fort McAllister taken?'

"'Not yet, but it will be in a minute.'"

Steeling his men for the attack, Lieutenant Colonel Henry L. Phillips of the Seventieth Ohio said: "Boys, do you see that pile of dirt over yonder? When we capture that we will get something to eat." This was encouragement enough for men who had been living on rice and little else for the past few days.[3]

The attack was launched shortly after 4 P.M. Ragged musketry and cannon fire from the fort's defenders dropped some of the Yankees as they neared the breastworks. Other explosions also ripped gaps in the blue line.

Hazen said of the assault: "Just outside the works a line of torpedoes had been placed, many of which were exploded by the tread of the troops, blowing many men to atoms."

Sharpshooters found cover behind the downed trees left by the Rebels and began picking off the fort's cannoneers.

"The Federal skirmish line was very heavy and the fire so close and so rapid that it was at times impossible to work our guns," Anderson said of the assault. "My sharpshooters did all in their power, but were entirely too few to suppress this galling fire upon the artillerists."[4]

From his vantage point Sherman saw Hazen's men emerge from the dark woods, "the lines dressed as on parade, with colors flying, and moving forward with a quick, steady pace."

Sherman continued his description of the assault: "Fort McAllister was then all alive, its big guns belching forth dense clouds of smoke, which soon enveloped our assaulting lines. One color went down, but was up in a moment. On the lines advanced, faintly seen in the white sulphurous smoke."[5]

Through the screaming lead and choking gunsmoke, the Yankee infantrymen broke alleys through the abatis and threw logs across the ditch to reach the mounded ramparts.

In spite of the raking fire and land mines, "the line moved on without checking, over, under and through the abatis, ditches, palisading and parapets," Hazen wrote.

On the far left of the Federal line the Forty-seventh Ohio of Colonel Wells S. Jones's brigade found an opening through the defenses. The Confederate obstructions extended to the river bank, but since the assault was made at low tide, the Ohioans charged along the river's edge, skirting the ditch and palisade.

Jones's men were among the first to swarm onto the embankments and engage the Rebels in hand-to-hand combat. In moments other Federals also were forcing their way into the works at various points.

"The Confederates were somewhat panic stricken as the Yanks were coming in on the fort in a dozen places on them with bayonets and the butt of our muskets, and the hand to hand fighting was terrible for a short time," recalled Captain J. H. Brown of the Forty-seventh Ohio.[6]

The Forty-seventh, the Seventieth Ohio, and the 111th Ohio all claimed to be the first to plant their colors on the fort's parapet.

Sherman remembered the assault's climax: "There was a pause, a cessation of fire. The smoke cleared away and the parapets were blue with our men, who fired their muskets in the air, and shouted so that we actually heard them, or felt that we did."[7]

The surviving Confederates scrambled into bombproofs, where the close-quarter fighting continued. The combat swirled for several minutes before the defenders were overwhelmed. The Southerners "only succumbed as each man was individually overpowered," Hazen reported.

"The fort was never surrendered," Anderson recalled. "It was captured by overwhelming numbers."[8]

"The National flag floated on the staff from which the Confederate ensign was pulled down, while the victors fired a feu-de-joie," a Union general wrote.[9]

Captain Nicholas B. Clinch, Anderson's artillery commander, personified the Rebels' mettle. Refusing to surrender, he became engaged in a personal duel with Captain Stephen Grimes of the Forty-eighth Illinois. "The two fought for some minutes after the firing had ceased," a soldier recalled. "Both were good swordsmen and they were permitted to fight it out." Grimes was "severely wounded about the head and shoulders" before other bluecoats intervened and subdued Clinch. Bayoneted six times, sabered three times, and shot twice, Clinch was captured and survived the war.

Realizing the day was won, Sherman was exultant in victory. He fired off a dispatch to General Slocum outside Savannah: "Take a good big drink, a long breath and then yell like the devil. The fort was taken at 4:30 P.M., the assault lasting but fifteen minutes."[10]

"No finer piece of military work has been done anywhere than was that of taking Fort McAllister," another Union officer said.

The human toll did not reflect the bitterness of the brief battle for the fort. Hazen lost twenty-four killed and 110 wounded, with most of his casualties resulting from the land mines. Confederate losses were fourteen dead, twenty-one wounded, and 195 captured.

As twilight deepened, Sherman and Howard boarded a skiff at the mill wharf and a volunteer group of young officers rowed them to Fort McAllister, passing the charred hulk of the blockade-runner *Rattlesnake* en route. Rowing against the tide, the trip took several hours.

Finally reaching the fort, the generals were taken to Hazen's headquarters at the McAllister house about a mile from the fort and congratulated him on his conquest. The three officers were joined by a despondent Major Anderson for dinner that night. During the meal Sherman apparently railed at Anderson for the use of the buried torpedoes, calling them "inhumane" and "barbarous," according to some accounts.

The evening was not totally confrontational, at least according to one Northern newspaper. A *New York World* reporter described an encounter between Anderson and Sherman after the meal. Anderson had a stock of fine cigars and knew of the Yankee's fondness for tobacco. Asking to be excused, Anderson told the Federals that he wanted them to try his Havanas. According to the *World*, Sherman replied, "Thank you, but I have some very good ones here. Permit me." With that, the Union commander handed Anderson one of the captured cigars.[11]

After supper the Federal officers walked back to the fort, which had been garrisoned by one of Hazen's regiments guarding the Rebel prisoners. The Confederate dead lay where they fell, "and they could hardly be distinguished from their living comrades, sleeping soundly side by side in the pale moonlight," Sherman remembered. He spoke briefly with some of the wounded Southerners.

The danger of the land mines remained, and while Sherman was in the fort a soldier searching for a comrade was killed by an explosion. Howard also described how an ambulance was "blown to pieces" when it rolled over one of the mines that night.

Sherman later angrily ordered details of Southern prisoners put to work locating and digging up the mines. Anderson strongly objected, saying "This hazardous duty . . . was an unwarrantable and improper treatment [of his men]." His objections were to no avail, but no Rebels were hurt.

Anxious to communicate with Washington, Sherman, accompanied by Howard, was rowed downriver in a yawl. His party reached the tender *Dandelion*, anchored at the Ogeechee's mouth, shortly before midnight. Naval officers briefed Sherman on the siege of Charleston and the general military situation in the Carolinas, as well as Grant's operations around Richmond and Petersburg, which had changed little since the march from Atlanta began.

Sherman dashed off messages to be read five days later by Grant, Secretary of War Edwin M. Stanton, and others. He also learned of Southern newspapers fancifully describing the defeat of his starving army and its wild flight to the coast. The real story appeared in his 11:50 P.M. message to Stanton: "The army is in splendid order and equal to any thing. ... The quick work made with McAllister, the opening of communications with our fleet, and our consequent independence as to supplies, dissipate all their boasted threats to head us off and starve our army. I regard Savannah as already gained."[12]

The Union generals were taken back to the fort in the wee hours of the morning and bedded down on the floor of Hazen's headquarters. Sherman's repose was brief. Soon he was awakened by an officer who told him that Major General John G. Foster, commander of the Union Department of the South, had arrived aboard a steamer and needed to see Sherman.

The tired general was again rowed down the river and met with Foster aboard the *W. W. Coit.* Foster apprised Sherman of his efforts to cut the Charleston and Savannah Railroad and discussed the best way to supply Sherman's army without delay. The generals then were taken to Wassaw Sound, where they found Rear Admiral John A. Dahlgren aboard his flagship, the *Harvest Moon.* The three worked out a supply plan and Sherman spent the rest of the night on the vessel.

News of McAllister's capture prompted waves of cheers, which rolled through the Union lines around Savannah. When Rebel pickets called over asking what the hoopla was about, some Yanks yelled back, "Let fort McAllister go to hell."[13]

Through the night bluecoats in the trenches taunted the Southerners about their victory. The sullen Confederates usually replied with muskets or cannon.

Rebel obstructions in the Ogeechee were removed, and on December 15 the first Union transports moved up the river bringing "supplies of food and clothing, and an immense mail, containing letters from home for nearly everyone in the army, from the commanding general down to the private soldier," an officer remembered. The occasion was "one of the happiest days experienced by the men of Sherman's army."

A few miles to the north the mood was much blacker. McAllister's fall meant that the backdoor of Hardee's Savannah defenses had swung wide open. And the Federal ships coming up the Ogeechee to the new Union base at King's Ferry were not only bringing food and mail but heavy-caliber rifled guns and ammunition for the reduction of Savannah. The Yankees were hard at work "making corduroy roads to connect the camps" with this new supply depot.

Hardee knew he was in deep trouble. "Unless assured that force sufficient to keep open my communications can be sent me, I shall be compelled to evacuate Savannah," he wired President Davis on December 15.[14]

XVII

"I Will Bombard the City"

"[Sherman] intends to throw a division across the Savannah to prevent the escape of Hardie [*sic*] from the city, and says he shall take his own time about reducing the city," Union Major John Chipman Gray wrote to a friend the day after McAllister's fall.

"He has 60,000 men with him and only wishes there were more men in Savannah; he says the city is his sure game and stretches out his arm and claws his bony fingers in the air to illustrate how he has a grip on it. There is a 'whip the creation' and an almost boastful confidence in himself."[1]

Only two letters were written by the rival generals regarding the possible surrender of Savannah in 1864—a demand and a refusal.

"They were both 'only talking' and both knew it," Major Thomas W. Osborn of Sherman's artillery wrote of the exchange.[2]

In a December 16 dispatch to Grant, Sherman expressed his intent to call for Hardee's capitulation: "If General Hardee is alarmed, or fears starvation, he may surrender; otherwise, I will bombard the city, but not risk the lives of our men by assaults across the narrow causeways, by which alone I can now reach it."[3]

Sherman was at Slocum's headquarters when he issued his surrender demand on Saturday, December 17, 1864.

The event was a family affair, as "Uncle Billy" sent his brother-in-law, Colonel Charles Ewing of Sherman's staff, under a white flag toward the silent Rebel lines.

Shortly afterward, this letter was read by Hardee:

"I WILL BOMBARD THE CITY"

HEADQUARTERS MILITARY DIVISION OF THE MISSISSIPPI, IN THE FIELD, SAVANNAH, GEORGIA, December 17, 1864.

General William J. Hardee, commanding Confederate Forces in Savannah.

GENERAL: You have doubtless observed, from your station at Rosedew [Rose Dhu Island] that sea-going vessels now come through Ossabaw Sound and up the Ogeechee to the rear of my army, giving me abundant supplies of all kinds, and more especially heavy ordnance necessary for the reduction of Savannah. I have already received guns that can cast heavy and destructive shot as far as the heart of your city; also, I have for some days held and controlled every avenue by which the people and garrison of Savannah can be supplied, and I am therefore justified in demanding the surrender of the city of Savannah, and its dependent forts, and shall wait a reasonable time for your answer, before opening with heavy ordnance. Should you entertain the proposition, I am prepared to grant liberal terms to the inhabitants and garrison; but should I be forced to resort to assault, or the slower and surer process of starvation, I shall then feel justified in resorting to the harshest measures, and shall make little effort to restrain my army—burning to avenge the national wrong which they attach to Savannah and other large cities which have been so prominent in dragging our country into civil war. I inclose [sic] you a copy of General Hood's demand for the surrender of the town of Resaca, to be used by you for what it is worth.

I have the honor to be your obedient servant,

W. T. Sherman, Major General.[4]

Hardee read Sherman's hand-written letter and conferred with Beauregard, who had arrived in Savannah from Charleston about 11 P.M. the night before. He then penned a reply to the demand, which did not reach Sherman until the next day.

HEADQUARTERS DEPARTMENT SOUTH CAROLINA, GEORGIA, AND FLORIDA, SAVANNAH, GEORGIA, December 17, 1864.

Major-General W.T. Sherman, commanding Federal Forces near Savannah, Georgia.

GENERAL: I have to acknowledge the receipt of a communication from you of this date, in which you demand "the surrender of Savannah and its dependent forts," on the ground that you "have received guns that can cast heavy and destructive shot into the heart of the city," and for the further reason that you "have, for some days, held and controlled every avenue by which the people and garrison can be supplied." You add that should you be "forced to resort to assault, or to the slower and surer process of starvation, you will then feel justified in resorting to the harshest measures, and will make little effort to restrain your army," etc., etc. The position of your forces (a half-mile beyond the outer line for the land-defense of Savannah) is, at the nearest point, at least four miles from the heart of the city. That and the interior line are both intact.

Your statement that you have, for some days, held and controlled every avenue by which the people and garrison can be supplied is incorrect. I am in free and constant communication with my department.

Your demand for the surrender of Savannah and its dependent forts is refused.

With respect to the threats conveyed in the closing paragraphs of your letter (of what may be expected in case your demand is not complied with), I have to say that I have hitherto conducted the military operations intrusted to my direction in strict accordance with the rules of civilized warfare, and I should deeply regret the adoption of any course by you that may force me to deviate from them in future. I have the honor to be, very respectfully, your obedient servant,

W. J. HARDEE, Lieutenant-General[5]

Hardee's besieged army was flanked on three sides and had a hostile fleet off the coast. But he still had the escape route via the plank road and the Charleston & Savannah Railroad. If he could get his men across the river and onto the causeway through the South Carolina swamps, he would survive to fight again. Sherman knew that a frontal assault against Savannah's formidable defenses likely would cost him many casualties. Yet even the highest-ranking Rebels in the city knew that a Union attack of any strength would puncture the thinly manned lines.

As Sherman neared the city, Hardee had not initially posted any units on the north side of the Savannah River, relying on the Confederate naval squadron to keep the Yankees in Georgia and away from the causeway. Besides, he believed an enemy force of any size landed on the river's north bank would be bogged in the South Carolina marshes and rice fields.

Wheeler's cavalry also had intercepted an enemy message on or about December 8, stating that Sherman would try to take Savannah by direct assault. With this information in hand, Hardee kept his men uncomfortably hunkered in their trenches.

Two days after the fall of Fort McAllister, Sherman again talked openly about putting a force on the South Carolina side of the Savannah to completely encircle Hardee. General Slocum urged immediate action: "Damn it, let us take this plank road and shut these fellows in!"

Not totally convinced by Slocum, Sherman cautiously decided to send a few troops across the river. From Argyle Island five Union companies crossed into South Carolina on December 15. Slocum pressed Sherman to send even more men, possibly an entire corps, over the river. But Sherman vacillated, deciding to shelve all plans to send any men across the Savannah—at least for the next few days. The beachhead was abandoned by early evening.

Sherman wanted to keep his army intact in case he was ordered to make a movement by sea to join Grant in Virginia.

Grant had written Sherman on December 3 asking him to consider establishing a garrison on the coast and to bring the army north to help defeat Robert E. Lee. Sherman balked at the idea, wanting to capture Savannah, and Grant would not press the issue.

As he studied the Savannah defenses, Sherman also knew that dividing his men by a wide river invited disaster. "I did not want to make a mistake like 'Ball's Bluff' at this period of the war," Sherman would later write, referring to the disastrous Union defeat along the Potomac River in October 1861.[6]

Rebel gunboats plied the river, posing another threat to his flank. And, besides, there was the great possibility that he could simply "starve out" the Confederates in Savannah, taking the town with little bloodshed.

"We have been here a week today under dreadful fire from the Enemy," a New Yorker in Slocum's wing wrote to his wife on December 18. "We are so close to them that our men can talk to them. . . . By the goodness of God I have been able to keep up but have on the march often thought I would have to give up but the prospect of seeing Savannah . . . taxed all my powers of endurance to its utmost."[7]

After Hardee refused his surrender demand, Sherman decided to try to snare his opponent in more direct fashion—he would launch an all-out attack.

On December 18 Sherman ordered preparations for a full-scale assault on Savannah tentatively set for December 21. Within a few hours, while his men were busy building scaling ladders, foot bridges, and rafts to reach and storm the Rebel defenses, Sherman changed his mind again. There would be no great attack, at least until Sherman played out his other options.

"The ground was difficult, and, as all former assaults had proved so bloody, I concluded to make one more effort to completely surround Savannah . . . in case of success, to capture his whole army," Sherman wrote in his memoirs.[8]

Finally Sherman committed to sending a strong body of troops to the South Carolina shore. On the morning of December 19 Colonel Ezra Carman's brigade was sent across the river at Argyle Island and established a two-mile line near Izard's plantation. Going against his earlier inclination to keep all of his troops south of the river, Hardee had dispatched a force to meet this threat.

Facing Carman's 1,500 Federals across the marshes and swampy woodlands was a portion of Wheeler's cavalry hastily reinforced by some of Hardee's infantry.

This Union toehold would be of secondary importance in Sherman's new plan. He decided to personally go to Hilton Head and confer with General Foster about the possibility of closing the door on Hardee in Savannah.

Examining his maps, Sherman believed Hatch's division of Foster's command could help him spring the trap. Hatch had been making an anemic attempt to sever the Charleston & Savannah at Pocotaligo, about forty miles north of Savannah. Still, Hatch's troops were in a prime position to strike south and seal Hardee in Savannah.

Leaving Howard and Slocum to continue preparations for a frontal assault as a last resort, Sherman embarked by sea for Hilton Head to meet with Foster.

Unaware that Sherman was away, Beauregard and Hardee played a desperate hand to save their forces in Savannah.

XVIII

"We Have Won a Magnificent Prize"

The constant tread of the troops and the rumbling of the artillery as they poured over those long floating bridges was a sad sound, and by the glare of the large fires at the end of the bridges it seemed like an immense funeral procession stealing out of the city at the dead of night.—J. B. Elliott, a Rebel soldier in Wright's division

Unlike the Rebels at Fort Pulaski in 1862 and the garrison of Fort Mc-Allister, "Old Reliable" Hardee was not bent on a death fight to defend Savannah.

Following Beauregard's orders, the Confederates were busy building the series of makeshift pontoon bridges in the eventuality that they would have to flee the city. The flamboyant Creole had made it plain to Hardee that he considered the army more valuable than retaining Savannah.

After meeting with General Jones, commanding the Confederates at Pocotaligo, Beauregard returned to Savannah about 11 P.M. on Friday, December 16. He was alarmed and irritated that the bridges were only about a third completed. "I well remember the anxiety you expressed when I stated the condition of affairs in consequence of this blunder," engineer Clarke wrote in a postwar letter to Beauregard.[1]

Garrison troops—including Hardee's few engineers under Captain Robert M. Stiles—militia, and sailors from the gunboats were aided by about a thousand slaves in stepping up the project.

The bridges would span the Savannah River in three sections from the

187

foot of West Broad Street (now Martin Luther King, Jr., Boulevard). The first section stretched from the city across the thousand-foot channel to Hutchinson Island, the second from Hutchinson to Pennyworth Island, and the third across the Back River to the South Carolina shore.

Boards and timber from the city wharves and some buildings were pried up to use for flooring, and Rebels scoured the area for rice flats to help float the bridges. These shallow boats, seventy- to eighty-feet long, were lashed end-to-end with ropes and chains. Railroad wheels were used to anchor the sections in place.

The Rebels piled straw over the flooring to deaden the sounds of the retreating army. Makeshift plank roads to support wagons and artillery were built over the dikes on boggy Hutchinson and Pennyworth islands.

Much of the work was done in cold and rainy weather. The laborers also were hindered by fog. But the bridge site was well within Hardee's lines and out of view of Sherman's units.

Beauregard's mood over the lack of progress on the bridges worsened when he learned that Wheeler's cavalry had destroyed a number of the much-needed rice flats, mistakenly believing they had been collected by the bluecoats.

Even so, the rattle of small-arms fire over the Carolina marshes and the sight of Yankees menacing the plank road spurred Beauregard and Hardee to quicker action.

Beauregard headed back to Charleston, but returned to Savannah on the night of December 18 to meet with Hardee and other officers and wrap up the evacuation plans.

Among those present was Commander Brent of the navy, who was given orders regarding the Savannah squadron. Brent's assignment amounted to a death warrant for the ironclads and little steamers that had defended Savannah, some since the war's early days.

The CSS *Georgia* was to be sunk; the ironclad *Savannah* would cover Hardee's exit and remain for two days, then try to reach Charleston; the *Isondiga* and tender *Firefly* would attempt to punch through the enemy lines and join Hunter at Augusta. If the river proved untenable, the *Isondiga* was to try to reach the Atlantic through Augustine Creek. Other vessels, including those under construction, were to be destroyed.

Brent forwarded the orders to his captains on December 18, concluding that the "foregoing plan was adopted on the advice and approval of Generals Beauregard and Hardee."

Secretary of the Navy Stephen Mallory was aware that Savannah could fall at any time, but did not know of Beauregard's orders for the squadron. Constantly blasted for the navy's lack of success, he expected Brent to try to make a fight of it.

By special messenger he sent a dispatch to Savannah: "Under any circumstances, it is better for the vessels, for the Navy, for a cause and country, that these vessels should fall in the conflict of battle . . . than that they should be tamely surrendered to the enemy or destroyed by their own officers. If fall they must, let them show neither the weakness of submission nor of self-destruction, but inflict a blow that will relieve defeat from discredit." The order did not arrive before Hardee's withdrawal.[2]

Beauregard also issued a "Memorandum for Location of Troops," dated December 18. After the evacuation the army's marshaling point would be the hamlet of Hardeeville, South Carolina, about seventeen miles north of Savannah and a stop on the Charleston & Savannah. From there the memorandum ordered Smith's division to travel by rail to Augusta via Charleston. Other units were to embark for James Island outside Charleston, while McLaws was to assume a defensive line along the Combahee River. Wheeler's cavalry north of the Savannah was to guard against any enemy interference of the evacuation and then operate in a defensive mode spread thinly between the South Carolina coast and Augusta.

With the work being pushed by Clarke and Colonel B. W. Frobel, the pontoon bridges were completed about 9 P.M. on December 19, and Beauregard ordered the garrison to evacuate as quickly as possible.

Following Beauregard's instructions, Hardee issued a "Confidential Circular" to his field commanders about the retreat and a timetable of when his divisions should leave the trenches and march for the river. The military evacuation would begin at dusk on Tuesday, December 20.

Written on December 19, but not distributed until the next day, the document over the name of Hardee's adjutant, T. B. Roy, began: "The troops in and around Savannah will be transferred to-night to the left bank of the Savannah River, and will proceed thence to Hardeeville."

Hardee's field artillery were to pull out of the lines at dark and head into town, crossing the Savannah with caisson and gun wheels muffled by blankets and rope. Wright's division was to depart at 8 P.M.

McLaws' command was to join the retreat at 10 P.M. and Smith's division at 11 P.M. Garrisons from the river batteries were to rendezvous at Fort Jackson by 9 P.M. and be taken across the Savannah by boat to Screven's Ferry, where they would join the column. Other troops from the coastal batteries were ordered to leave their lines at dusk and cross at the ferry. Hardee's heavy guns would launch a bombardment beginning at sundown to cover the withdrawal.

On Tuesday, Beauregard sent a telegraph to President Davis updating him on the situation at Savannah and the river crossing of the Union troops. "General Hardee reports that about fifteen hundred of the enemy's infantry crossed yesterday [the] Savannah River from Argyle Island to Izard's plantation. Wheeler holds them in check. General Hardee will probably evacuate Savannah to-night. His first defensive line will be in rear of the Combahee. Wheeler's cavalry will guard country thence to the Savannah River."

The retreat actually began that morning with a stream of civilians heading over the bridges. Union troops on the north bank of the Savannah watched "wagons, family carriages, men and women on foot. . . . The stream of fugitives and number of carriages and wagons increased as the day wore on." The ironclad *Savannah* and the *Isondiga* silently floated nearby, ready to provide protective fire.

From across the river came the distant snapping of revolvers and carbines as Brigadier General P. M. B. Young of Wheeler's command led a brief cavalry attack against Carman's force. The Rebels wanted to dissuade these Federals from making any movement toward the plank road.

In his postwar memoirs Sherman wrote that he "knew Hardee would have a pontoon bridge across the river." But most Federals in the trenches before Savannah apparently had no clue that the Confederates were building such a structure before December 20. Even if they had, they were in no immediate position to stop Hardee unless Sherman proceeded with his great assault or Carman's brigade was strongly reinforced.

Beauregard took other measures on December 20 to ensure the operation would be successful. He sent orders that the remains of the Charleston & Savannah Railroad bridge and trestle on the South Carolina side of the river should be burned immediately. The span had been burned on the Georgia shore, but it possibly could be repaired and used by the Yankees. Beauregard also sent word to Flag Officer Hunter at Augusta to bring the gunboat *Macon* as far downriver as possible to help hold the bluecoats at bay.

Just after sunset Hardee's army began its evacuation. Before leaving their lines, the men disabled any remaining guns and destroyed ammunition and other stores as quietly as possible so as not to attract the enemy's attention. Orders were that the ordnance was to be disposed of by "throwing it into the river or otherwise, and not by blowing it up." Unit by unit the Confederates marched into the city and joined the rest of the army.

"There was no confusion and all movements were executed promptly and in silence," a Southern officer recalled.

Assembling on West Broad Street, the Confederates tramped down to the river and onto the first bridge, stepping carefully on the unsteady span. About the time these first squads began crossing, Hardee's cannoneers opened their bombardment. The gray artillery had been freely slamming away all day, the Rebs trying to expend their shells to keep them out of Union hands.

This evening bombardment of about two hours was sporadic, but it kept the Federals pinned down. Most of the firing was done by the heavy coastal guns Hardee had shifted to the inland defenses. Unable to move these cannon quickly, the Rebels spiked them before fleeing.

All along the westside trenches, the Confederates continued their pullout through the night.

"I have no words to picture the gloomy bitterness that filled my breast on that dreary march through water, mud and darkness," a Confederate marine wrote to his mother a few days later. "We started from the trenches at dark and reached the city at 12 o'clock midnight, halted an hour and then fell into the long line of silent men who were pouring in a continuous stream over a pontoon bridge."

Occasionally a supply wagon veered off one of the bridges and tumbled into the black water, thrashing horses and all disappearing beneath the surface.

Confederate casualties were few, but because of a lack of ambulances, Hardee was forced to leave behind a number of his wounded and ill.

In the cold, dark woods outside the city, Union lookouts had this exchange with a soldier in the Fifth Georgia Reserves:

"Whatcha doin' there Johnny? Thought you was getting out tonight?"

"We loves you too good, Yanks. We can't leave you."

"We're gonna blow you away, Johnny."

"Blow up yer ass, Yank. Blow to hell!"

A Rebel band somewhere in the lines struck up "Dixie." From the Union trenches, bluecoats yelled derisively, "Played out! Played out!"[3]

A platoon of less than fifty Confederate marines occupied trenches near King's Ferry for twelve days, sniping with the Yankees before evacuating that night. Led by Lieutenant Henry L. Graves, these men reached Savannah about midnight and joined the dreary march across the river.[4]

Details were left to stoke campfires in the Rebel lines to make the Federals believe the opposing trenches still were occupied. These pickets were among the last to evacuate.

The night's horrors were magnified by the looting that broke out in Savannah even before the last of Hardee's troops had left.

"It was the white scum of the city that came out of their dens like nocturnal beasts to the work of pillage," wrote George Blount, a young Georgian in Hardee's rearguard. These soldiers heard "the roar of the robbers and the breaking of doors" as they vainly tried to maintain order before following the rest of the army. "If you want to know what brutes human beings can become, wait and watch them in such a time as this was," Blount wrote.[5]

Hardee and most of his staff crossed the river aboard the steamer *Swan* about 9 P.M. A number of stray soldiers also were carried across with Hardee's entourage.

"I will never forget passing through the city," wrote W. H. Andrews of the First Georgia, which left its lines about 11 P.M. "Doors were being knocked down, guns were firing in every direction, the bullets flying over and around us. Women and children screaming and rushing in every direction. All combined made it a night never to be forgotten by them who witnessed it."[6]

The funereal march over the bridges was sporadically bathed in hot light as ships of the Rebels' naval squadron died in flames.

Although the army's evacuation was a success, almost everything went wrong with the navy. Unable to get upstream, the *Isondiga* was abandoned, set afire, and exploded before dawn. Smaller river craft used by the Rebels also were torched.

"The cheeks of the men were warmed by the heat from burning vessels," a Confederate wrote. "Their eyes were weary with looking at the flames, which the river like a mirror, reflected from beneath. The men were subdued in spirit, quiet in voice and sad at heart."

Andrews added that the "burning of the Confederate gunboats" was "Sad to look at, but at the same time made a beautiful picture on the water."[7]

Her guns spiked, the *Georgia* was scuttled by her crew in the river near Fort Jackson. Anticipating her abandonment, Confederate authorities had earlier sent her marines north by train to reinforce Fort Fisher off Wilmington, North Carolina.

Flames also licked the Savannah sky from the navy yards set afire by the Rebels and from the burning CSS *Milledgeville*, a sister ironclad of the CSS

Savannah, which was afloat but not yet completed. At the Krenson & Hawkes shipyard, a large, unnamed ironclad under construction was also burned.

The Rebel seamen of the Savannah squadron, among them old Josiah Tattnall, sullenly turned their backs on these blazing hulks and joined Hardee's column. The CSS *Savannah* stood alone to defend the city.

Beauregard's timetable for the evacuation did not go precisely as he had planned. Smith's division did not begin its crossing until about 1 A.M., two hours behind schedule. In battle, this time discrepancy likely would have been a catastrophe, but it had little, if any, effect on the Rebels' withdrawal.

Before dawn the Confederate army was safely in South Carolina on its trek to the railroad junction at Hardeeville.

Along the siege lines, the Yankees began to sense something was amiss in the Rebel trenches. In fact, the Rebels were missing.

Alone or in small bands, the Federals crept forward, braced for the Johnnies to open up at any moment. They never did.

On the eastern horizon the bluecoats saw a reddish glow over Savannah and heard explosions coming from the city's environs.

Cautiously the Yanks climbed through ditches and up earthworks, close to the maws of silent Confederate guns. Peering into the Rebel defenses, they found simmering campfires but no graybacks, other than a few wounded or deserters.

Some of the Yankees gleefully scampered about examining the empty forts and looking for souvenirs. Others, with muskets ready, quietly marched toward undefended Savannah.

In the City Exchange on Bay Street Mayor Richard D. Arnold and the city's aldermen spent a nerve-racking night debating their course of action. They met with several of Savannah's more prominent citizens to get additional advice.

Hardee's army was gone, and the city fathers reasoned that it was their responsibility to surrender Savannah. It was a purely symbolic gesture, as Sherman's troops could now enter the city unopposed.

Arnold and the councilmen decided to travel in buggies out to meet the Yankees, but the retreating Rebels, particularly Wheeler's cavalry, took most of the horses with them. With only one carriage available, the little party headed to meet the enemy. They quickly became separated in the predawn darkness.

The Union brigade of Colonel Henry A. Barnum was the first organized Federal unit to enter Savannah after Hardee's departure.

Aldermen John F. O'Byrne and Robert Lachlison were halted by a Union patrol on Augusta Road and taken to Brigadier General John W. Geary, whose Twentieth Corps division had reached the city's outskirts. The aldermen surrendered Savannah with little fanfare, but the official capitulation did not occur until Arnold was brought before Geary shortly afterward.

According to Geary, Arnold respectfully requested "protection of the lives and private property of the citizens and of our women and children." Geary consented, and Arnold later would describe the general as "the noble Geary."

The mayor then guided the brigade of Colonel Henry A. Barnum, led by the 102nd New York, into the city. These were the first organized Federal units to enter Savannah after the evacuation. They were soon followed by the rest of Geary's division.

"Savannah was left to the Terrible Sherman Yankees," a New York soldier remembered.

Barnum almost did not live to gain glory at Savannah. During the battle of Malvern Hill in 1862, he was severely wounded leading a charge and was left for dead on the field. In the confusion the body of another officer was buried with Barnum's name on the headboard. Barnum meanwhile was found and captured while recuperating from his wound. He was exchanged in time to fight at Gettysburg, Chickamauga, and Lookout Mountain, where he was again wounded. Now, with Arnold as a guide, he was marching into the heart of Savannah.

"With lusty cheers at every step the column pressed forward," Barnum recalled, "and entered the city on West Broad street from Augusta road, marched down West Broad to Bay street, and down Bay street to the Exchange or City Hall, from the balcony of which was displayed the national colors of the regiments."[8]

It was about 6 A.M., and Barnum's New York and Pennsylvania troops exultantly celebrated their victory.

A few minutes earlier, engineer Captain Stiles, watching from the pontoon bridge closest to Savannah, saw Union troops running down West Broad Street toward the riverfront. Stiles and other engineers were cutting loose the pontoon bridges so that the enemy could not follow the retreating army. The engineers freed the pontoon bridges from the Savannah side of the river and scampered across them as the crude spans broke apart and drifted downstream.

Looting continued through the night and early Wednesday morning before the occupying U.S. troops restored order at bayonet point. Geary declared martial law and sent patrols through the streets to maintain the new peace.

"The Yankees entered our peaceful little city in a much more orderly way than I anticipated, although of course there were many robberies committed, the lower classes and the negroes, whom they came to befriend, being the greatest sufferers," Fanny Cohen Taylor wrote from her Lafayette Square home that morning. Mrs. Taylor's husband, Henry, was a Rebel soldier. Her father, Octavus, was a Savannah cotton merchant and exporter.

"[The Federals] gave three very orderly and unimpressive cheers when they raised the Flag in the Barracks' yard."[9]

Printed with the knowledge that Hardee was gone, the *Republican* this day was dejected in a front-page editorial: "By the fortunes of war we pass today under the authority of the Federal military forces. The evacuation of Savannah by the Confederate army, which took place last night, left the gates to the city open. . . . It behooves all to keep within their homes until Gen. Sherman shall have organized a provost system and such police as will insure safety in persons as well as property."

Yet there were still some armed Confederates who remained at their guns. Defiantly, the ironclad CSS *Savannah* ruled the river as Wednesday's daybreak revealed her namesake city teeming with bluecoats.

Commander Brent lobbed a few rounds at Fort Jackson after a U.S. flag was raised over her ramparts, the only time the fort ever came under hostile fire. Geary had sent a four-hundred-man force to occupy the fort shortly after he entered the city. During the day the *Savannah* also engaged Federal artillerymen who unlimbered a battery near the east end of Bay Street.

Brent had made an effort to escape to sea as Hardee evacuated, but found the way barred by submerged torpedoes in the Wilmington River. These and other river obstructions emplaced by the Rebels to keep the Yankees out kept the *Savannah* from at least reaching the Atlantic and dueling for her survival with the Union fleet.

A party under Lieutenant Sidney McAdam had tried to remove the torpedoes at Turner's Rock so that the *Savannah* could reach Wassaw Sound. But McAdam did not have the equipment necessary to clear the passage.

With little choice short of surrender, Brent decided to destroy the ironclad. After sundown he and his men abandoned the *Savannah* and began their march to rejoin Hardee's army. They reached the South Carolina shore in small boats. Behind them they left the iron warship in flames and black powder charges aboard, ready to explode.

A few hours later, as the exhausted sailors and marines were making camp for the night about 11:30 P.M., the ironclad disintegrated in a cataclysmic blast. "It lit the heavens for miles," a crewman noted. "We could see to pick up a pin where we were and the noise was awful."[10]

"You have no idea what a sad blow it was to me," a CSN marine recalled. "Thinks I, there goes my pleasant quarters, my good clothes, my good warm overcoat, and I am forever cut off from Savannah and the hope of making myself agreeable to the Savannah girls."[11]

The ironclad's eruption turned night into day in what a Yankee near Fort Pulaski described as a "fiery column with a ball of thick black smoke at its summit." The proud ironclad was no more.

Thirty-seven days after Sherman's columns left Atlanta, Savannah was in Union hands amid a panorama of wild excitement and despondency, the acrid smoke from burning Confederate ships and stores swirling in the sky.

The March to the Sea had cost the Federals total casualties of ten officers and ninety-three men dead, twenty-four officers and 404 men wounded, and one officer and 277 men missing. Of these casualties, Kilpatrick's cavalry reported thirty-eight dead, 159 wounded, and 168 missing. For the campaign the Northerners reported the capture of seventy-seven Rebel officers and 1,261 of lesser ranks. It is not known how many Confederates were killed or wounded in the numerous clashes with Sherman's army on the road to Savannah.

"We have won a magnificent prize.... We are in Savannah, in the full enjoyment of superb quarters, fish, oysters, and other good things," wrote Sherman's aide-de-camp, Major George W. Nichols, "and our army relishes the condition of affairs."

More than three hundred Confederate prisoners being held at Fort Pulaski heard the news of Savannah's fall late in the day. "At sunset, there were unmistakable signs that the Yanks had good news," a Virginia captain confided in his journal. "Presently the band began to play, three cheers were given and they soon brought us news that Savannah had fallen.... We still can't believe this. It seems preposterous."

Sherman was miles away from his army when Savannah fell. After conferring with General Foster on Hilton Head, he headed back toward the city on the night of December 20 aboard the *Harvest Moon*, Dahlgren's flagship.

Sherman expected to return to Savannah and possibly launch the land assault for which he had earlier ordered preparations. Foster had assured him that day that he would "give his personal attention" to closing in on Hardee from the north.

The short sea journey was an eventful one. High winds and waves rocked the steamer, and she lodged on a mud bar at low tide. The crew worked for hours to free her before Sherman boarded Dahlgren's personal barge. He was to be rowed through the Romney Marshes toward King's Ferry. The sailors struggled against the wind and choppy surf and made slow progress.

Late on the afternoon of December 21, the barge was approached by the tugboat *Red Legs* carrying messages for Sherman, including word of Savannah's capture.

"I was disappointed that Hardee had escaped with his army, but on the whole we had reason to be content with the substantial fruits of victory," Sherman recalled.[12]

Sherman was less self-assured in a December 24 letter to General Halleck: "I feel somewhat disappointed at Hardee's escape, but really am not to blame. I moved as quickly as possible to close up the ... causeway, but intervening obstacles were such that, before I could get troops on the road, Hardee had slipped out."[13]

Colonel Alexander R. Chisolm, one of Beauregard's aides, criticized Sherman in a postwar account: "The real point is that, having an over-whelming force, his movement should have been a prompt and vigorous one to the rear of Savannah, and not a voyage to Hilton Head. . . . It is clear that, had Slocum's suggestion been adopted, or had even the single brigade of his corps . . . been vigorously pushed against the thin line of Confederate pickets covering the causeway, all escape from Savannah must have been cut off."[14]

Other Federals felt Sherman had erred in allowing Hardee to bolt. "I do not find fault with Genl. Sherman for this mistake for I know there must be a reason for it yet I cannot but feel that in the end it will prove disastrous to us," a Union officer confided in his diary.

Major Osborn felt Sherman intentionally let Hardee go: "We concluded General Sherman wanted the enemy to leave and not make a fight necessary. What was wanted was the city and the route by the Savannah River open to the sea. This was secured without a fight."[15]

Secretary of War Stanton was clearly disappointed by Hardee eluding the trap: "It is a sore disappointment that Hardee was able to get off," he wrote to Grant. "It looks like protracting the war while their armies continue to escape."[16]

At least one of Sherman's staff officers praised the Confederates' decision to pull out. "Hardee acted wisely and well," said Major Nichols. "He withdrew his troops at a critical moment, and saved his command, at the expense, it is true, of valuable material; but there is a large balance in his favor to the credit of good sense and humanity."[17]

"The escape of Hardee was a disappointment, but as we now know that he had been carefully watching the roads since the first approach of the National army, with the determination to abandon the city before the investment could have been made complete, the only question was whether he should make the evacuation a few days sooner or later," Union Major General Jacob Cox wrote after the war.

The shivering and exhausted gray defenders of Savannah trudged into Hardeeville and fell into camp in and around the village throughout the day on December 21. Most bivouacked near the Charleston & Savannah depot. The first troops to arrive had to smash thick ice in the water tanks and form relays to carry water to waiting locomotives—Hardee wanted trains to be ready to move quickly if needed.

The march was not without controversy—and death. That morning some of the Rebels were caught in a rain shower. Several soldiers fired their muskets into the air so their powder would not become wet and clog their weapons. Officers riding along the line of march angrily ordered the firing stopped.

W. H. Andrews wrote that a lieutenant on the staff of Brigadier General John K. Jackson snatched a rifle from a young Reb who had fired his gun and promptly shot the soldier, killing him on the spot. The grey column snaked past the scene as a detail dug a roadside grave for the youngster.

"Had it been one of the Regulars [the officer] shot, he would have struck the ground nearly as soon as his victim did," Andrews remembered. "It was simply an outrage, and he deserved death at the hands of the boy's comrades."[18]

As his men rested in their camps, Hardee busily assigned destinations to various units and released volunteers who had virtually been forced into service on account of Sherman's advance. Among these men were Savannah civilians and workers from war factories in Macon and Augusta.

"General Hardee reports to-day from Hardeeville that evacuation of Savannah, as instructed by me, was successfully accomplished last night," Beauregard wrote to Jefferson Davis from Pocotaligo on December 21. "All the light artillery and most of the stores and munitions were brought off. The heavy guns were spiked and otherwise disabled. Line of defence behind Combahee River will be taken as soon as possible."[19]

Beauregard also sent Hardee a telegram of congratulations the same day "on the success of the evacuation."

"This was one of the neatest achievements of the war, rivaling in decision, resource, and skill the evacuations of Corinth and of Morris Island by the same commander," Beauregard's aide, Colonel Chisolm, wrote after the war, taking some of the credit for his general.

Hardee headed to Charleston on December 22 to prepare a defensive line across the lower portion of South Carolina to welcome Sherman. This was in response to the detailed orders sent from Beauregard on December 20 regarding the disposition of the army after the evacuation. Forty-nine pieces of light artillery that the Confederates had removed from Savannah were dispersed among Wheeler's troopers, and Rebel forces in the vicinity of Hardeeville, Pocotaligo, and Coosawhatchie.

"The Southern troops which had guarded Savannah retreated to our neighborhood, and we cared for them for several weeks," recalled Nancy Bostick DeSaussure. The wife of a Confederate surgeon, Mrs. DeSaussure, at the time, was staying with her elderly father on the family's estate near Beaufort.

"There were at least five thousand troops on our plantation. . . . Barbeques of whole beeves, hogs, and sheep were ordered for them. The officers were fed in the house, there being sometimes two thousand a day. The soldiers had their meals in camp."[20]

Hardee considered Savannah's evacuation one of the finest accomplishments of his wartime career. Writing to President Davis, Hardee stated that the landing of enemy troops on the South Carolina side of the Savannah was "so near my communications that to save the garrison it became necessary to give up the city. Its evacuation was successfully accomplished."[21]

Colonel Jones, Hardee's artillery chief, recalled that the commander told him he "sadly deplored the loss of the city" but that he "was persuaded nothing had been neglected which could have contributed to the honor of our arms; and that under the circumstances he regarded the safe withdrawal of his army . . . as one of the most signal and satisfactory exploits in his military career."[22]

Hardee came under scrutiny for leaving the valuable and vast stores of cotton intact for Sherman to seize. Confederate officials wanted to know why he had not destroyed the bales. Suspicions were heightened by the fact that Hardee's brother, Andrew, was a cotton merchant in Savannah and might find a way to profit from these war spoils.

Hardee contended that the cotton was widely distributed over the city and that he simply did not have the manpower to gather it for destruction, much less torch it. His soldiers were in the lines, and all wagons, drays, and carts were needed to supply them rather than to haul cotton.

Indeed, Hardee was quite proud of the smoothness with which the evacuation was carried out: "Tho' compelled to evacuate the city, there is no part of my military life to which I look back with so much satisfaction."[23]

Hopelessly outnumbered, Hardee's army did not seriously threaten Sherman in the closing months of the war. But these Confederates formed the nucleus of the Southern forces that daily bled Sherman's columns in the Carolinas campaign, primarily in battles at Averasboro and Bentonville in North Carolina.

In the war's grand scheme, however, Hardee's escape remains an overlooked footnote to one of the most famous campaigns in American history. In less than eight months since spearing into Georgia from Chattanooga in May 1864, Sherman had taken Atlanta and Savannah while making "Georgia howl" as he had promised Grant. By mid-January 1865 Sherman opened the second act of his march, plowing through the Carolinas and forcing the surrender of Johnston's army on April 26, 1865.

In his book *A Present For Mr. Lincoln*, A. A. Lawrence describes a postwar encounter between Sherman and Colonel Ezra Carman, whose brigade almost closed the last road out of Savannah before the Rebels fled. Here, Sherman put the whole episode into perspective: "Well, Carman, we didn't catch Hardee did we? But it is all right, anyhow; the war ended all right and just as it ought."[24]

(In spite of popular belief, the town of Hardeeville, South Carolina, is not named for General Hardee—although it may have been established by some of his relatives. Hardee's family migrated to south Georgia from North Carolina during the Revolution. Other North Carolina Hardees continued the movement south in the coming years, including Thomas and Pearson Hardee. They settled in South Carolina's St. Peter's Parish in the early 1800's and were instrumental in settling the town that now bears their name.)

XIX

Lincoln's Christmas Gift

Savannah, Ga. Dec. 22, 1864

To His Excellency,

President Lincoln,

Dear Sir,

I beg to present you as a Christmas Gift, the City of Savannah with 150 heavy guns and plenty of ammunition; and also about 25,000 bales of cotton.

W. T. Sherman
Maj Genl.

Sherman rode into conquered Savannah early on the morning of Thursday, December 22, 1864, more than a day after his troops marched into the city. His victorious entry had been delayed by his arduous roundtrip to Hilton Head. Hardee's escape while he was away was embarrassing, but Savannah's occupation was an objective gained with relatively few casualties.

After arriving at King's Ferry on the night of December 21, Sherman rode toward Savannah early the next day. Passing almost unnoticed through the blue columns on the roads, Sherman and his entourage trotted north down tree-lined Bull Street to the Customs House on Bay Street. He climbed to the roof for a bird's-eye look at Savannah.

"We had an extensive view over the city, the river, and the vast extent of marsh and rice-fields on the South Carolina side," Sherman wrote in his memoirs. "The navy-yard, and the wreck of the iron-clad ram *Savannah*, were still smoldering, but all else looked quiet enough."[1]

This was not Sherman's first trip to Savannah. As a green lieutenant he

Sherman's blue legions march down Bay Street on the morning of
December 22, 1864. The U.S. Customs House is to the left, the City
Exchange to the right. (Courtesy of the Georgia Historical Society.)

had visited the city and stayed at the Pulaski House hotel on Johnson
Square.

Leaving the Customs House, Sherman went to the Pulaski House,
which he had "known in years long gone." He described the hotel
proprietor as "a Vermont man with a lame leg" who previously had been a
New Orleans hotel clerk. Sherman's staff inquired about using the hotel as
headquarters; and the Vermonter "was anxious to have us for boarders," the
general wrote, adding that "we were not in the habit of paying board."[2]

Dispatching officers to look for more suitable quarters with a nearby
stable for the horses, Sherman waited at the Pulaski House. It was here that
he was approached by Charles Green, the prosperous British cotton broker,
who offered his house for use as the commander's headquarters. Sherman
accepted and headed to the beautiful mansion on Madison Square.

Green, who had been imprisoned by Federal authorities earlier in the war
on account of suspected Confederate activities, owned a substantial amount
of the immense stores of cotton confiscated by the Yankees in Savannah.
Obviously his motives for offering his house to Sherman were questionable.

The Britisher answered his critics, explaining that he extended his

Entrance hall of General Sherman's headquarters in Savannah, the mansion of English cotton broker Charles Green on Madison Square. (Courtesy of the Georgia Historical Society.)

invitation to save some other resident the embarrassment of having his home seized by the Federals. (Whatever his reasons, Green didn't get back his cotton.)

"I accepted his offer, and occupied that house during our stay in Savannah," Sherman wrote in his memoirs. "He [Green] only reserved for himself the use of a couple of rooms above the dining-room, and we had all else."[3]

Sherman's private quarters would be the southwest bedroom on the second floor. "The house is elegant and splendidly furnished with pictures and statuary," he wrote in a Christmas Day letter to his wife. "My bedroom has a bath and dressing room attached which look out of proportion to my poor baggage."[4]

In another note to Ellen, Sherman said, "I am now in a magnificent mansion living like a gentleman but soon will be off for South Carolina."[5]

The general was just settling in to the Green house when he was visited by A. G. Browne, a U.S. Treasury agent for the Department of the South. Browne's official business was to "claim possession, in the name of the Treasury Department, of all captured cotton, rice, buildings, etc."

The weary commander was not so quick to comply with the government agent. His army had just completed one of the legendary campaigns in U.S. history and had paid in death and blood for this prize. The pair negotiated and Sherman agreed to turn over the property (or at least anything for which he had "no special use") to the Treasury after the army had conducted a thorough inventory.

Unwittingly Browne would play a key role in one of the most famous

A modern-day photo of the Green-Meldrim House,
Sherman's headquarters

messages to be sent in the Civil War. In his memoirs Sherman described Browne as "a shrewd, clever Yankee" from Salem, Massachusetts. During the meeting the agent suggested that Sherman "make it the occasion of sending a welcome Christmas gift to the President, Mr. Lincoln, who peculiarly enjoyed such pleasantry." Browne also related that Sherman's message could be sent by a ship leaving for the North within a few hours and that the vessel could reach Fortress Monroe in Virginia by Christmas Day if the weather cooperated. There the message could be telegraphed to Lincoln.

Sherman agreed and promptly sat down to pen his dispatch. The message contained one error: the Federals had seized more than thirty-eight thousand cotton bales rather than the twenty-five thousand Sherman reported.

Lincoln received the telegram on Christmas Eve, and the transmission soon was on the front pages of newspapers across the Union. On December 26 Lincoln wrote a letter of thanks to Sherman:

My dear General Sherman:

Many, many thanks for your Christmas gift, the capture of Savannah. . . . The undertaking being a success, the honor is all yours. . . . It is indeed a great success. . . . But what next?"[6]

Lincoln's reply was brought to Savannah by Major General John A. "Black Jack" Logan, who was returning to command of the Fifteenth Corps. Peter Ostherhaus had taken over the corps when Logan was wounded at Dallas, Georgia, outside Atlanta.

During the first days of Sherman's occupation, Mayor Arnold received a petition signed by fifty to seventy-five residents asking to discuss the city's situation and the future. As a result, an estimated seven hundred people attended a public meeting on the night of December 28.

Almost four years of war, the horrible deaths of loved ones on distant fields, and personal deprivations had put these citizens in the mood for a return to normalcy. The state of mind in Savannah was correctly forecast by a C.S.A. congressman who wrote that "a little bad influence would make [the city's residents] forsake the Confederate cause and make what peace they can with the Yankee government."

He was right. Those gathered voted in the spirit of "burying bygones in the grave of the past" to submit to the "national [U.S.] authority under the Constitution." While the comatose Confederacy staggered to its death, Savannah had basically put an end to its war with the Union.

The unprecedented peace vote probably gained some support because Sherman's occupying force had not been the child-eating vandals that they had been described as prior to the city's fall.

"The city authorities have seen fit to declare the city once more in the Union," Frances Thomas Howard wrote on December 31.[7]

Still, Savannah's shocking stance infuriated others. "These miserable Sycophants," was how the *Augusta Constitutionalist* described Savannahians in March 1865. "If there is one sink lower than any other in the abyss of degradation the people of Savannah have reached it."

"Savannah has gone down on her knees," wrote a fervent Confederate belle, "and humbly begged pardon of Father Abraham, gratefully acknowledging Sherman's clemency in burning and laying waste their State! Oh it is a crying shame, such poltroonery!"[8]

"Sallie, I see the citizens of Savannah has held a Union meeting and passed resolutions in favor of going back into the Union," Georgian J. H. Jenkins wrote to his wife from his post at Coosawhatchie on January 21. "They say they are going to send one copy to the Mayor of Augusta, one to the Mayor of Atlanta, one to Macon, one to Columbus and one to the President of the United States. I suppose they treat them very well in Savannah!"

General Sherman raises a toast during a Christmas day dinner at his
Savannah headquarters in 1864. (*Harper's Weekly*, Jan. 28, 1865,
courtesy of the Georgia Historical Society.)

Shortly after the meeting, Sherman ordered food stores left by the
Confederates to be turned over to the local officials for distribution to the
population. And a Northerner of Polish descent proved to be a savior for
hundreds of destitute Savannahians.

Julian Allen of New York arrived in Savannah after Sherman's occupation. Taken with the city's strong ties with Casimir Pulaski (who died
fighting for the patriots in the Revolutionary War siege of Savannah in
1779) and the vote to return to U.S. governance, Allen became an advocate
for the city. Returning north, he made impassioned appeals on behalf of
Savannah's hungry, ragged women and children. Allen's eloquence touched
the hearts of even hardened "Union forever" zealots in New York and
Boston. Within a few weeks three ships ladened with food from the North
were approaching Savannah.

An ugly confrontation marred the goodwill mission when Sherman's
commissary chief, Colonel Amos Beckwith of Vermont, met with a
Savannah citizens delegation about distribution of the supplies. When the
committee asked for Union soldiers or sailors and wagons to unload the

cargo, Beckwith exploded: "No! A hundred times no! What lazy, miserable curs slavery made of men! A few years more of it and you would have had a [Negro] to open your eyes in the morning and to work your jaws at breakfast!" With that the enraged Beckwith angrily dismissed the delegation. The supply vessels were unloaded by local laborers.[9]

Savannah savored the dressed geese, turkeys, chickens, and ducks sent from their Northern benefactors. And Allen returned to the city in January 1865 to a hero's welcome and everlasting thanks.

Apparently due in part to her effort at reconciliation, Savannah received particular attention from Northern relief agencies in the early weeks of 1865. Merchants met in Philadelphia and other supporters gathered at Boston's Fanueil Hall to discuss how best to get supplies to Savannah. By mid-January a relief fund in Boston had reached $30,000.

In one of the last speeches before his death the famed orator Edward Everett stirred a Boston audience on January 9 speaking in favor of aid for Savannah. Relief ships soon were en route from New York and other cities.

Some $40,000 in government-supplied provisions arrived aboard the *Daniel Webster*. Goods were distributed at the City Market, with black and white Savannahians standing in line for donated flour, meat, salt, beans, bread, and other staples.

About a thousand loaves of bread collected for Sherman's army was turned over to the Poor Association of Savannah.

With the gloating tone of the victor, a *New York Times* correspondent described the chaotic distribution scene after the arrival of one of the first relief shipments:

> Rome, in time of the carnival, can exhibit no such spectacle. There are two doors to the store, one on Bay and the other on Barnard street, affording entrance and exit. Several hundred persons of both sexes, all ages, sizes, complexions, costumes; gray-haired old men, with canes, with bags, bottles and baskets; old "Uncle Neds," who just before death gives them liberty from hardship and suffering, are made freemen by the mighty march of events; well-dressed women wearing crepe for their husbands and sons, who have fallen while fighting against the old flag, with pale and sunken cheeks, stand there patiently awaiting their turn. There are women with tattered dresses— old silks and satins, which were laid aside as useless, but which have become valuable through destitution. There are women in linsey-woolsey, demi-white women wearing negro cloth, negro women dressed in gunny cloth; men with Confederate uniforms, men with butternut clothes. There is a boy in a crimson plush jacket, made from what was once the upholstering of a

sofa. There are old men in short jackets, little boys in long ones—the cast-off overcoats of soldiers, the rags which have been picked up from garrets—wearing the boots and shoes which have been kicked off and thrown aside, down at the heel, out at the toes, open on the instep. There are old bonnets of every description, some with white and crimson flowers, some with ribbons once bright and flaming, but faded now and worn. There are Shaker bonnets, "sugar scoops," "coal scuttles," hats of every description, size and shape worn by both sexes—women wearing men's hats of palm-leaf or felt, men wearing stove-pipes battered and bruised, felt, slouched and torn, ventilated by accident and not by patent ventilators. There is one which had no crown, worn by a man who had red hair, reminding one of a chimney on fire and flaming out at the top. It is the ragman's fair—rather the ragman's jubilee and day of rejoicing, for Charity, like a kind angel, has suddenly stepped in to ward off the wolf which is howling at their doors.

There are teams in the street—old, dilapidated wagons—weak, broken down horses—sorry mules, with rope harness. It is a collection of odds and ends. . . . It is literally a distribution of the bread of life. In no profane sense, but in truth and reality, it is a sacrament, given freely, and I doubt not thankfully received. The recipients, at any rate, are eager to partake of it—so eager that the sentinels at the door at times are compelled to present their bayonets to the crowd to keep the passage clear. There will be some who fail to receive the aid they need—persons who have never known want, who will suffer silently rather than mix in the crowd which throng at the door. Others will obtain provisions when they have an abundance at home.

In spite of the Northern generosity, there were shortages of everything in Savannah in early 1865. Coal for heating and cooking was in high demand, and some residents, as well as soldiers, burned fences, furniture, and beams from houses to stay warm. The unscrupulous sold cords of firewood at exorbitant prices. Many freedmen, including hundreds who drifted into Savannah from the rural counties, suffered for a lack of clothing. While the men might pick up discarded shirts or pants from the soldiers, many of the women and children had little to wear and suffered in the winter chill.

XX

Sherman and "The Negro Question"

Sherman's victory at Savannah would be haunted by a witch hunt from his own government that would forever taint his hour of triumph. Even while his army was resting and reveling in the glory of its historic march, political trouble for Sherman was boiling in Washington.

By late December elation swept the North with the news that Sherman's "lost army" had emerged on the Georgia coast and captured Savannah. Many trumpeted Sherman as a Union lion surpassing even the revered Ulysses S. Grant.

Yet amid the national hoopla, Sherman and his generals, especially Major General Jefferson C. Davis of Indiana, came under close scrutiny from Radical Republicans for their handling of "the Negro question."

The bedrock issue stemmed from a December 3, 1864, incident at Ebenezer Creek, some twenty miles northwest of Savannah. As Sherman's columns neared the city, they were increasingly hampered by ever-growing bands of liberated slaves. Davis, who led the Fourteenth Corps in Slocum's wing, found himself slowed by these refugees clogging the roads.

On December 2 Davis' corps was delayed after Rebels burned a bridge at Ebenezer Creek near Springfield, Georgia. Indiana troops worked all night to put a pontoon span over the creek by the next morning. Sensing a chance to rid himself of about five hundred camp followers who were hindering his advance, Davis ordered them held back while his corps crossed. After the last soldiers reached the opposite bank, the pontoon bridge was cut loose, leaving the blacks stranded.

U.S. Major General Jefferson C. Davis, commander of Sherman's Fourteenth Corps, stirred a cauldron of controversy for his alleged mistreatment of former slaves on the march to Savannah.

"There went up from that multitude a cry of agony," an army chaplain wrote. Suddenly someone shouted "Rebels!" and the ex-slaves panicked. Some men, women, and children rushed into the water.

Soldiers threw tree branches and logs into the creek to help them and pulled other refugees ashore. A group of black men quickly built a make-shift wooden raft and began ferrying people across. Others were swept away and drowned as the Union column turned east and pressed on toward Savannah. Shortly thereafter, gray troopers from Wheeler's cavalry trotted up and captured the remaining band left behind.

Davis was roundly criticized—even by his own men—for his handling of this affair. "This barbarous act has created a deep feeling against Davis in this division," a Minnesota private wrote.[1]

Northern newspaper accounts stated that many of the blacks were killed by the Confederates, which apparently was untrue.

Even before Ebenezer, Davis already was one of the more controversial and colorful figures in the Union service. A Mexican War veteran and Indian fighter, he was a first lieutenant in the Fort Sumter garrison and was among those Union officers who unanimously voted against a Southern surrender demand on April 11, 1861. The Rebels opened their historic bombardment the next morning.

Appointed colonel of the Twenty-second Indiana, he rose to brigadier general of volunteers by December 1861. Davis led a division at the battle of Pea Ridge in March 1862 and during the siege of Corinth. Although he had a distinguished war record and was one of Sherman's favorites, Davis' loyalties were questioned by some of his fellow officers.

A Democrat, Davis was described by one Union officer as "an infernal copperhead" who posted soldiers to guard the property of wealthy Rebels. The butt of perpetual jokes in the army due to his decidedly "Secesh" name, Davis also was criticized for threatening to shoot Union troops for looting during Sherman's march and for his friendliness with Southern belles he encountered.

By late 1864 Davis was a well-known figure in the Federal armies, not only for his war record but for the killing of another Union general. On September 29, 1862, Davis had quarreled with Union Major General William "Bull" Nelson of Kentucky in the lobby of the Galt House hotel in Louisville. Nelson was Davis' former commander, and Davis apparently felt he had been insulted on a prior occasion. In the confrontation Nelson slapped Davis' face. Davis retaliated by drawing his revolver and killing Nelson.

Davis was arrested, but because of his friendship and ties with the powerful Governor O. P. Morton of Indiana, he never faced charges related to the murder. Within days he was back with his command. Davis fought well at Stones River, Chickamauga, and, as a corps commander, in Sherman's dissection of Georgia. If the Nelson slaying made Davis infamous, the events on the Ebenezer only intensified his notoriety.

The Radicals also criticized Sherman for not bringing more freed slaves from Georgia's interior to the coast. Some seven thousand blacks traveled with the army to Savannah. Thousands of others, in addition to those forced to turn back at Ebenezer Creek, wearily returned to their homes after several days on the road, still unsure of what to do with their newfound freedom.

Sherman learned of the possible trouble he faced from Washington in a letter from General Halleck on December 30. Halleck wrote that while Sherman's "great march through Georgia" was being praised by almost everyone, "there is a certain class having great influence with the President ... who are decidedly disposed to make a point against you. I mean in regard to 'inevitable Sambo.' They say you have manifested an almost criminal dislike to the Negro." Halleck continued that Sherman's opponents accused him of driving the blacks from the army, cutting bridges to prevent them from following the troops, and "thus caused the massacre of large numbers by Wheeler's cavalry" at Ebenezer Creek.[2]

Sherman fired off a response to Halleck the next day, calling the accusations a "cock and bull story." He defended Davis' conduct at Ebenezer, stating that Davis "took up his pontoon bridge, not because he wanted to leave them [the refugees], but because he wanted his bridge. He and Slocum tell me they don't believe Wheeler killed one of them."

In all probability Davis' actions at the creek were precisely to rid himself of the freed slaves who were slowing his advance, whether Sherman admitted it or not. Stories of Davis' rumored pro-South and pro-slavery leanings stoked the fire.

For Sherman the inquisition officially began on January 11, 1865, when Secretary of War Stanton arrived in Savannah unannounced aboard a revenue cutter to meet with the general. Although a Democrat, Stanton shared some ideals of the Radical Republicans, including their strong abolitionist beliefs.

The secretary had come after conferring with Grant about Sherman's reluctance to enlist black soldiers, at least to use for garrison duty. Such a move would free white troops for combat.

Ostensibly, Stanton had traveled to Savannah in hopes that the mild climate would improve his health. He also wanted to deal with the issue of who had legitimate claim to the captured cotton, valued at some $25 million. Among the papers Stanton brought with him was a commission by brevet of major general of volunteers for Judson Kilpatrick.

Yet foremost among the wily Stanton's reasons for the Savannah trip was the question of Sherman's attitude toward blacks. Even Grant had suggested that Stanton might want to try to personally persuade Sherman to use U.S. Colored Troops. From earlier correspondence Stanton knew that Sherman was strongly opposed to putting blacks in the ranks with whites, favoring their use in subordinate roles. His reasoning was that "our prejudices, yours as well as mine, are not yet schooled for absolute equality."

At Savannah, Sherman reaffirmed his position, telling Stanton that "in our army we had no Negro soldiers, and, as a rule, we preferred white soldiers," a sentiment shared by many Union generals to whom the concept of black troops still was unacceptable. Sherman added that his army "employed a large force of them as servants, teamsters, and pioneers, who had rendered admirable service."[3]

Stanton wasted little time in getting to the point. He bluntly asked Sherman about Davis and his opinion of Davis' views regarding blacks. Sherman assured Stanton that Davis "was an excellent soldier" who did not harbor "any hostility to the Negro." Stanton then showed Sherman a newspaper story about the affair at Ebenezer Creek, and Sherman called in Davis to defend himself.

Davis gave his account of the event, admitting that some of the refugees drowned trying to cross the creek. He added, however, that he did not believe any of the refugees were slaughtered by the enemy cavalry.

In his memoirs Sherman stuck to his defense of Davis at Ebenezer and aimed a verbal volley at Stanton. "At all events, the same thing might have resulted to General Howard or to any other of the many most humane commanders who filled the army." Davis "was strictly a soldier and doubtless hated to have his wagons and columns encumbered by these poor Negroes, for whom we all felt sympathy, but a sympathy of a different sort from that of Mr. Stanton, which was not of pure humanity, but of politics."

After the one-on-one meeting with Sherman, Stanton requested a conference with the ministers and lay leaders of Savannah's black community. Twenty of these men assembled at Sherman's headquarters, their spokesman being Garrison Frazier, a sixty-seven-year-old Baptist preacher who had bought his own freedom. About half of the other members of the delegation were former slaves freed by Sherman's forces. Stanton scribbled notes to himself as he listened to Frazier. The meeting was held in Sherman's personal quarters on the second floor of the Green house.

Stanton asked Frazier several questions, including his interpretation of the Emancipation Proclamation and what it meant to the new freedmen. He also questioned Frazier about how the blacks could earn their living. To this the minister replied that his people would flourish if they had land to farm and could eventually become landowners.

To Stanton's question of whether the black Savannahians felt more comfortable living with whites or in separate communities, nineteen of the community leaders said they believed segregation was right. Frazier summed up the majority opinion, saying they believed white Southern prejudice against them "would take years to overcome."

The lone dissenter was James Lynch, a twenty-six-year-old missionary originally from Baltimore, who said blacks and whites should live together.

Stanton was impressed by Frazier's eloquence, later describing him as "shrewd, wise and comprehensive." He added that the minister could discuss racial issues "as well as any member of the Cabinet."

Sherman was present for the conference, but at one point was asked by Stanton to leave the room. After the general's departure, Stanton asked the clergymen their opinions of Sherman's outlook on their race and his treatment of them.

"We unanimously feel inexpressible gratitude to him," Frazier told Stanton. "Some of us called upon him immediately upon his arrival, and ... he met us ... as a friend and a gentleman. We have confidence in General Sherman and think that what concerns us could not be under better hands." Again only Lynch abstained in this vote of support, saying he had not known Sherman long enough to form an opinion.[4]

Stanton and Sherman put together a plan to give ex-slaves in South Carolina and Georgia a helping hand in their new freedom. The plan, issued in Special Field Order No. 15 on January 16, 1865, called for an expanse along the coast of South Carolina, Georgia, and Florida to be given to blacks.

Each family of freedmen would be given forty acres, clothing, seed, and farm equipment. Land titles were granted to the blacks by Brigadier General Rufus Saxton, who had been appointed inspector of settlements and plantations. Saxton reported that by the end of summer 1865, from twenty thousand to forty thousand homesteads had been created for freedmen and their families on the sea islands and other coastal lands.

Saxton spoke to an assemblage of several hundred blacks who gathered at the Second African Baptist Church on Greene Square to hear about the plan. His explanation of the order was met by wild enthusiasm and praises for Sherman and Lincoln.

Sherman's "40 acres and a mule" order appeared to be a success—at least in its initial stages. In Georgia, black communities sprung up on Ossabaw, St. Catherine's, and Sapelo islands, and ex-slaves laid out a village on Skidaway Island near Savannah. Unfortunately the project was soon submerged and lost in the violence, confusion, and politics marking Reconstruction.

In Special Field Order No. 15, Sherman also agreed to address the need to enlist black soldiers. By March 1865 veteran regiments of U.S. Colored Troops were garrisoned in Savannah.

Sherman was obviously bitter about the way he was treated by Stanton, especially after just completing his great campaign. "It certainly was a strange fact that the great War Secretary should have catechized Negroes concerning the character of a general who had commanded a hundred thousand men in battle, had captured cities, conducted sixty-five thousand men successfully across four hundred miles of hostile territory, and had just brought tens of thousands of freedmen to a place of security," Sherman wrote in his memoirs. "Because I had not loaded down my army by hundreds of thousands of poor Negroes, I was construed by others as hostile to the black race."[5]

On January 15, the day Stanton left Savannah, Sherman wrote a lengthy letter to Ellen in which he referred briefly to the issue: "Mr. Stanton has been here and is cured of that Negro nonsense which arises not from a loss of the Negro but a desire to dodge service. Mr. [Treasury Secretary Salmon P.] Chase and others have written to me to modify my opinions. . . . I want soldiers made of the best bone and muscle in the land, and won't attempt military feats with doubtful materials. I have said that slavery is dead and the Negro free, and want him treated as free and not hunted and badgered to make a soldier of, when his family is left back on the plantations. I am right and won't change."[6]

Without doubt, Sherman would be labeled a racist by modern standards. After watching his troops capture Fort McAllister on December 13, 1864, he had danced about, calling to General Howard, "There'll be no sleep for dis nigger dis night." He was mimicking the reaction of an old slave who had come out to see him ride past a Georgia plantation a few days earlier. Amid the war and fratricide of the 1860's, this mindset was commonplace among soldiers in blue and gray.

Although he clearly believed the ex-slaves to be inferior, there appears to be no hatred in Sherman's treatment of blacks who followed his army to Savannah in 1864.

After the Union occupation, Northern recruiting agents descended on Savannah, rounding up blacks of military age. These men were detained until they agreed to join the army. With these agreements in hand, the agents could basically sell the ex-slaves as substitutes for wealthy draftees in the North. Sherman ordered the release of the unwilling conscripts and threatened the recruiting agents with arrest.

"In truth, I honestly believe the General entertains a more profound respect and love for these loyal blacks than for the rebellious white men who formerly called themselves masters," Major Nichols wrote.

Throughout his time in Savannah, Sherman was the center of attention, not only from the white populace, but from throngs of former slaves who viewed him as their liberator. He was mobbed by them on the streets.

"They gather round me in crowds, and I can't find out whether I am Moses or Aaron . . . but surely I am rated as one of the congregation, and it is hard to tell in what sense I am most appreciated . . . in saving him [the Negro] from his master or the new master that threatens him with a new species of slavery. I mean the state recruiting agents."

Sherman also received an unending stream of admiring freedmen at his headquarters in the Green house.

No charges were ever filed against Sherman or Davis based on the Ebenezer Creek accusations, but Stanton and Sherman would remain bitter enemies for the rest of their lives.

Sherman wrote that he believed Frazier's delegation "convinced [Stanton] that he was in error, and that they understood their own interests far better than did the men in Washington who tried to make political capital out of this Negro question. . . . But as regards kindness to the race, encouraging them to patience and forbearance, procuring them food and clothing, and providing them with land whereon to labor, I assert that no army ever did more for that race than the one I commanded in Savannah."[7]

XXI

"The Army Is
Acclimatized in Savannah"

The city of Savannah was an old place, and usually accounted a handsome
one. Its houses were of brick or frame, with large yards, ornamented with
shrubbery and flowers; its streets perfectly regular ... and at many of the
intersections were small inclosures in the nature of parks. These streets and
parks were lined with the handsomest shade-trees of which I have knowledge ... and these certainly entitled Savannah to its reputation as a
handsome town more than the houses, which, though comfortable, would
hardly make a display on Fifth Avenue or the Boulevard Haussmann of
Paris. ... In rear of Savannah was a large park, with a fountain, and between
it and the court-house was a handsome monument, erected to the memory
of Count Pulaski. ... Outside of Savannah there was very little to interest a
stranger, except the cemetery of Bonaventur[e], and the ride along the
Wilmington Channel by way of Thunderbolt, where might be seen some
groves of the majestic live-oak trees, covered with gray and funereal moss,
which were truly sublime in grandeur, but gloomy after a few days' camping
under them.—William T. Sherman in his *Memoirs*, 1875.[1]

Savannah had an estimated population of some twenty thousand whites
when Sherman arrived, "all of whom had participated more or less in the
war, and had no special claims to our favor," the general recalled. Now the
pro-Southern populace had to submit to occupation by Sherman's troops
for some four weeks and a Union garrison for even longer.

"Already the public squares which checker the city are filled with the
wooden houses built by the ingenious hands of our soldiers," Major Nichols
wrote. "Very few of the citizens have left their homes, and officers and

These Union officers enjoy a leisurely look at Fort Jackson after
Savannah's capture. (*Harper's Weekly*, Jan. 21, 1865, courtesy of the
Georgia Historical Society.)

soldiers are in close affiliation with the people. The army is acclimatized in
Savannah."[2]

The uninvited blue guests were scattered in camps all over the town and
its environs. Many of Sherman's boys who were bivouacked in Savannah's
squares erected temporary huts and other shelters of ununiform design. The
soldiers used tent halves, fence boards, and timbers from houses in their
construction. Begun before the war, the unfinished home of General Hugh
Mercer on Bull Street fell victim to bluecoats who pried off some of
the timbers.

"All of our Squares [are] built up with wooden houses so that I scarcely
recognized the streets," Fanny Cohen Taylor wrote on December 27.[3]

On a walking tour of the camps in January, Stanton and Sherman
stopped and marveled in particular at one Yank's ingenuity. Sherman
recalled the moment: "I remember [Stanton's] marked admiration for the
hut of a soldier who had made his door out of a handsome parlor mirror,
the glass gone and its gilt frame serving for his door."[4]

The soldiers were busy with a number of other tasks related to the war
effort. Captain Orlando Poe, Sherman's chief engineer, was surveying the
Rebel fortifications, deciding which were to be destroyed and which were
to be retained for the army's use. Other units were taking inventory of the
Confederate supplies and other property left in Savannah.

Squads of bluecoats were dismounting coastal guns and stockpiling them at Fort Pulaski. Aided by the navy, troops also were removing the many river obstructions emplaced by the Rebels. An Illinois private who examined Savannah's strong defenses wrote, "I often wonder yet, how many of us would have been left alive if the Rebs had stayed there and fought as we expected."

Quartermaster and commissary officers took stock of warehouses and other buildings for use as storerooms for mountains of supplies. Sherman wanted his army outfitted and fed "abundantly and well" in the coming campaign.

An Iowa sergeant related how some of his comrades had found bundles of Confederate money outside a Savannah printing office. The Federals generously had offered fistfuls of the bills to Savannahians for a loaf of bread or for someone to groom their horses. Dejected civilians wouldn't take the all but worthless currency.

The Yankees relished the story that a Savannah clergyman had asked Sherman's permission to pray for Jefferson Davis. "Hell yes," the general replied, "Jeff Davis and the Confederate government need all the prayer they can get." The account elicited roars of laughter around many an army campfire.

Like his soldiers, Sherman received back pay for November and December, in his case, amounting to $550 per month. He kept $300 and sent Ellen a check for $800, writing that "It is good for you that I keep in the woods where my expenses are small."

General Geary was appointed military commander of the city and proved to be an energetic administrator. After four years of war, Savannah needed help to restore sanitary conditions as well as her overall appearance. Geary filled the bill, cleaning up the streets, posting guards to protect private property, and generally sprucing up the city. The massive project would take several weeks to complete, however.

Kilpatrick's cavalry rested in camps along the Ogeechee River near King's Ferry, guarding the supply depot. They spent several days prying up sections of the railroads leading into Savannah. Kilpatrick also posted a picket line between the Ogeechee and Savannah rivers in case of any Rebel surprises. With no foe to fight, Kilpatrick issued orders to his brigade commanders to "detail one battalion each day . . . with their officers, to proceed to . . . Savannah to see the city and enjoy themselves generally. It is to be hoped that these officers and men while in the city will so conduct themselves as to reflect no discredit upon the command."

The wear of the campaign and the weather had taken its toll on the cavalry's armament and horses. Kilpatrick requested three hundred Spencer carbines in early January, writing: "The Joslyn carbine, with which the Ninth Pennsylvania is armed, and the majority of my Sharps carbines are utterly worthless." He added that his men were "worse armed at present than Wheeler's irregular cavalry," which was likely far from the truth.

Colonel W. D. Hamilton of the Ninth Ohio Cavalry reported that his command was ineffective in the latter stages of the march due to a lack of ammunition for his Smith carbines. The rainy weather had ruined hundreds of rounds. "I regard the weapon for that reason, and for its liability to get out of repair, as one which should not be used in the service."

In spite of their proximity to the vast depot, Kilpatrick's mounts apparently did not receive enough forage. "Our animals had been nearly starved at Savannah and only by the most untiring efforts were our horses kept in anything like serviceable condition," an Indiana officer wrote.

This view was in raw contrast to the experiences during the march as described by trooper Jacob Bartmess of the Eighth Indiana in a letter written to his wife from Savannah: "We always had plenty of meet [*sic*] and ham, and honey and butter when we could get it, and sweet potatoes without end and chickens much the same. It have [*sic*] been the time in the service for me. We burned cotton enough to nearly buy the state of Indiana."

Some of Sherman's generals followed their commander's lead in appropriating Savannah houses for their headquarters. Fanny Cohen Taylor wrote on December 21 that General Howard tried to seize her family's home that afternoon, but that her father had persuaded the general's staff to take a vacant house across the street.

General Hazen called at the Cohen home on Christmas Eve afternoon in search of quarters. The general took the front parlor and a bedroom. "It is a hard trial but I suppose we must submit," Mrs. Taylor wrote in her diary that day. She had known Hazen before the war. "I trust for that reason he will treat us with more consideration than some of our friends have received who have been obliged to receive Yankees in their homes."[5]

Hazen only occupied the house for a few days in early January, sending the Cohens a supply of firewood in advance. Mrs. Taylor visited with the general on January 2, later relating: "He was very considerate during his stay and said nothing offensive."[6]

Major General William T. Ward established himself in several rooms of a home occupied by the wife of General G. W. Smith in Hardee's army. General Geary set up headquarters in the Railroad Bank building, while Brigadier General Amos B. Eaton, the army's commissary general, was lodged in a "fine house on the corner of West Broad and South Broad streets."

General Howard eventually was posted in the beautiful home of Edmund Molyneux, the British consul in Savannah. The house, located at the corner of Bull and Gaston streets, was the former residence of Brigadier General Henry R. Jackson, who had been captured at Nashville days earlier.

The seizure of Molyneux's home in no way bothered Howard or Sherman. The Englishman also dealt in cotton, and a large quantity of his bales were confiscated by the Federals. His appeals for their return were met with hostility from Sherman, who said he was "unwilling to fight [for the release] of cotton for the benefit of Englishmen openly engaged in smuggling arms and instruments of war to kill us."[7]

"I have now been in the vicinity of this beautiful city since the 21st," Howard wrote to his wife on December 26. "I am living in the house of an old English consul: A magnificient establishment."[8]

After the Yankees left Savannah, Molyneaux filed a claim against the U.S. government for $11,000 in damages to his home sustained during the occupation. Howard's staff apparently helped themselves to Molyneaux's expensive collection of brandy and wines and also sacked his library.

Union Captain Wimer Bedford admitted that many of the missing bottles, books, and other valuables from the house somehow turned up later at Howard's headquarters on the march through the Carolinas. He was quick to rationalize, however, that since Molyneaux represented the pro-Confederate British, the thievery could be overlooked: "We had no respect for the English government, and hence none for its flag."[9]

Under the occupation Savannah took on a renewed vibrancy, even if staunch Confederates among the citizenry remained depressed over their defeat. The riverfront, virtually barren of Rebel commerce ships during the blockade, now hummed with activity as it had in prewar times.

"The wide piers, or wharves, at our feet are thronged with thousands of laborers in army blue," Major Nichols wrote on January 2. "They are loading supplies with the long tiers of wagons which stretch through the admirably-built causeways to the main street above. Hundreds of them, thousands come here daily on a similar errand. Certainly in the most prosperous times there could not have been more life and movement in Savannah than we see here to-day."[10]

This house at the corner of Bull and Gaston streets was the headquarters
of Union General Oliver O. Howard during Sherman's occupation.

The Savannahians' unconventional December 28 vote to "submit to
national authority" showed the willingness of many war-weary residents to
put the conflict behind them. Even if this vote represented only a small
majority of the populace, the citizenry as a whole did nothing to upset the
peace.

Sherman issued general orders that civilians wishing to leave the city
could do so and be escorted under a truce flag to Charleston or Augusta,
which the Rebels still held. About two hundred people, mostly families of
Confederate soldiers, accepted the offer and were taken by steamer to
Charleston. Indeed, Sherman had the authority from a standing order to
relocate all women married to Confederates outside the city, but he chose
not to enforce it.

Sherman remembered that "the great bulk of the inhabitants chose to
remain in Savannah [and] generally behaved with propriety, and good social
relations at once arose between them and the army."

Among the many visitors to Sherman's headquarters were civilian relatives
of Confederate generals requesting protection. General Gustavus Smith's
wife appeared with a letter from her husband, whom Sherman had known

at West Point. In the note Smith asked Sherman for the "courteous protection" of his spouse.

General Hardee's brother, Andrew, the Savannah cotton broker, also saw Sherman and presented a note from "Old Reliable." Hardee's letter requested protection for Andrew as well as for his family and cotton. Sherman assured the merchant that "no harm was designed to any of the people of Savannah who would remain quiet and peaceable, but that I could give him no guarantee as to his cotton."[11]

The wife of Lieutenant General Alexander P. Stewart, a corps commander in Hood's army, was in Savannah and asked that Sherman come see her. Sherman complied and found her not only concerned about her personal safety, but anxious over the unknown fate of her husband in Tennessee. Sherman assured her that, to the best of his knowledge, Stewart was alive and well. Learning that Mrs. Stewart was a native of Cincinnati, he urged her to return there through the lines and await the war's outcome.

While he dealt with these requests as best he could, Sherman was rankled by the letters from Hardee and Smith: "Before I had reached Savannah, and during our stay there, the rebel officers and newspapers represented the conduct of ... our army as simply infamous; that we respected neither age nor sex; that we burned every thing we came across—barns, stables, cotton-gins, and even dwelling-houses; that we ravished the women and killed the men.... Therefore it struck me as strange that Generals Hardee and Smith should commit their families to our custody.... These officers knew well that these reports were exaggerated ... and yet tacitly assented to these false publications, to arouse the drooping energies of the people of the South."[12]

Savannah's women displayed a variety of emotions and attitudes in their contact with the Yanks. They either hated the Northerners with a passion, flirted with the handsomer soldiers, swallowed their defiance to ask for food and safety, or baked cookies and cakes for money. Eliza Thompson won admirers among many Yanks with the treats she created in the kitchen of her home on West Jones Street.

Infuriated by four years of loathing Yankees and the hardships wrought by the enemy, many of the city's fairer sex watched the blue invaders through shuttered windows as they paraded in the streets. Others were petrified by accounts of rape, theft, and other atrocities blamed on Sherman.

Whatever their outlook, Savannah's belles were admired by Sherman's troops, who had been away from home for a long time. "The ladies are the tastiest Secesh I have ever seen and I rather think would get to like

Yankees," said Union Colonel Oscar Jackson. "The majority do not look a bit mad now."[13]

"In truth, there is a delightful entente cordiale between the officers and ladies," Major Nichols remembered.

Sherman also described good relations between his men and the city residents: "The guard-mountings and parades, as well as the greater reviews, became the daily resorts of ladies, to hear the music of our excellent bands; schools were opened, and the churches every Sunday were filled with most devout and respectful congregations; stores were reopened, and markets for provisions, meat, wood, etc., were established, so that each family, regardless of race, color, or opinion, could procure all the necessaries and even luxuries of life."[14]

Other Savannahians still loyal to the Confederacy despised Nichols and his comrades. General Howard threatened to arrest one lady who daringly refused to walk beneath a U.S. flag hung over a sidewalk. The woman was brought before Howard who, when other tough talk failed, told her that he would hoist a flag over her front door. She replied that she would send her servants out for day-to-day business and avoid walking beneath the banner. Frustrated, Howard released her.

On a visit to Sherman's headquarters, another Savannah woman saw the handsome bed where the Union commander slept. "I wish a thousand papers of pins were stuck in that bed and that he was strapped down on them," she remarked.

Other events also caused tension. About the time of Sherman's departure, Frances Thomas Howard, whose father was in Hardee's army, wrote of Union soldiers despoiling one of Savannah's burial grounds: "Our cemetery is desecrated with their fortifications. The Yankees have broken open the doors of vaults, and, in one instance that I know of, the coffin of a lady was opened and a cross and chain stolen from her body. Surely such men are not human."[15]

Enticed by tales that families had buried silverware and other valuables in Colonial Cemetery, numerous graves and vaults were looted by soldiers or civilians who left "bones and skulls scattered about."

Savannah's first burial ground was used as an encampment and makeshift horse stables by the Federals. Among the soldiers' amusements, they altered tombstones to read that the deceased died before they were born.

As visitors have been doing ever since, the Yankees spent much of their time sightseeing. Among the most popular stops were Forsyth Park, Laurel Grove and Bonaventure cemeteries, and the Pulaski Monument in

Monterey Square. "The most attractive spot was the beautiful cemetery of Bonaventure, with its majestic live-oaks and wooded paths," wrote Union Captain Luis F. Emilio.[16]

A Cincinnati newspaper correspondent visited Francis Bartow's tomb in Laurel Grove and left with this observation about the Savannah hero: "A brave man, no doubt, but now that he fills a traitor's grave it ought to be so marked, if marked at all."[17]

While many Federals were impressed with Savannah's squares, fine homes, and oak-shaded avenues, Nichols was less than flattering in his description of the city: "Savannah is not so beautiful a city as Portland, in Maine, or Rome, in Georgia, where Nature has shown her graces with prodigal hand. . . . The city is not celebrated for its works of art, nor for fine architectural displays . . . it would be an extravagance of words to say that Savannah is beautiful."

Other Northerners were smitten by the mild climate, even in the winter. "You hardly know what a really pleasant place this is," General Howard wrote to his seven-year-old daughter, Grace Ellen, on January 6. "While you have snow & cold, bleak fields with the wind whistling through the trees, we have it warm & sunny."[18] Howard also described Savannah as "a beautiful city."

The soldiers also delved into more worldly diversions. Having marched and fought hard for months, Sherman's boys finally received their back pay and were more than ready to raise a little hell.

Savannah's whorehouses grew in number and did a thriving business. Gambling dens, where dice and card games ruled, sprung up in the camps in spite of Sherman's prohibition on betting. A horse track was set up, and Yankee jockeys raced captured Georgia thoroughbreds for high stakes. Sherman closed the track after several riots broke out there.

The William W. Gordon home at the corner of Bull Street and what is now Oglethorpe Avenue was frequented by many Union officers, including Sherman and Howard.

Gordon was a Confederate captain with Wheeler's cavalry, but his wife, Eleanor Kinzie Gordon, a Chicago native, had ties on both sides. Mrs. Gordon's father, John H. Kinzie, and two of her brothers were in the Union army, while a third served in the U.S. Navy.

Mrs. Gordon, however, was fervent in her support for the Confederacy. Her stand remained firm even when other Savannah belles told her they hoped that her Union relatives would be killed in battle. Further complicating matters was her relation, by marriage, as the niece of Union General David Hunter, one of the most hated Yankees in the South.

Mrs. Gordon knew many of the highest ranking officers in Sherman's army. Some of them, including Major General Alpheus Williams, did not call on her because of her very well-known Southern sympathies. The Gordon children, four-year-old Juliette "Daisy" Gordon and her sister Nelly, were awed by the presence of the invaders.

A few days after the occupation, some units of Sherman's command marched through the streets. "Everyone's shutters were tightly closed," Mrs. Gordon wrote. "Nelly and Daisy, however, stood on chairs looking out of the parlor windows through the blinds, and watched the troops marching past."

Occasionally one of the girls would ask, "Oh, Mama, is that Old Sherman?"

Sherman first visited the Gordon home to deliver letters from one of Mrs. Gordon's brothers, a Union colonel and one of Sherman's old friends.

"I was seated by the fire, while the two little girls played together," Mrs. Gordon recalled. "Suddenly the parlor door was flung open, and the maid announced 'General Sherman!'"

Mrs. Gordon wrote that she was surprised but welcomed the general. She then noticed that the children had "retreated" behind her. "I took hold of Nelly and drew her forward, saying, 'General, here is a little girl who was very anxious to see Old Sherman the day of the parade.'"

"'I declare,' exclaimed Nelly in tremulous tones, 'I never said old Sherman. It was Daisy.'"

"'Well you said it too, Nelly,' retorted Daisy, equally alarmed.'You did say Old Sherman!'"

The general "roared with laughter" and replied: "'Why of course you never said Old Sherman,' he continued, 'because you and I used to play together when I was a little boy, and now we are going to sit right down and talk it all over.'"

"With Daisy on his knee and his arm around Nelly, he kept them in shouts of laughter till long past their bedtime and when the nurse came for them I had hard work to make them go," Mrs. Gordon remembered.[19]

Sherman seemed to enjoy "the home fireside and the children" and shared several amusing anecdotes and accounts of his march to Savannah. "Old Sherman" returned to the Gordons on several occasions, delighting in the antics of the sisters.

One of the other visitors was a staff officer for General Howard who asked if Howard, the father of four little girls "whom he had not seen for many months," might visit the Gordons' daughters.

Howard, whose right arm had been smashed at the battle of Seven Pines in 1862, called on a late winter afternoon.

"The children at once made friends and General Howard took Daisy on his knee," Mrs. Gordon recalled. "Instantly she noticed he had lost an arm. 'Oh,' she cried, 'you have only got one arm!'

"'Yes, little girl,' he answered. 'Are you not sorry for me?'"

When Howard told her the Rebels had shot it off, the youngster nonchalantly replied, "'Well, I shouldn't wonder if my Papa did it. He has shot lots of Yankees!'"[20]

Juliette "Daisy" Gordon Low would grow up to establish the Girl Scouts of America.

Word of Union officers in his home reached Captain Gordon at the front. Angered, he wrote a January 14 letter to his wife: "The fact of your being in the Federal lines is of course very difficult to bear, but I accept that as the fate of war and will endure it as I would any sacrifice that may be called for. But really what galls me is that you should associate with my enemies upon any terms than those of politeness demand from every lady."[21]

On Christmas Eve, Sherman received official word that Thomas had demolished Hood's army at Nashville, although the Federals had been hearing rumors about the triumph for several days. The Yankees celebrated with a review of the Fifteenth Corps that day and parades of the other corps in the week to come.

Christmas Day found the soldiers ordered out to hear their sergeants read a congratulatory note from Sherman for their part in the success. The victories at Nashville and Savannah also prompted Sherman to issue a special field order on January 8 to all troops in the Military Division of the Mississippi.

"So complete a success in military operations, extending over half a continent, is an achievement that entitles it to a place in the military history of the world," the general wrote. Amid his compliments, Sherman added that each regiment "may inscribe on its colors, at pleasure, the word 'Savannah' or 'Nashville.'"[22]

*   *   *

"This is the saddest Christmas that I have ever spent and my only pleasure during the day has been in looking forward to spending my next Christmas in the Confederacy," Fanny Cohen Taylor wrote that night.[23]

"The men of our Army had a lean and hungry Christmas in Savannah," remembered Sergeant Rice Bull of the 123rd New York. "While the Armies nearer home in Virginia and Tennessee were having their turkey dinners, furnished and forwarded them by the people of the North, we at Savannah, were so far away we could not be reached. We had boiled rice, Georgia fresh beef that was left from those driven along with us on our march through the state, and coffee."

Sherman hosted a dinner party of about twenty at the Green House on Christmas night, the guests enjoying several turkeys and bottles of wine.

Some of the Yankees in Savannah decided that a visit from old Kris Kringle would brighten the day for the city's children, according to Dr. Spencer B. King, who wrote a series of Civil War centennial columns for the *Macon Telegraph and News* in the 1960's. In a January 5, 1964 column, King described how a company of bluecoats, homesick and missing their own youngsters, decided to bring the Christmas magic to Savannah. They created dolls from rags, fashioned other toys, and gathered what rations they could for the "sleigh," a wagon decorated in gay colors. The mule team serving as reindeer was fitted with improvised antlers. By lot, a sergeant from the company was selected to dress as Santa Claus and drive through the streets, delivering the gifts to youngsters.

In the week after Christmas, Sherman learned of the death of his six-month-old son, Charles, whom he had never seen. The heartbreak was intensified since the general received the news in a New York newspaper dated December 22. He had not heard from Ellen since early November because the army had been cut off from communications while marching through hostile Georgia.

The personal tragedy cut even deeper since the Shermans had lost their first young son, Willy, to typhoid fever early in the war. The December 22 *New York Herald* ran Charles Sherman's obituary. The baby died of natural causes.

"He too is lost to us and gone to join Willy," Sherman wrote to Ellen on December 31. "I should have liked to have seen the baby of which all spoke so well, but I seem doomed to pass my life away so that even my children will be strangers."[24]

Sherman wrote to his wife again on January 5, mourning "the little baby

I never saw. All spoke of him as so bright and fair that I had hoped he would be spared to us to fill the great void in our hearts left by Willy, but it is otherwise decreed and we must submit."[25]

Whether brooding over the loss of his son, dealing with Stanton, or appeasing his many visitors, Sherman remained focused on one goal. He and Grant were actively planning for Sherman's army to march north through the Carolinas and link with Grant's forces in Virginia.

"Your confidence in being able to march up and join this army pleases me, and I believe it can be done," Grant wrote Sherman on December 27. "The effect of such a campaign will be to disorganize the south, and prevent the organization of new armies from their broken fragments. . . . Without further directions, then, you may make preparations to start on your northern expedition without delay. Break up the railroads in South and North Carolina and join the armies operating against Richmond as soon as you can."[26]

Sherman needed no prodding. On January 2, 1865, he sent Grant a detailed plan for the invasion of South Carolina and "concluded at once" to march into the Palmetto State. By land and sea Sherman's troops were on the move within days. The offensive was ordered in spite of heavy winter rains that swelled rivers, creeks, and swamps in the Yankees' path.

Sherman himself was "quite impatient to get off . . . for a city life had become dull and tame, and we were all anxious to get into the pine-woods again, free from the importunities of rebel women asking for protection, and of the civilians from the North who were coming to Savannah for cotton and all sorts of profit."

General Foster was left in overall command at Savannah and placed Brevet Major General Cuvier Grover of Maine in charge of the city's garrison troops.

On January 21 Sherman boarded a steamer bound for Beaufort, South Carolina, to join Howard for the northern thrust. South Carolina, which had led the secession parade, was to feel the vengeful lash of a Union army intent on making her pay "a debt to justice and humanity."

In farewell, a New York lieutenant in Barnum's brigade kissed the baby of a family with whom he had stayed in Savannah. The mother "was very indignant and has nearly scrubbed the poor little mortal's face off," a relative wrote in her diary.[27]

Sherman himself predicted that the march through South Carolina would be "one of the most horrible things in the history of the world," adding that "the Devil himself couldn't restrain my men."[28]

"THE ARMY IS ACCLIMATIZED IN SAVANNAH"

U.S. Major General Cuvier Grover of Maine commanded Union troops garrisoning Savannah after the departure of Sherman's army in January 1865.

While Savannah benefitted, overall, by the presence of Sherman's army, the city faced a long, arduous journey to recovery. "The potent spell of poverty, idleness and a singular lethargy broods over everything," one observer wrote during this time. "Groups of citizens could be seen some in the dirty grey of the rebel army, others in the coarse butternut colored cloth of country manufacture and still others in dilapidated old-fashioned garments, thread-bare and glossy—recalling better days."[29]

If a Massachusetts visitor to Savannah is to be believed, General Geary's task to clean up the city was far from fulfilled in late January 1865.

"My expectations in regard to finding a mild and delicious climate, and a beautiful Southern city, have been far from realized," wrote John M. Glidden of Boston. "I don't know what the condition and appearance of Savannah was, before the rebellion; but at present it is in the most dilapidated and miserable condition.

"The effects and ravages of war are noticeable everywhere, business is almost entirely suspended, and nearly every store is closed, the houses are also carefully closed, and very few civilians and ladies are to be seen, fences are broken down, sidewalks and wharves are going to ruin, and Sherman's dead horses are laying about the streets by the dozen. . . . The fact is, this is a most miserable hole."[30]

Sometime around Christmas, Hardee's army in South Carolina was reinforced by the Orphan Brigade's Fifth Kentucky, which had been cut off and fighting independently around Savannah for about a month. On picket duty west of the town, this mounted command of Colonel Hiram Hawkins had been unable to break through the ring of besieging Federals before Hardee evacuated.

Hawkins, who had married a young Alabama belle in September, brought his unit within five miles of Savannah, but had to turn back because Sherman's troops were everywhere. Riding south through Hinesville to the Altamaha River, the Kentuckians set about ambushing Sherman's "bummers" and isolated blue patrols.

On one occasion these Orphans encountered an old man and his two daughters, all of whom were greatly distressed. Union soldiers of an enemy squad just up the road had tried to assault the girls, they were told. Enraged, Hawkins' men galloped in pursuit and caught two of the alleged offenders, hanging them in short order.

Another Orphan killed a Federal and reported finding some $5,000 in looted diamonds in the Yank's pockets.

To the defenseless Georgia civilians, Hawkins was "an angel of mercy and peace" before his command crossed the Savannah to rejoin its brigade.

In the terribly efficient campaign of Sherman's march through Georgia and the Carolinas, the pyres of two flaming cities rise above the other destruction. Atlanta and Columbia burned in the wake of Sherman's warpath. There is no doubt that Sherman's destruction of Atlanta was deliberate. As to the February 1865 conflagration in Columbia, Sherman always denied intentional arson, blaming the fire on fleeing Rebel horsemen who ignited cotton bales. But what of the little-known burning of Savannah, which occurred within days of Sherman's departure from the city?

By late January most of Sherman's troops already had moved into South Carolina, anxious to exact revenge on the state whose firebrands touched off the secession fire.

In Savannah since December 21, Sherman's veterans were rested, paid, and eating well. There had been almost none of the destruction that marked the Federals' trek from Atlanta to the coast. Savannahians gave Sherman's men little reason to burn the city. The occupation had been without serious incident.

"While we occupied Savannah, nothing occurred to interrupt the quiet and order which belongs to a large city," Major Nichols wrote. "A foreigner visiting the city would not suppose that it was so lately a prize of battle."

Federal soldiers began printing pro-Union newspapers in Savannah
within days of Sherman's occupation in December 1864. (Courtesy of
the Georgia Historical Society.)

Regardless of opinions and causes, no one in Savannah was prepared for
the conflagration, accidental or intentional, that occurred on the night of
January 27–28, 1865. An inferno of flames and smoke consumed the city, fire
licking from building to building in the downtown districts. A captured
Confederate naval arsenal at West Broad and Zubly Street virtually
exploded, sending artillery rounds and ammunition of every description
flying in all directions.

Shell fragments were hurled all over the city as an estimated fifty
tons of black powder and hundreds of cannonballs ignited. "Never while I
live shall I cease to remember this night of horror," one Savannahian
recalled. Some reports state that the fire actually began when the magazine
exploded.

The *Savannah Daily Herald*, a Northern newspaper that sprouted during
Sherman's occupation, said the blaze was "evidently an incendiary one" set
about 11 P.M. in a stable behind the arsenal, which was located in a building
called Granite Hall.

Fire companies were quickly on the scene, and Union officers frantically
organized bystanders to remove shells and other ordnance before the flames
swirled in.

"Before midnight the ammunition was reached, and then commenced a series of terrific explosions," the *Herald* reported. Panicked servants believed the Rebel army had returned to bombard the city, and lodgers at the Pulaski House also were convinced that "the rebels were upon us."

"Between twelve and one, the scene was sadly, savagely grand," said the *Herald*. "The flames from the burning piles of buildings had [thrown] an eerie, lurid sheet over the city with a black cloud of smoke like a funeral pile [*sic*], hovering over them. Every moment hissing, shrieking shells would mount in the air, dashing their hurtling fragments around."[31]

With rounds splashing nearby, some ships docked at the river wharves were forced to retreat to safety. Another shell crashed into the city water tower in Franklin Square. A jet of water gushed from the reservoir, "rivalling in beauty any fountain, and looking in the fiery glare like a shower of molten silver."

Amid the "scene of ruin and conflagration," panic-stricken citizens rushed about in confusion, trying to escape the fire or save some belongings. "Women and children were huddled in groups under shelter of walls and houses, trembling both with cold and fear."

Before it was over, the blaze destroyed more than two hundred buildings (some accounts say a hundred) and may have killed as many as seven people.

"We saw a few dead and some wounded men lying on the street or being carried away," the *Herald* said.

"The scene the next morning was heart-rending," wrote John Glidden, who was asleep aboard a ship in the river when the fire broke out. "Hundreds of people turned out of house and home, and were carrying off what little they had saved from their burning houses."

By about 2 A.M. most of the shells had exploded, but the inferno rampaged through the rest of the night.

"This morning the appalling extent of the ruin and devastation could be fully realized," the *Herald* said on January 28. Buildings on West Broad, Ann, St. Gaul, Congress, Pine, Broughton, and Zubly streets were "all in a heap of ruins, with nothing but tall, spectre looking chimnies and smoking piles remaining."

Trees on West Broad were shattered by the exploding ordnance, and shell fragments littered the streets. A charred corpse was found in the rubble near West Broad and Broughton, and authorities tried to determine whether or not it was one of the city's firemen.

"It was a sad sight to see homeless women and children weeping over the ruins of their late homes," the *Herald* reported. "They were now outcasts as poor and shelterless as Lazarus."[32]

Who, if anyone, was to blame?

The *Savannah Republican* (now being published by a pro-Union staff under John Hayes, a *New York Tribune* correspondent) stated the fire was started by "an incendiary" that caused a grim vista of "awful grandeur and sublimity." Union General Foster blamed the massive blaze on Rebel soldiers or Southern sympathizers.

Glidden reported that "this was an attempt, by some of Wheeler's Cavalry, three of whom have been captured in the city in Federal uniform, to destroy the city." It is unlikely that Wheeler's men were involved, although Wheeler was in the area of Lawtonville, South Carolina, only a few miles north of Savannah at the time.

Sherman was gone, but many Savannahians believed the fire was set by Yankee troops, whether in Sherman's army or in the Savannah garrison commanded by General Grover.

Some of Sherman's men were still in the city at the time. Indeed, Barnum's brigade, the first Federals to enter Savannah on December 21, departed a few hours before the fire, Barnum exhorting his men "as patriots to write their names indelibly upon the soil of South Carolina."[33]

The mystery of Savannah's burning remains unsolved.

XXII

Arrival of the U.S. Colored Troops

On a brisk March Saturday in 1989, reenactors portraying the Fifty-fourth Massachusetts regiment of U.S. Colored Troops paraded over the ballast stones of River Street. A segment of the motion picture *Glory* was being filmed in Savannah. The scene was a recreation of the Fifty-fourth's march through the streets of Boston on its way south to join the war effort. Amid the camera lighting and on-cue confetti, actor Matthew Broderick led the procession, portraying Colonel Robert Gould Shaw.

Not far from the movie set, the original Fifty-fourth came ashore at Savannah on March 13, 1865, facing a much harsher reality. Colonel Shaw and a good portion of his original volunteers were long dead, falling in a spearhead assault on Battery Wagner outside Charleston on July 18, 1863.

A steamer carrying the Fifty-fourth docked at the city wharf, and the troops soon were marching down Bull Street. They reached "the edge of the place," probably Forsyth Park, and set up quarters in board shelters vacated by Sherman's soldiers.

Joining the Fifty-fourth were two other black infantry regiments, the Thirty-third and the 102nd, which bolstered the Union garrison's white troops.

"Savannah was a most attractive city, with wide, shaded streets, numerous parks, and many good buildings, and elegant residences," wrote Captain Emilio of the Fifty-fourth.[1]

The Fifty-fourth and 102nd were not long in Savannah. On March 27 they boarded ships for Charleston and thence to Georgetown, South

Carolina. These troops joined a force under Union Major General Edward E. Potter, which embarked on a destructive march through central South Carolina in the war's closing weeks.

Like the rest of the occupying force, the black troops were well behaved while in Savannah. But diehard residents, including many who had lost loved ones in the war, resented the presence of these soldiers.

Two days after St. Patrick's Day 1865, the pro-Union *Republican* scolded citizens for their attitude toward the USCT regiments: "These black troops are here in this city as United States Soldiers ... and as such all parties are bound to respect their uniform, if they do not the men who are clothed in them, no matter what their complexion may be."[2]

The newspaper went on to state that the black soldiers were being "jostled and sneered at by both soldiers and citizens, while walking peaceably through the streets.... It is of no use to permit the sight of a colored man bearing a shining musket to ruffle our temper and sour our countenance."[3]

Alexander Lawrence relates another incident that showed a different side of the issue. Confederates returning home from the war were initially forbidden to wear their uniforms. Since few of them had any other clothes, the order was amended so that the gray could be worn, but the military buttons had to be removed.

During the Union occupation, Josiah Tattnall, the old Rebel naval commander, was seen walking in his gray uniform on a Savannah street. Tattnall, who had served with distinction in the U.S. Navy from the War of 1812 until Georgia's secession, had refused to cut off his CSN buttons. As he hobbled past a black sentry, other passersby feared a confrontation. The soldier, however, smartly snapped to attention in salute to the ancient mariner.[4]

When the Thirty-third regiment of black troops reached the city, they were accompanied by Susie King Taylor, whose story is among the most remarkable of Savannah's war tales. Raised a slave in Savannah, Mrs. Taylor served as a laundress, teacher, and nurse for United States Colored Troops during the war.

Born in coastal Georgia in 1848, she and two siblings were raised by their grandmother in Savannah and secretly taught to read and write. (At the time, it was against state law for slaves to be educated.)

Shortly after Fort Pulaski was captured by Union forces in 1862, Mrs. Taylor and other members of her family fled the city. Led by an uncle, the family made its way to St. Catherine's Island, which was in Union hands. She was among slave refugees taken to St. Simons Island, where she taught school for a brief time. In late summer 1862 Mrs. Taylor went to Beaufort, South Carolina, where she became a laundress for the First South Carolina Volunteers, a black regiment that would become the Thirty-third U.S. Colored Infantry.

She taught a number of the soldiers to read. She also met and married her first husband, Sergeant Edward King of Company E. After almost drowning in a sea accident, Mrs. Taylor was with the Thirty-third when it arrived for garrison duty in Savannah in March 1865. Her return marked the first time she had seen her grandmother in almost three years.

When the war ended, she and her husband returned to Savannah, where Mrs. Taylor opened a school at her home on South Broad Street. This was one of several black private schools in the city at the time. She taught almost a year before the opening of the Beach Institute took away most of her students.

After King's death in September 1867, Mrs. Taylor opened a school in Liberty County. She later returned to Savannah and worked as a teacher, laundress, and cook. Moving to Boston, she did similar work for several families and, in 1886, helped form Corps '67, Women's Relief Corps, an auxiliary to the Grand Army of the Republic veterans organization. While in Boston she fell in love and married Russell Taylor.

In 1902 Mrs. Taylor published her war memoir, *Reminiscences of My Life With the 33rd United States Colored Troops Late 1st S.C. Volunteers.* This journal offers a seldom-seen perspective of slave life and a description of life among the Union's first black soldiers.

"Justice we ask," she wrote, "to be citizens of these United States, where so many of our people have shed their blood with their white comrades, that the stars and stripes should never be polluted." Mrs. Taylor died on October 6, 1912, and was buried in Boston's Mount Hope Cemetery.

XXIII

Death of the Confederacy—1865

Where's Bragg, Hardee and Beauregard,
Who lately figured here.
They're studying now Topography—
An outlet in their rear.

Our gallant boys will gain the day,
We've nothing then to fear;
For Gen'l Sherman now my boys,
Has got them by the ear.

Excerpt from U.S. Army Surgeon T. J. Farrell's poem, "Has Got Them by the Ear," *Savannah Republican*, February 1, 1865.

Dirges for the Confederacy and the hosannas of freed slaves were being sung in Savannah and across the South in spring 1865. Sherman was long gone, tearing through South Carolina and battling Joe Johnston's little army, including the remnants of Hardee's Savannah garrison, in the pine thickets of North Carolina.

The brutal ironies of this war were personified in the death of Rebel Major General W. H. C. Whiting. When Fort Pulaski was seized by Georgia troops in January 1861, Whiting was a U.S. Army captain in charge of the fort and other government property at Savannah. Four years later the Mississippian had risen through the Confederate ranks to earn a general's stars and had seen much combat in the eastern campaigns.

The principal architect of powerful Fort Fisher off Wilmington, North

Carolina, Whiting was severely wounded in a Union land and sea assault that resulted in Fisher's fall in January 1865.

Incarcerated at Fort Columbus in New York Harbor, Whiting died on March 10, 1865, one of many Confederates who gave their lives fighting against the flag they once served.

General Grover would endure the hatred of Southerners for decades to come for his actions at Savannah in March 1865. Grover began enforcing a standing Federal order to escort all women married to men in Confederate service outside Union lines. A number of wives were forced out of their homes and sent up the Savannah River to Rebel-held Augusta.

Some Savannahians blamed Sherman for this "cruel and barbarous order," but Sherman had chosen not to enforce it during his time in the city. "We are kept entirely in the dark as to Confederate movements, and are taught to believe that we are to be crushed without fail in a very short time," Mrs. William H. Stiles wrote to her husband in Virginia on March 2. "Still, with General Lee at our head, and with the blessings of the Almighty, we shall not be made slaves to these wretches."[1]

As he predicted, Sherman's march through the Carolinas was indeed a canvas of fiery destruction, the army's trail marked by hundreds of blazing homes, barns, and gins. After watching "the well-known sight of columns of black smoke" from burning buildings, Major Nichols wrote: "This cowardly traitor state, secure from harm, as she thought, in her central position, with hellish haste dragged her Southern sisters into the cauldron of secession. Little did she dream that the hated flag would again wave over her soil."[2]

Much of the vengeance was wreaked on Columbia after Union troops took it in February. A good portion of the capital went up in flames on the night of February 17–18.

Although he is often blamed for burning Columbia, Sherman vigorously maintained that the blaze was sparked by Confederate cavalry torching cotton to keep it from being captured. In particular, Sherman blamed C.S. cavalry general Wade Hampton of South Carolina, whose troops were in the city at the time and whom Sherman considered "a braggart" who "professed to be the special champion" of the state. Hampton replied that "History will brand him [Sherman] as a robber and incendiary and will deservedly damn him to everlasting fame."[3]

Cutting through the Carolinas, Sherman accepted the surrender of

Johnston's army at Durham Station, North Carolina, on April 26, 1865, more than two weeks after Lee's capitulation at Appomattox.

Lee's final defeat and April 9 surrender was the biggest news. The *Savannah Daily Herald* called Lee's debacle the "Most Glorious News of the War." It added that the Confederacy "will speedily be but a dark shadow of the past."[4]

Savannah's Volunteer Guards were among the last Rebels to fight and die in Lee's army. Led by Major William Starr Basinger, the Savannahians fought a valiant rearguard action at Sailor's Creek, Virginia, on April 6. Trying to save the army from annihilation, the battalion fought with fixed bayonets across the little stream and through the pine woods. With heavy losses, the Guards were soon "overcome by the larger Union forces." Basinger was shot and captured, his once proud unit destroyed. Of the eighty-five or so guardsmen who had gone into battle, fifty-two were killed or wounded, the rest taken prisoner.

Basinger was a Union captive when he wrote his mother from Petersburg on April 14: "I cannot think of the splendid conduct and of the losses of my noble little command without mingled emotions of admiration and grief. . . . I escape with a slight wound, but was grazed many times. My coat was pierced, my sword belt struck, my pistol shattered in one hand, my sword in another. We drove a regiment with the bayonet and took their colors.

. . . For the conduct of the command, let it suffice to say that everyone I met from [Lieutenant General Richard S.] Ewell down to the privates congratulates me upon it."

The assassination of President Lincoln further bled a nation just beginning to salve the deep wounds of civil war. Lincoln was shot on the night of April 14 while attending a play at Ford's Theatre in Washington. He died early the following morning.

The startling news crackled across the North and through the war-savaged South over the next few days. With Johnston's army in North Carolina, Colonel Olmstead wrote that most of the Confederates, far from celebrating the death of the Yankee president, actually mourned his loss: "There was a very general feeling in the army that the South had lost in Mr. Lincoln a friend who would have guarded our section from the malignity of such men as Thad Stevens, Edwin M. Staunton [*sic*] and Benjn F. Butler which afterwards found expression in the awful reconstruction period."[5]

"We know not the motive of the assassins—whether over-weening zeal for the wicked cause of Rebellion, or some private hostility incomprehensible to us, or the strange freaks of insanity," said the April 19 *Daily Herald.* "The disloyal class are deprived of a friend who has always pleaded their cause, and extended to them such clemency as is rare among rulers towards subjects in rebellion."[6]

In Savannah an estimated four to five thousand people attended a "mass meeting" of mourning for Lincoln on Saturday, April 22. On the river, gunboats including the USS *Pontiac* fired hundred-gun salutes while their flags flew at half mast. Black bunting was draped along the fronts of many buildings and bells tolled.

Johnson Square, where secessionists rallied in the old days, was the center of the somber proceedings. Atop a large stage erected just east of the Greene Monument sat General Grover, other Union army and navy officers, and city officials.

Many of those in the crowd were there "in obedience to the call ... to make suitable demonstrations of the sincerity of our citizens in exhibition of our sympathy with the nation in its late melancholy bereavement," the April 24 *Republican* stated. "The scene was truly an imposing one, and will ever be a memorable epoch in the history of Savannah, and her condemnation of the atrocious crime which has deprived us of so good, so pure a ruler."

The pro-Union correspondent added: "We noticed a large number of ladies present who seemed to feel the importance and solemnity of the occasion, many of whom are old citizens of Savannah."[7]

A series of resolutions was read and adopted, condemning "the cruel, barbarous and unparalleled atrocities" of Lincoln's death and the attempted assassination of U.S. Secretary of State William H. Seward.

One resolution read "that from the depths of our hearts we regret that our chief Magistrate could not have lived to realize the consummation of his labors, the earnest wish of his heart, the restoration, re-union and perfect harmony of all the States—One Flag, One Country, One People."[8]

The country was absorbing the news of Lincoln's assassination when a well-known Savannahian was among the last to die in battle. Colonel Charles A. Lafayette Lamar of the Twenty-fifth Georgia Cavalry was killed on Easter Sunday. Lamar was among the Confederates defending Columbus, Georgia, when a mounted Union force attacked the city.

The April 16 night battle was one of the last significant engagements of the war. A former slave trader who was a godson of Marquis de Lafayette, Lamar was buried at Laurel Grove.

Leaving his triumphant army to march north for a grand review in Washington, Sherman briefly returned to Savannah in the first week of May. He arrived at Hilton Head on April 30 with news of Johnston's surrender.

"A despatch [*sic*] from our correspondent at Hilton Head informs us that Gen. Sherman is to visit us to-day," said the May 1 *Daily Herald*. "Gen. Sherman comes to Savannah as before, after a great and successful campaign but under how different circumstances otherwise? Now as then, he appears as the conqueror of Confederate armies, but with what different feelings will he be received in . . . Savannah?[9]

"His march through Georgia, and the fall of Savannah were then looked on as humiliating disasters to the Confederate arms in a still actively progressing war. But the surrender of Johnston and the capitulation of all the forces in Florida, Georgia, and the Carolinas must be regarded as the real termination of the war. . . . This consummation is undoubtedly most grateful to all, at whatever cost obtained; and General Sherman, as the bringer of peace to a war-worn State, will receive the welcome of a friend from the people of Savannah."

Sherman arrived that Monday and oversaw the dispensation of food and clothing to civilians. He also sent transports up the Savannah River to Augusta with supplies for Union Brigadier General James H. Wilson based in Macon.

Savannah Theatre patrons were surprised when the scruffy conqueror made an entrance during a performance of *Evadne* that night. "The General entered the house accompanied by but a single friend," the *Daily Herald* said. "The audience at once rose and spontaneously greeted the veteran with cheer after cheer" until Sherman reached his private box.[10]

With his staff Sherman left Savannah the next afternoon on the steamer *Russia* bound for Hilton Head. By May 9 the general had rejoined his command in Virginia and accompanied the army to the capital.

Mid-May saw the return to Savannah of Jefferson Davis. In a notable change from his triumphal visit in 1863, Davis this time was under Union guard, a humbled and ridiculed man possibly facing a date on the gallows. Forced to flee Richmond in the Confederacy's dying days, Davis had headed south with members of his family, government executives, and a military escort.

Early on the morning of May 10, 1865, his entourage was camped just north of Irwinville, Georgia, when it was surprised by Wisconsin and Michigan cavalrymen. In the confusion and darkness Davis vainly fumbled to find his hat. Either to keep him warm or to hide his identity, Davis' wife, Varina, threw her shawl over his head.

After the president's capture minutes later, the story quickly spread through the North that Davis had tried to disguise himself as a woman in order to escape. Northern newspapers trumpeted accounts and cartoons portrayed the Rebel leader in hoopskirts. But a Union officer who was there told the real story. "I defy any person to find a single officer or soldier who was present at the capture . . . who will say upon honour that he was disguised in women's clothes," wrote Captain James H. Parker. "I am a Yankee, full of Yankee prejudices, but I think it wicked to lie about him."[11]

Davis was to be sent north for possible trial on treason charges. Under guard, he was taken to Augusta and boarded a tug bound for Savannah and the Union fleet off the coast. Among the other prisoners with him were Confederate Vice-President Alexander Stephens and General Joe Wheeler.

After a brief stop in Savannah, the Confederates were taken down the river and reached Port Royal, where they were transferred to a steamer for the voyage north. Davis would be jailed at Fortress Monroe, Virginia, for two years, but was never brought to trial.

During his imprisonment Varina Davis and the children returned to Savannah, where daughter Maggie attended St. Vincent's Academy. Young Jeff Davis, Jr., also was schooled at St. Vincent's, going to the Sisters of Mercy convent daily to recite his lessons. These nuns earlier had visited the destitute Davis family and offered them money, which the proud Varina refused. The children's education was a much greater gift.

"The people of Savannah treated me with the greatest tenderness," Mrs. Davis wrote in October 1865. "Had I been a sister long absent and just returned to their home, I could not have received more tender welcome. Houses were thrown open to me, anything and everything was mine. My children had not much more than a change of clothing after all the parties who had us in charge had done lightening our baggage, so they gave the baby dresses and the other little ones enough to change until I could buy or make more."

Varina learned from a Savannah *Republican* article that her husband had been ordered shackled in his cell. The revelation caused her the "most acute agony" and grief for Davis and "stops my heart's vibration," she wrote. "It was piteous to hear the little children pray at their grace, 'That the Lord would give father something which he could eat, and keep him strong, and bring him back to us with his good senses, to his little children, for Christ's sake;' and nearly every day, during the hardest and bitterest of his imprisonment, our little child Maggie had to quit the table to dry her tears after this grace, which was of her own composition."

Union guards assigned to the Davis family and other occupation troops amused themselves with the Davis children. "Little Jeff was constantly told that he was rich; that his father had 'stolen eight millions,' etc," Varina wrote. "Little two-year-old Billy was taught to sing, 'We'll hang Jeff Davis on a sour apple-tree,' by giving him a reward when he did so."

Two women from Maine contemplated whipping Jeff Jr. when they found out his identity. A man escorted the women away "just in time to avoid a very painful scene to them as well as to me," Varina remembered.

In another tense situation a black Union sentry leveled his musket at young Jeff for calling him "uncle."

The abuse and jokes probably would have been much worse if the children had not been escorted by Robert Brown, a black servant who remained loyal to the Davis family. Brown accompanied Varina Davis on late-night evening walks, about the only time she left her room.

The Savannah nuns sent Jefferson Davis a Roman Catholic scapular and a medal of the Blessed Virgin Mary, which Davis kept with him during his incarceration at Fort Monroe. Father Peter Whelan of Savannah also visited Davis during this time.

Thanks in large part to Varina's campaign to convince influential politicians to free her husband, Davis was released in May 1867 and went into exile in Canada, still facing a federal indictment for treason. He was among former Confederate leaders granted amnesty from prosecution by President Andrew Johnson in December 1868.

Alexander Stephens was imprisoned for five months before he was freed. He served nine years as a U.S. congressman and returned to Savannah in 1883 as the state's governor.

Wheeler had been captured by Union troops near Atlanta after opposing

Sherman's march through the Carolinas. He spent little time in prison, being released from Fort Delaware on June 8. Always popular, he would be elected to eight terms as a U.S. congressman. The old cavalryman also would don the blue uniform again as a major general of volunteers in the Spanish-American War before his death in 1906.

XXIV

The Postwar Years

Even though scarred by the suspicious fire of January 1865, Savannah did not endure the rebuilding task faced by other Southern cities like Atlanta, Columbia, and Charleston. The miles of railroad torn up by the Yankees would be repaired over time. Stores reopened with replenished stocks. River steamers and creaking wagons again began bringing cotton and other harvests to the port.

Schoolboys would play at war and look for bullets and uniform buttons in the old rifle pits. Gray veterans, some who had manned the same trenches, returned to Savannah to pick up the pieces of shattered lives.

"It would be difficult to paint in words the change which has come over Savannah," George Mercer wrote on June 11, 1865. "Externally the city is the same, but the iron has entered its soul, its whole social organization has been subverted. . . . At present I see no future for the South. All is dark and hope itself seems to have abandoned my unhappy section."[1]

A *New York World* reporter walking through the streets in July 1865 reported oceangoing vessels docked at the wharves and Northern newspapers, magazines, and novels being hawked by vendors. He was irritated, however, because he could not find a good hotel.

The Confederacy's downfall presented a bonanza of opportunities for Northern businessmen who flocked to Savannah in the months after the war. The lumber trade proved to be especially lucrative.

New freedmen from rural counties and white refugees continued to flood the city, looking for work or a handout. Savannah's subjugation had been relatively bloodless, but amid the return to normalcy ran a coarse thread of raw loathing. "My heart is filled with an intensity of hatred toward the authors of our misery that I cannot mollify," Rebecca Mims wrote at

Savannah in July 1865. "If we go to our street doors to catch a breath of fresh air we are annoyed by the sight of armed Yankees (white and black). I cannot reconcile myself to this wretched state of servitude. How can Southerners for a moment forget the wrongs they have suffered." Her views were shared by many, not only in Savannah, but across Dixie.[2]

Reconstruction embroiled Savannah in violence just as it did every other major Southern city dealing with the clash of new societies—a defeated antebellum chivalry versus a black underclass striving for equality. The emergence of the pro-North Union League chapters and the Ku Klux Klan escalated tensions, as did the unethical practices of Northern "carpet-baggers" and Southern "scalawags."

Murders, whippings, beatings, and other assaults grew in number across Georgia with the approach of the 1868 presidential election. In Savannah and throughout the South there was direct intimidation by Democratic factions to keep blacks from voting for the Republican candidate, U. S. Grant. This presidential election would be the first in which Southern blacks went to the polls to cast their ballots.

John B. Gordon, the former Confederate general who unsuccessfully ran for governor in April 1868, expressed the views of many white Southerners (as well as Northerners) toward blacks in a September 1868 speech. Speaking to a crowd at Charleston, Gordon directed these remarks to the freedmen among his listeners: "If you are disposed to live in peace with the white people, they extend to you the hand of friendship. But if you attempt to inaugurate a war of races you will be exterminated. The Saxon race was never created by Almighty God to be ruled by the African."[3]

Election day in Savannah would be a bloody one. A group of freedmen were assembled at the courthouse when a number of white railroad workers approached the polling site. The whites tried to force their way in to vote so that they could return to work, but the blacks refused to let them ahead of everyone else. Police arrived and, in support of the railroad men, tried to push through the freedmen.

A riot quickly erupted, punctuated by gunshots; yells and screams echoed through the streets. After a brief flurry of shooting, clubbing, and stabbing, the blacks retreated. Sprawled on and around the gory avenue were police officers Samuel Bryson, R. E. Read, and two unidentified blacks, all fatally injured. Five other freedmen were wounded.

The Confederacy died in 1865, but Savannah was a crossroads for some of the conflict's most illustrious figures for years to come. Jefferson Davis,

One of the Confederacy's most famous generals, Joseph E. Johnston settled in Savannah after the war and became a successful insurance executive.

Robert E. Lee, and Joseph E. Johnston were among those who either lived in Savannah or visited the city after the guns fell silent. Even former general and U.S. president Ulysses S. Grant accepted an invitation to come to Savannah in the winter of 1879 and received an enthusiastic welcome.

Yet for every Grant, Lee, or Hardee, there were hundreds of other people, unknown to the masses, who were also returning to peacetime, their lives forever tormented by the war's specters.

Father Peter Whelan returned to Savannah in 1864 suffering from a lung illness contracted at Andersonville. He would never fully recover.

After the war, Union authorities arrested Captain Henry Wirz, former CSA commander at Camp Sumter, and tried him for alleged war crimes committed at the prison compound. Whelan was among 160 witnesses ordered to testify at the trial. The priest was allowed to visit Wirz during the proceedings, which ended in Wirz being convicted and hanged.

His health declining, Whelan served as pastor of St. Patrick's Cathedral in Savannah until 1868. He was sixty-nine when he died on February 6, 1871. With veterans of the Fort Pulaski garrison in the funeral procession, the Rebel chaplain was laid to rest in the Cathedral Cemetery.

Major W. S. Basinger, whose Savannah Volunteer Guards had been all but wiped out at the battle of Sailor's Creek, spent several months in a Union prison camp. After his release the peacetime attorney traveled to New York, where, still in his Confederate uniform, he set about collecting on debts he was owed in prewar days.

Basinger later returned to Sailor's Creek, where he had the bodies of his fallen comrades exhumed and paid for them to be returned to Savannah. Most of the soldiers' remains were claimed by relatives, but eleven unidentified Guards were buried together at Laurel Grove.

General Henry Wayne was in the lumber business in Savannah from 1866 to 1875. In his last years Wayne gave an unlikely account of a December 9, 1864, conversation he had with General Beauregard as Sherman's army closed in on Savannah. Wayne, Beauregard, and Hardee had known each other for years, all graduating in the West Point class of 1838.

Wayne said he told Beauregard that Sherman had some seventy thousand men and was aiming at Savannah. According to Wayne, Beauregard replied, "My God, Harry! What has come over you? You did not use to be so nervous." Based on Wayne's version, Beauregard went on to say that he had received intelligence from General Bragg at Augusta that Sherman had no more than twenty-one thousand troops and was in retreat.

From all indications, Beauregard had a much greater grasp on the grave situation faced by the Confederates in Savannah. Wayne died in Savannah on March 15, 1883, and is buried in Laurel Grove Cemetery.

Colonel Charles Jones, the former Savannah mayor, established a successful law practice in New York. He returned to Georgia in 1877 and began writing from Montrose, his newly acquired estate near Augusta. Jones wrote exhaustively and became nationally known for his works on Georgia history, many centering on Savannah. He died in July 1893 at age sixty-one.

General Joseph E. Johnston was the most famous Confederate to settle in Savannah after the war. Johnston commanded armies from First Manassas to Atlanta and in the South's death throes at Bentonville, North Carolina.

Johnston had the distinction of fighting longer than Lee and surrendering a larger army when he capitulated near Durham Station, North Carolina, on April 26, 1865.

A Virginian born near Farmville in February 1807, Johnston was a West Point classmate of Lee. (Lee ranked second in the class of 1829; Johnston was thirteenth.) After four years among the hierarchy of the Confederate military, the old generals would meet again one last time in Savannah.

Thrust back into civilian life in 1865, Johnston was associated with a railroad company based in Alabama and Georgia from 1866 to late 1867. When the rail line failed, he went into the insurance business. Recognizing the respect and fame Johnston enjoyed, a British-based insurance firm contracted with him to become manager of its Southern Department.

Johnston came to Savannah in 1868 to establish Joseph E. Johnston & Company, agent for the Liverpool and London and Globe Insurance Company.

The general worked from offices on Bay Street and lived in a townhouse at the corner of Oglethorpe Avenue and Whitaker Street. He and his wife, Lydia, traveled extensively, spending most of their summers at Warm Springs, Virginia, on account of Mrs. Johnston's fragile health. They also spent the Christmas holidays with relatives in Baltimore. Johnston was visited by Lee when the latter came to Savannah during a vacation in April 1870.

In 1874 Johnston published his war memoirs, *Narrative of Military Operations, Directed, During the Late War Between the States*. The lengthy work brimmed with criticism of Jefferson Davis, Braxton Bragg, and John Bell Hood, all of whom had been his detractors during the war.

Himself highly maligned for his defensive strategy in most of his campaigns, Johnston also tried to give his side of the story. In the end the book failed financially and infuriated many of Johnston's old comrades. Through letters, memoirs, and magazine articles, the commanders would wage a war of words for years.

Tiring of the defense of his military reputation, Johnston gradually became more interested in politics. The insurance firm was thriving and he had more than 120 agents in Georgia, Alabama, and Mississippi by 1872.

The Johnstons moved from Savannah to Richmond in the winter of 1876–1877, but left a lasting legacy that still influences many Savannahians. The firm he established evolved into Palmer & Cay/Carswell, Inc., one of the largest insurance brokers in the nation.

Johnston served as a U.S. representative from Virginia in 1879–1881. He was U.S. commissioner of railroads from 1885 to 1891, appointed by President Grover Cleveland.

Another notable Confederate who moved to Savannah in the postwar years was Major General Jeremy F. Gilmer. Considered one of the finest military engineers in the Confederacy, Gilmer served as president of the Savannah Gas Light Company from 1867 until his death in December 1883.

Gilmer had overseen the first series of fortifications erected at Savannah in 1861. He was chief engineer to General Albert S. Johnston and was wounded at Shiloh in April 1862. Afterward he became chief engineer for the Department of Northern Virginia and served in the same capacity for the CSA War Department. The North Carolinian was also the architect of intricate defenses guarding Atlanta and Charleston.

Some historians have criticized Gilmer for his alleged lack of attention to strengthen forts Donelson and Henry in autumn 1861. Guarding the Tennessee and Cumberland rivers, these strongpoints were crucial if the Rebels were to keep Union forces from penetrating Tennessee's interior.

Gilmer's wife and many friends were in Savannah during this time; and he longed to be with them, preferring the warmer coastal climate to a winter in the rugged hill country. His lack of enthusiasm and concentration on improving the forts, along with the weak Confederate command structure, lack of equipment and heavy guns, and poor location of the bastions, contributed to their capture in February 1862, a catastrophic loss to the South. Whatever the reality of his war record, Gilmer rests in Laurel Grove.

In 1883 Georgia celebrated its 150th birthday with Savannah, the first colonial capital, serving as hostess. Governor Alexander H. Stephens, former vice-president of the Confederacy, made a Founder's Day speech among the festivities on February 12.

The sickly governor arrived in Savannah that morning after a lengthy train trip. The day was cold and damp, and Stephens was trundled about the city in a carriage that had a broken window.

In spite of being swathed in layers of clothing, the governor suffered chills from the blasts of winter air pouring into the coach. Stephens delivered his speech and returned to Atlanta but within a few days was taken ill. He died on March 4 at age seventy-one.

Stephens had been in Savannah on at least two other major occasions in his life. Stephens gave his famous "Cornerstone Speech" at Savannah in March 1861. He was next in Savannah as a Union prisoner in 1865, en route to imprisonment in Boston.

After being granted amnesty by President Johnson, Jefferson Davis settled in Memphis in 1869 as an insurance executive. When the company failed in 1874, Davis returned to Mississippi to write a book about the inner workings of the Confederacy. This work, *The Rise and Fall of the Confeder-*

ate Government, was published in 1881. Accompanied by daughter Winnie, Davis made his final trip to Savannah in 1886 to help celebrate the centennial of the Chatham Artillery. Davis arrived in Savannah on May 3 in a railroad car adorned with flowers and banners, one of which read, "He Was Manacled for Us," referring to his imprisonment after the war.

Savannah was the latest stop in a tour of Southern cities also including Atlanta and Montgomery, the Confederacy's first capital. On the special train traveling with the Davises from Atlanta to Savannah was a local delegation including Hugh M. Comer, president of the Central of Georgia Railroad, and General Gilbert Moxley Sorrel.

The Davises were guests at Comer's home on Monterey Square and attracted large crowds of admirers. Winnie Davis and her father also visited St. Vincent's Academy, which Davis' other daughter, Maggie, had attended in 1865. The Davises praised the Sisters of Mercy for their kindness and generosity during the family's postwar adversity.

Davis spent his last years on his Mississippi plantation and died in New Orleans on December 5, 1889, a few days after his eightieth birthday.

Confederate General Lafayette McLaws went into the insurance business in his hometown of Augusta after the war. In 1875 he was appointed collector of internal revenue in Savannah and was named the city's postmaster a year later, serving two terms.

McLaws died suddenly at his home at 306 East Anderson Street shortly after midnight on July 24, 1897. Already in poor health, he had complained of indigestion earlier in the evening. Described as "a thorough confederate," McLaws was buried in Laurel Grove Cemetery.

Juliette Gordon, who had charmed General Sherman as a child, married William "Billow" Low of Savannah, the only son of British cotton magnate Andrew Low, in 1886. The couple moved into the Low home on Lafayette Square. After the collapse of her marriage in 1901, Juliette spent several years traveling the globe until 1911, when she met English General Robert Baden-Powell, founder of the Boy Scouts.

She was strongly influenced by his work and that of his sister, Agnes, who organized the Girl Guides, the female version of the Boy Scouts. Juliette returned to the U.S. from England with a new-found commitment to helping girls through such an organization. She established America's first Girl Guide patrol in Savannah on March 12, 1912, with her niece, Daisy Gordon Lawrence, as its first member. The small troop would be the seed that grew into the Girl Scouts of America under Juliette Gordon Low's nurturing hand. "Daisy," who had shaped her own destiny decades after entertaining General Sherman, died in 1927. Her accomplishments live on through the thousands of Girl Scouts who annually visit her childhood home as a national shrine.

Ambrose Wright, one of Hardee's division commanders, continued his law practice and bought two Augusta newspapers in 1866. Renewing his political aspirations, Wright was elected to the U.S. House of Representatives but would never take office. He died in Augusta on December 21, 1872, the eighth anniversary of Savannah's evacuation.

After his wound at Antietam ended his fighting days, Alexander Lawton recovered to assume command of the Confederate quartermaster general's department, a post he held until the surrender. Lawton resumed his law practice in Savannah after the war and again became engrossed in politics.

He served in the state legislature from 1870 to 1875 and was defeated in a bid for the U.S. Senate in 1880. Lawton was appointed minister to Austria by President Grover Cleveland in 1887 and died in Clifton Spring, New York, on July 2, 1896. He was returned to Savannah for burial at Bonaventure Cemetery.

Henry Jackson, the Confederate politician and general captured at Nashville, also returned to the bar in Savannah. He was named U.S. minister to Mexico by President Cleveland in 1885. For almost twenty-five years before his death in May 1898, Jackson was president of the Georgia Historical Society. He is among the Confederates buried at Bonaventure Cemetery.

General Hugh Mercer continued his banking career in Savannah before moving to Baltimore in 1869. In ever-declining health, he relocated to Baden-Baden, Germany, where he died in 1877.

Robert H. Anderson was a CSA brigadier who returned to his native Savannah after the war. Anderson, a longtime captain of the Republican Blues, had seen combat in the Fort McAllister bombardments in 1863 and also served with Wheeler's cavalry.

Anderson is credited with reorganizing the city police force and establishing the Savannah Police Department in November 1865. He was chosen as its first chief and employed officers composed mostly of veterans from the Confederate and Union armies. Anderson served as chief until his death on February 8, 1888. He was buried in Bonaventure Cemetery.

A granite and copper monument, crowned with a bust of the general, was erected over his grave in February 1894. An estimated seven thousand people attended the unveiling.

Gilbert Moxley Sorrel was wounded in the leg at Petersburg and was also shot in the lung a few weeks later, in February 1865, at Hatcher's Run. After a quick recuperation during the next two months, the general was returning to his troops in Virginia when he learned of Lee's surrender.

Sorrel became a merchant and steamship company entrepreneur in Savannah. He also wrote a book on his war experiences, which he did not live to see published. He died near Roanoke, Virginia, in August 1901, and rests in Laurel Grove. Sorrel's book, *Recollections of a Confederate Staff Officer*, was published in 1905.

George Paul Harrison, Sr., a brigadier general of Georgia troops, lived in Savannah for more than twenty years after the war. Harrison had been a state representative and a rice planter on the Savannah River before the conflict. He was appointed a general of state forces by Governor Brown in September 1861. Harrison spent the winter training and organizing regiments near Savannah, but his command was dissolved in 1862. Harrison returned to service in 1864 as a colonel of militia. He was captured by Sherman's troops at Monteith, his plantation.

Harrison was elected to the state legislature in 1865 and later served as clerk of city court and clerk of Chatham County Superior Court. He died at Monteith in May 1888 and was buried at Laurel Grove.

Harrison's son, G. P. Harrison, Jr., was a hero at Olustee and is mentioned as a general in some historical accounts. The colonel commanded the post at Florence, South Carolina, including a prison stockade for Union POW's, in late 1864 and later led a brigade of Georgia infantry and reserves contesting Sherman's march through the Carolinas. After the war he settled in Alabama and distinguished himself as a lawyer and politician. He also was elected major general of the Alabama Division of the United Confederate Veterans. Death took him at Opelika, Alabama, in 1922 and he is buried there.

Described by some as the last brigadier general appointed by Jefferson Davis, Peter A. Selkirk McGlashan was a Scottish immigrant who lived in Savannah before the war and returned there afterward. A veteran who fought at the Seven Days' battles, Gettysburg, Chickamauga, and the Wilderness, he was promoted to colonel of the Fiftieth Georgia in 1863. Seriously wounded at Cedar Creek, he was captured at Sailor's Creek in April 1865.

Twenty years after the war, he moved to Savannah and opened a harness shop. In the postwar era, McGlashan was appointed a general of the United Confederate Veterans, but apparently did not reach this rank in the war. He served as the city's plumbing inspector before his sudden death from a heart attack in June 1908. McGlashan lies in Laurel Grove.

Josiah Tattnall, the naval commander most associated with Savannah, surrendered with Johnston's army. Living in Nova Scotia for a short time after the war, Tattnall returned to Savannah, where the post of port inspector was created for him. Suffering from "congestion of the brain caused by general debility," Tattnall died at his home on the night of June 14, 1871.

"During the past several months the health of the Commodore has been failing rapidly, and his death was not unexpected," the *Morning News* said on June 15. "The news of the sad event will be received with sorrow throughout the South, his gallant deeds in behalf of the Lost Cause being still fresh in the memory of those who hold the deeds of those valiant days in sacred remembrance."[4]

Tattnall was buried in Bonaventure Cemetery, the site of his ancestral home. Among those who would eventually join him at rest there was his son, John R. F. Tattnall, a captain of Confederate marines stationed at Savannah.

Robert E. Lee emerged from the war as a brilliant and beloved general who had gambled and usually won against long odds. He also would be the unassuming standard bearer of "the Lost Cause" for generations to come.

After leaving Savannah in March 1862, Lee was appointed military adviser to Jefferson Davis and served in that capacity until the battle of Seven Pines in May 1862. When Joseph Johnston, commander of the main Confederate army, was severely wounded on May 31, Lee was given command the next day. With lieutenants such as "Stonewall" Jackson, James Longstreet, and "Jeb" Stuart, Lee deftly molded the Army of Northern Virginia into one of the world's finest armies.

Lee's combat record is a litany of the war in the east—Gaines' Mill, Second Manassas, Antietam, Fredericksburg, Spotsylvania, Petersburg. His greatest triumph was Chancellorsville; the worst debacle, Gettysburg. Almost always he fought against an enemy of greatly superior numbers who was better armed and provisioned. Almost always he emerged the victor.

Lee was appointed general-in-chief of the Confederate States armies in January 1865, but could not curtail the South's collapse. His surrender of the Army of Northern Virginia at Appomattox was a blow the Confederacy could not endure.

In June 1865 he was indicted for treason by the U.S. government. His old antagonist, General Ulysses S. Grant, intervened on Lee's behalf, threatening to resign from the army if Lee was arrested. Grant influenced the administration of President Johnson to suspend prosecution of Lee.

Lee was named president of Washington College in Lexington, Virginia, in September 1865. He spent much of his postwar years urging reconciliation among hard-core Rebels, but preaching pride in their Confederate service.

Lee made his last trip to Savannah in April 1870 accompanied by his daughter, Agnes. The visit was part of a swing through several Southern cities for Lee, vacationing to help improve his deteriorating health. He arrived by train from Augusta on the night of April 1 for a few days of leisure, but was smothered by admiring crowds at the depot.

The Lees were taken to the home of their host, former general Alexander Lawton, at the corner of York and Lincoln streets. Bands playing wartime tunes and a flood of visitors caused Lee to leave the home by a back entrance in order to get a peaceful night's rest. He found refuge at the Andrew Low home on Lafayette Square.

Later in his sojourn, Lee paid a visit to the home of his old West Point classmate, Joe Johnston, at 105 East Oglethorpe Avenue. He had not seen Johnston since the war. The aging Confederate chieftains spent time reminiscing about the glory days and were persuaded to go to Ryan's photography studio, where they posed together.

Lee also spent time with his old friends, the Mackay family at their Broughton Street home.

The Lees remained in Savannah until April 12, when, accompanied by Low, they boarded a southbound steamboat. They docked at Cumberland Island, Georgia, where they visited the grave of Lee's father. Returning from Florida, the Lees stopped again in Savannah on April 25 before returning to Virginia.

One of the last photos of Robert E. Lee (*left*) was taken in a Savannah studio in April 1870 while he was visiting former general Joseph E. Johnston. Lee succumbed to poor health six months later at his Virginia home.

Lee did not live out the year. After murmuring his last words, "Strike the tent," he died in Lexington on October 12, 1870. Only sixty-three, he apparently suffered from heart problems that first struck him in 1863. The illness was aggravated when he was taken sick after a school meeting on a cold, rainy night several weeks earlier.

Lee is entombed in Lee chapel, with other members of his family, on the campus of Washington and Lee, the college renamed in his honor. Without question he is one of the greatest soldiers ever to wear the gray and blue.

General Sherman's friendship with Grant served him well in the postwar era. After Grant was elected president, Sherman was promoted to full general and commander-in-chief of the army. Disliking the political climate in Washington, he moved his headquarters to St. Louis in 1874, but returned to the capital two years later.

Sherman retired from the service in 1884, but his public life was far from over. He was constantly bombarded with requests for appearances and speeches, even being considered as a presidential candidate in 1884.

Sherman lived in New York City from 1886 until his death on Valentine's Day 1891. He was buried at Calvary Cemetery in St. Louis. Among those

Confederate Memorial in Forsyth Park

who marched in his funeral procession was his old adversary Joe Johnston, an honorary pallbearer, who marched bareheaded. The weather was bad and friends urged Johnston to put on his hat. The eighty-two-year-old general refused. Out of respect for Sherman, he replied, "If I were in his place, and he were standing here in mine, he would not put on his hat."

Johnston would be dead in little more than a month, apparently catching a cold that worsened after the sad day in St. Louis. He died in Washington on March 21, 1891, and is buried in Baltimore's Green Mount Cemetery.

The verdict will always be out on Sherman as a commander. He was a battle-toughened soldier who believed in all-out war, but his combat record at Shiloh, on the slopes of Missionary Ridge, and in the Vicksburg campaign was that of a leader who suffered setbacks when faced by an enemy of equal or superior force.

In the Atlanta campaign he displayed great instincts and tactics by flanking Johnston out of defensive positions that could have been slaughter pens for his men. Still, Sherman's one hundred thousand men greatly outnumbered the Confederate army facing him, whether it was led by the defensive-minded Johnston or the bullish John Bell Hood.

The capture of Atlanta was a great achievement for Sherman and a critical loss to the South. In deciding to have Thomas wrangle with Hood, Sherman knew there were substantially more Union troops in Tennessee than the Confederates could muster.

With Hood, his main adversary, out of the picture, how much daring did it take for Sherman to strike for the Georgia coast with sixty-two thousand seasoned fighters and no comparable enemy army in the vicinity?

True, Sherman cut off his communications and supply lines to plunge three hundred miles across enemy country, dividing his army for most of the campaign. The fact that "Uncle Billy," or "Old Cump," was genuinely admired and had the confidence of his soldiers played a major role in the campaign's success.

Sherman has been criticized by some historians for being too cautious, particularly in the war's early campaigns. If he suffered from this flaw, his inability to trap Hardee's army in Savannah might serve as a prime example of his hesitancy.

Although he was a brilliant administrator and quick-thinking battle commander, others contend that his version of "modern war," waged against civilians and home-front industries, had been around since "Attila or Genghis Khan."

Sherman biographer Albert Castel gave this summation of Sherman's march through Georgia and the Carolinas: "In short, his military skill and character remained untested in the sense of having to cope with an opponent of comparable strength and talent. But there can be no reasonable doubt that Sherman was an exceptional man who developed into an excellent general."[5]

General Hardee surrendered with Johnston's army in North Carolina in April 1865, finally brought to bay by Sherman. For about nine months after the war, Hardee supervised operations of two plantations owned by his wife's family near Demopolis, Alabama. In early 1866 the Hardees moved to Selma, Alabama, where Hardee was named president of the Selma & Meridian Railroad. During this time the general applied for a pardon from the U.S. government. It was granted, but not before Hardee requested and received an endorsement from his old foe, William T. Sherman.

The railroad venture folded in 1869, and the company was eventually sold in 1882. Hardee remained in Selma, where he was popular in social circles

"Silence" watches over the Confederate dead at Laurel Grove Cemetery.

and entertained former enemies and old Confederates with equal grace.

He made several visits to Savannah in the postwar years to visit relatives living in the area. The Hardees also made annual pilgrimages to White Sulphur Springs, West Virginia, each summer to escape the stifling Alabama heat. Hardee was on one of these excursions in 1873, when he became ill and was confined to bed for the rest of the summer.

Placed on a train for the return to Selma, Hardee reached Wytheville, Virginia, where he was too sick to continue the journey. Carried to a hotel near the station, he died there on November 6, 1873. Hardee's body was returned to Selma for burial, his battle horse, Black Auster (also called Shiloh), a part of the funeral procession.

Hardee's demise elicited no great outcry of public mourning in Savannah. The *Morning News* on December 10 ran an inside story about the general's death based on a telegram dispatch from Selma two days earlier.

In Selma, businesses were closed and "a vast concourse of citizens" watched the funeral procession. "Thousands were at the cemetery, for the people loved Hardee, Selma to-day had him in mourning," the report said. "There was a spontaneous outpouring of our whole people ... to the memory of our illustrious dead."[6]

XXV

Short Stories—1861–1865

Blue and Gray St. Patrick's Days

Savannah's St. Patrick's Day celebration has grown into a party that annually draws thousands of revelers from around the world. During the war years, the March 17 observance was tinged in Rebel gray or Union blue more than the Irish green for which it was meant.

In a martial frenzy after Georgia's secession two months earlier, Savannah's 1861 St. Patrick's Day was a triumphant affair, especially since militiamen from the city had seized Fort Pulaski in January.

Promptly at 10 A.M. the Irish Jasper Greens and the Irish Volunteers militia units formed in parade ranks on Bay Street and, preceded by a band, marched to Lincoln Street. There they were joined by members of the Irish Union Society, and the procession continued to St. Andrews Hall on the northwest corner of Jefferson and Broughton streets. After a speech by Father O'Neill, the men marched back to Bay Street, where they were dismissed.

At 5 P.M. the Hibernian Society gathered for dinner at the City Hotel. The sixth toast (following a hoisting of glasses to St. Patrick, Ireland, and others) honored Jefferson Davis, president of the Confederacy. Members of the Irish Union Society had their dinner and celebration at the Gibbons House on the corner of West Broad and Broughton.

The war raged in full fury by St. Patrick's Day 1862. A Union blockading squadron stood off the coast, and Federal ground forces were closing in on

Fort Pulaski. The Irish Jasper Greens and the Irish Volunteers had been called to the front. For only the second time since the city's first St. Patrick's celebration in 1824, there was no parade. The Hibernians and the Irish Union Society held meetings, but the most colorful event took place at Fort Pulaski. There soldiers of the Montgomery Guards were presented a silk flag made for them by the Sisters of Mercy. The Guards, composed of Irishmen from Savannah, were a part of the First Georgia and assigned to the Pulaski garrison.

Fringed with green and gold tasseling, the beautiful flag bore a gold cross and the motto "In Hoc Signo Vinces" on one side. The other side displayed a harp and shamrock, twelve stars, and the company's name.

The banner waved proudly through the heavy Union bombardment on April 10, 1862, and was only lowered when the Rebels were compelled to surrender the fort the next day. Private Bernard O'Neill hid the flag to keep it from being taken by the Yankee captors.

The gray captives were searched several times during their journey to Northern prisoner of war camps. While being held at Fort Delaware, some members of the Montgomery Guards learned that O'Neill was considering taking an oath of allegiance to the United States. They managed to get the banner shortly before O'Neill changed sides.

For the next several months six guardsmen took turns hiding the flag. When they were exchanged in September 1862, the Savannahians reached the safety of Confederate lines along the James River in Virginia. Immediately they improvised a makeshift staff and flung the battle flag to the breeze again.

The Guards served through the remainder of the war and surrendered with Johnston's army. Today their beloved flag has been restored and is on display at Fort Pulaski National Monument.

The highlight of the 1863 observance was the dedication of St. Patrick's Catholic Church. Located on the southeast corner of West Broad and Liberty streets, the church had been converted from a cotton warehouse. A solemn ceremony to dedicate the building and lay a cornerstone began with a procession from the Church of St. John the Baptist on Drayton Street. For the Confederacy as a nation, this was a sad day as Major John Pelham, a favorite of J. E. B. Stuart, and who was much admired by Robert E. Lee, was killed in action at Kelly's Ford, Virginia.

Forty years after Savannah's first St. Patrick's Day observance, there apparently was no celebration or event of any kind to mark the Irish holiday in 1864. The war was going badly for the South, and everyone was feeling the economic pinch or, even more terrible, the losses of loved ones. The worst was yet to come.

By March, 17, 1865, the city was under Union occupation. Sherman's army, which captured Savannah in December 1864, was burning a swath of destruction through the Carolinas.

Still, the Federals in Savannah celebrated grandly with a parade down Bay Street of the Ninth Connecticut, recently arrived from campaigns with Phil Sheridan in Virginia's Shenandoah Valley. The parade was marred by a minor confrontation between black and white youths hurling sticks and rocks at each other.

The city's Irishmen quietly held their own observances with meetings by the Hibernians and the Irish Union Society along with high mass at St. Patrick's Church.

With the war over, St. Patrick's Day in Savannah slowly began to flourish, growing in size each year. Today it rivals holiday observances in New York, Boston, and Chicago as one of the largest celebrations of the green in the country.

Old Tybee Enemies

In late summer 1921, a letter arrived at the Georgia Historical Society in Savannah from an old Union sailor with a unique request. Francis Mc-Carten of San Diego believed he had been the first Yankee to raise a U.S. flag on Georgia soil during the Civil War.

McCarten had been a sailor on the USS *Augusta* and participated in a November 25, 1861, amphibious landing on Tybee Island. He had planted the flag on the beach and wanted to know if this was the first time the Union colors had flown over Confederate Georgia since the war began. The letter was forwarded to Colonel Charles Olmstead, who had commanded Confederate-held Fort Pulaski at the time.

Olmstead replied that McCarten's claim could very well be true. He also related that, watching Yankee troops wade ashore that winter day, he felt "natural anxiety" in seeing the Stars and Stripes fluttering in the wind over Tybee.

In closing, Olmstead wrote, "Trusting that the world has used you well through all these long years."[1]

"The Monkey" Lee

In command of Southern coastal defenses, General Robert E. Lee made an inspection tour along the Georgia shore in late 1861. After checking fortifications near Brunswick, Lee, traveling by train, stopped near a camp of Georgia troops.

The soldiers clamored about the general's car, shouting for him to make a speech. When Lee did not comply, they crowded in to at least catch a glimpse of the stately Virginian. Lee apparently did not protest and was "duly inspected," according to diarist George Mercer.

Not exactly basking in Lee's presence, one of the Rebels up front pushed his way back through the crowd saying loudly, "Gim me room boys. I'se seed the monkey."[2]

"Inundated With Swarms of Yankees"

Like most Southern newspapers during the war, the *Savannah Daily Morning News* was a journalistic flamethrower, spewing hatred for the "Yankee race."

A great example of this came in March 1863, when the *News* speculated on how Northerners would act whenever peace finally came: "We have sometimes thought that the Yankees would be shy about coming among us after the war, fearing the just indignation of our people.... They will contaminate and pollute and debauch us morally and mentally.... After peace, unless prevented, we may look to be inundated with swarms of Yankees with their nasal whine, their vile notions, their viler manners, all at heart our enemies, but wearing the hypocritic mask of friendship."[3]

A few days earlier the *News* had targeted the Union's concentration on building ironclad warships for its sarcasm: "If the war continues we shall expect to see a Yankee sheet-iron life preserver invented to be worn by their troops, who will be encased from head to foot in their iron armor as seashore fiddlers are in their shells. For our part, we wish they would invent an immense iron canopy that would cover in the universal Yankee nation so securely that the artillery of heaven could not break their shell, and that the outside world might never see or hear more of the detested race."[4]

Gray Angel of Mercy

Savannah's Phebe Levy Pember was to the Confederacy what Clara Barton was to the Union. Both of these courageous and pioneering nurses were honored in June 1995 with the issuance of a U.S. Postal Service series of stamps depicting Civil War personalities and events. Mrs. Pember was the aunt of Fanny Cohen Taylor, whose 1864 diary describes Sherman's occupation of Savannah.

Born Phebe Levy in Charleston in August 1823, Mrs. Pember was the fourth of seven children, including six girls. Her parents' immigrant roots were in Poland and England. The family moved to Savannah about 1853 and joined Temple Mickve Israel.

Early in 1861 Phebe married Thomas Pember, a Bostonian of whom little is known. He died of tuberculosis in July 1861. Mrs. Pember returned to her family and moved with them to Marietta when it appeared that Union forces were poised to capture Savannah in early 1862.

On a recommendation from the wife of Confederate Secretary of War George Randolph, Mrs. Pember was appointed chief matron of a division at Chimborazo Hospital outside Richmond in December 1862. Chimborazo was the largest and possibly the finest military hospital on either side and was practically an independent city. The massive complex had some 8,400 beds in about 150 buildings sprawling over forty acres. During the war years, it treated about seventy-six thousand soldiers, more patients than had been served by any other hospital in the world to that time.

Mrs. Pember was unique in that she was in an assignment traditionally filled by male nurses. Women, particularly whites, were not supposed to work in military hospitals because it could be "injurious to the delicacy and refinement of a lady," she later wrote.

While a number of physicians caused her problems, Mrs. Pember was supported by Surgeon-in-Chief James B. McCaw, who oversaw the hospital's operations. During her tenure she did everything from baking gingerbread in the hospital bakery to tending to thousands of the most grievously wounded.

As the South's war fortunes waned, more and more women became nurses. When Confederate forces evacuated Richmond in April 1865, Mrs. Pember stayed behind, caring for her patients.

After the war, she returned to Savannah for a short time before moving to Baltimore, where she wrote her memoirs. Her book, *A Southern Woman's*

Story, (1879) has been described as "the best first-person account of Confederate hospitals."

Mrs. Pember died on March 4, 1913, while visiting a friend in Pittsburgh. Her body was returned to Savannah, and a private funeral was held at the home of her sister, Mrs. Octavus Cohen of 321 Abercorn Street. Mrs. Pember was buried next to her husband at Laurel Grove.

A Yankee Architect in Dixie

New York architect John S. Norris figures prominently in Savannah's elegance, especially its Civil War–era buildings. Norris came to Savannah after winning a contract for the design of the Customs House completed in 1852. While in Savannah, Norris also created the plans and constructed the home of cotton magnate Charles Green on Madison Square. Renowned for its Gothic majesty, the mansion would serve as Union General W. T. Sherman's headquarters during the war.

Norris also designed the Andrew Low House on Lafayette Square. Low was another cotton entrepreneur who married Juliette Gordon. Years after his death Mrs. Low founded the Girl Scouts of America in this house. Robert E. Lee stayed there during a visit to the city in 1870.

One of Norris' last projects in Savannah was building a mansion for Hugh Mercer on Monterey Square. Construction began in 1860, but was not completed until after the war.

With the country moving toward conflict in 1860, Norris went home to New York, never to return to Savannah. His legacy, however, endures in his architectural grandeur.

The Rebel Baker

The story of a young Confederate soldier who opened a modest Broughton Street bakery after the war lives on today in a multimillion dollar Savannah business. As a teenager, John Derst immigrated with his family to America from Germany and settled in Savannah. Derst undertook a bakery apprenticeship in 1857 and kept a careful record of his training and recipes in notebooks.

When the Civil War opened, he volunteered with Savannah's De Kalb Riflemen. As a private he helped construct and defend Fort McAllister.

Suffering from ill health, Derst was transferred to Atlanta, where he became chief baker for a military hospital.

After the war's end, Derst came back to Savannah and established a bakery opposite the Marshall House hotel on Broughton Street. Advertising himself as a "variety baker," he offered fresh bread, cakes, and pies "made at Short Notice."

The bake shop flourished, and Derst joined the German Volunteers militia unit as a private. He rose to the rank of captain and commanded the company for eleven years, also serving as a city alderman.

Captain John Derst died in 1928, but his baking company had become a Savannah institution, which generations of his family would continue to nurture.

"Tom Cat"

An unsung hero that gave his nine lives for the Confederacy is memorialized on a historical marker at Fort McAllister near Savannah.

"Tom Cat," the garrison mascot, was killed in a Union bombardment of the fort on March 3, 1863. At the time of the battle, the cat's death was noted in a Savannah newspaper account of the action and in an official dispatch sent to P. G. T. Beauregard, Confederate commander of the department.

"The death of the cat was deeply regretted by the men," the marker reads. Recorded history has no description of this feline, but he was a fixture at the fort when a squadron of Union gunboats confronted McAllister in early 1863. Tons of shells rained on the Rebel works, but none of the Southerners, huddled in their bombproofs, was hurt.

Tom Cat, however, scampered into the path of a Yankee cannonball and was killed. In spite of the feline's loss, McAllister withstood the naval attack and was not captured until overrun by Sherman's army in December 1864.

Nicknamed "Tom Cat II," another feline took up residence at the fort in the early 1980's. When Tom Cat II died in 1982, he was buried at the base of the marker honoring his predecessor.

"The Pathfinder"

On a sweaty July day in 1890, a Savannahian better known to the nation as "The Pathfinder" lay on his death bed in New York City. The story of John Charles Fremont—trailblazer, soldier, and politician—is related to

Savannah only because he was born there on January 21, 1813, in a house near the present-day intersection of Bay and Montgomery streets.

Basically forgotten in the city of his birth, Fremont remains one of the most extravagant and eccentric characters of the American frontier, his biography reading like a dime western novel.

His parents were a French dancing instructor who had immigrated to the United States and a Virginia housewife with whom he had eloped. Expelled from Charleston (South Carolina) College in 1831, Fremont taught math before receiving an army appointment with the topographical engineers in 1838.

In 1841 he married Jessie Benton, daughter of influential Senator Thomas Hart Benton. From the early 1840's until the Mexican War's outbreak, "The Pathfinder" led several important expeditions into the western frontier and figured prominently in the Bear Paw Revolution, which resulted in the U.S. acquisition of California from Mexico.

Fremont's refusal to obey army orders and his personal designs to build a western empire, however, quickly ended with a court-martial in which he was convicted of mutiny and insubordination. Somehow escaping a harsh sentence, and resigning from the army in 1848, Fremont soon found fortune when gold was discovered on his California ranch. His new wealth payrolled a turn to politics. Fremont's fortunes rose with his election as a U.S. senator from California in 1850 and as the new Republican Party's first candidate for President in 1856, although he lost to James Buchanan.

Using his political connections, Fremont was appointed major general in May 1861 and assigned to command the U.S. Department of the West. He earned few war laurels, however, and Fremont's fortunes declined rapidly as he showed ineffectiveness in several posts.

His 1862 failure against Stonewall Jackson in the Shenandoah Valley was the killing blow to his military career, and he was relieved of command at his own request. Fremont was briefly considered as a possible third-party presidential candidate in 1864, but soon faded.

He served as territorial governor of Arizona from 1878 to 1887 and was restored to the army roster as a retired major general shortly before his death. Fremont was living in New York City on a temporary basis when he died on July 13, 1890.

"The Immortal Six Hundred"

On the morning of October 23, 1864, a column of haggard, ragged Confederate officers trudged off a Union transport and entered Fort Pulaski. These Rebel prisoners, representing every state in the Confederacy, will forever be known as "The Immortal Six Hundred." Their story is one of the most tragic of Savannah's Civil War saga.

During the bombardment of Charleston that summer, Federal authorities learned that U.S. officers captured by the Southerners were imprisoned at locations in the city. Because of the Union shelling, these POW's were considered to be vulnerable to "friendly fire" by U.S. Major General John G. Foster, headquartered at Hilton Head.

Foster demanded that the captive Yanks be sent elsewhere, but the Confederates could not comply. Their dying war effort had drained them of manpower, sufficient rations, railroad connections, and even other prison camps where the Northerners could be sent.

"The truth is they are so short of men as guards they have no place to put their prisoners in except Charleston and Savannah," Foster wrote to his superiors on August 18. "As far as injury goes to them there can be none, for I know their exact position and direct the shells accordingly."

Foster's mood changed quickly. On September 4, he sent a dispatch to Confederate Major General Samuel Jones in Charleston, accusing Jones of keeping prisoners where they were exposed to Union artillery fire. "I have therefore to inform you that your officers, now in my hands, will be placed by me under your fire as an act of retaliation," Foster wrote.

Jones vigorously denied that any Union officers were intentionally placed in harm's way. But Foster requested and received permission to bring six hundred imprisoned Confederate officers from Fort Delaware to be pawns in his retaliation. By the first week in September he was using them as human shields to temper Rebel cannon fire against Union positions on Morris Island.

About forty of the most sick and severely wounded Southerners were sent ashore at Beaufort on October 3 after an agonizing sea voyage toward Charleston. The rest had already been herded into a stockade on Morris Island. Built between Union-held forts Gregg and Wagner, the Federals knew this area of the island was the most heavily bombarded by Charleston's defenders.

In addition to shells from both armies rocketing overhead or exploding nearby, the Rebel officers soon had their meager rations cut. The Federals were in the mood for revenge—if the damned Rebels couldn't supply their blue prisoners with adequate food and medical care then to hell with the captive Johnnies!

In reality, front-line Confederates were almost as bad off as any Yankee prisoners, if not worse. The Richmond government no longer had the ways or means to feed, clothe, or care for any of them.

Even though their stockade was in the line of fire, the Rebel prisoners on Morris Island miraculously escaped injury. A few, however, died of previous wounds, illness, or their exhausted physical condition.

The Union POW's in Charleston were removed to other locations in early October on account of the threat of a yellow fever outbreak, but their Southern counterparts on Morris Island were held in their pen until October 21.

The Yanks had decided to ship them south to Union-held Fort Pulaski. Foster no longer needed the ragged officers as flesh and blood defenses for his troops.

The first of two shiploads of the gray prisoners disembarked at Pulaski's wharf on the morning of October 23, 1864. With the 157th New York Infantry as their guard, the men were herded into the brick casemates on the south side of the pentagonal fortress.

At least two of the Rebel officers had Savannah connections. Lieutenant Sanford Branch of the Oglethorpe Light Infantry had comforted his dying brother, John, at First Manassas. Captured during the battle, "Santy" had been later exchanged, only to be seriously wounded at Gettysburg and made a prisoner again.

Also among the prisoners was Captain Harris K. Harrison, a relative of Georgia Brigadier General George Harrison, both of Savannah.

According to the prisoners' accounts, they were better treated by Union Colonel Philip P. Brown, commander of the New Yorkers, than they had been by Colonel Edward N. Hallowell, whose Fifty-fourth Massachusetts had been their keepers on Morris Island. The casemates were jammed with prisoners, and blankets and warm clothing were scarce, but rations were improved. The men also were allowed to trade with a sutler outside the fort and to receive letters and packages from home.

Still, the damp, cold brick quarters and one of the rawest winters in years contributed to the captives' woes. Malnutrition and the lingering effects of the unsanitary conditions of Morris Island contributed to the men's health problems.

The overcrowded conditions in the casemates caused the Union authorities to act. On November 19, about two hundred Confederates were transferred by ship to Hilton Head. The remaining prisoners spent their time trying to keep warm and obtain sufficient food, gambling, reading, and speculating on the war's course.

Thirty-one of the officers were taken to Charleston and exchanged on December 14. Six of the released officers wrote a letter thanking Colonel Brown for his benevolence. This act of gratitude dearly cost the remaining members of the "Immortal Six Hundred."

When the letter was published in a Charleston newspaper and seen by the Federals, Brown drew the wrath of General Foster, the department commander. The outraged general ordered a strict crackdown on the Pulaski prisoners to include ration cutbacks and other measures.

Meanwhile captors and captives were hearing the rumble of guns signaling Sherman's march on Savannah. Several companies of the 157th New York reinforced Foster's attempt to cut the railroad at Coosawhatchie, South Carolina, and sustained casualties.

Any morsel of war news was manna for the prisoners. The bread was seldom sweet. "The Yanks insist that Forts McAllister and Beaulieu have been taken," Captain Henry Dickinson of the Second Virginia Cavalry wrote on December 16. "They say Sherman's force left Atlanta 61,000 strong, and have lost from all causes 1,400 men, and that he dined yesterday at Hilton Head, having sent rations for 60,000 men to Nassau [actually Ossabaw] Sound. They assert that he has his battery within one and a half miles of the Charleston & Savannah railroad and is permitting all cars to go in but none to go out, and that the city must capitulate. We believe none of this and it leaked out today that nothing could be heard from Slocum with two corps. We are awfully impatient and all are excited and disturbed by Sherman."

The city's downfall caused a celebration by the Union garrison and despondency among the prisoners. "I fear it is a painful truth that our forces have evacuated Savannah," Virginia Captain David Grayson penned in his diary.

The torturous winter cold and icy wind wailing in from the sea afflicted many of the Southerners. Even though plentiful, some medicines were withheld from the ailing prisoners on account of Foster's policies.

Foster ordered retaliation rations of ten ounces of corn meal a day and unlimited pickles to go into effect for the Rebels on December 26. The incoming packages and letters to the Johnnies were stopped, as was their trade with the Union sutlers.

The corn meal was old and worm ridden, virtually inedible, and the Confederates suffered terribly. Scurvy and other maladies raged through the casemates. The starving men soon were feasting on rats or any hapless cat or dog they could catch.

"We cooked ours two ways," a Virginia cannoneer recalled of three unlucky felines. "One we fried in his own fat for breakfast—another we baked with a stuffing and gravy made of some of the corn meal—the other we also fried. The last was a kitten—was tender and nice." One of the furry victims belonged to the little daughter of Colonel Brown, the Union garrison commander.

Several of the men died during the winter. A handful of others were pushed beyond endurance and, taking the oath of allegiance to the Union, were released. They were scorned as traitors by their former comrades. The situation was just as bad or worse for the Confederates who had been transferred to Hilton Head.

Driven to desperation, seven Rebels at Pulaski decided to tunnel to freedom. Using an old dinner knife and a stove poker, they spent the weeks from Christmas to late February 1865 burrowing through the brick walls and the fort's foundation. Their back-breaking labor resulted in a tunnel some 330 feet long through solid brick. On the night of February 27–28, the men slipped into the tunnel and crawled outside the fort's walls. Wet, cold, and muddy, they were set to overwhelm a sentry at the wharf and commandeer a boat in the darkness.

Suddenly one of the escapees, Private Rufus Gillespie, inexplicably yelled for the guard not to shoot. Discovered, the tunnelers were recaptured in minutes and returned to confinement. They would never know why Gillespie called out, but the private was shunned and soon took "the oath" to get away from the other prisoners.

In early January, Foster received permission to exchange the "Immortal Six Hundred." He took no action and continued to hold them under retaliation status. Only when Foster was replaced in department command by Major General Quincy A. Gillmore, the victor at Fort Pulaski in 1862, was there a change in fortune for the prisoners. While Gillmore was en route to his new assignment, General Grover, in charge of the Union garrison at Savannah, assumed temporary command of the department. Members of his medical staff made an inspection of Fort Pulaski and found conditions deplorable. The captive Rebels "are in a condition of great suffering and exhaustion for want of sufficient food and clothing," Grover reported on February 7. Within a week of Gillmore's arrival, the Confederates were receiving better rations. The Federals also made arrangements for the exchange of the gray officers.

By March 12, 1865, what was left of the "Immortal Six Hundred" arrived back at Fort Delaware, which they had left almost seven months earlier. "Our hard fare and rough treatment . . . has been princely compared with that inflicted upon these scurvy-afflicted Fort Pulaski sufferers," remembered an imprisoned Alabamian who watched the officers limp ashore or be carried in on stretchers.

The Confederacy's slow death that spring eventually convinced even the staunchest Rebel among the Immortals to take the oath of allegiance. Among the last diehards to be released was Lieutenant Colonel Tazewell Hargrove of the Forty-fourth North Carolina Infantry, who was paroled on July 24.

The graves of the Immortals who didn't survive the war are scattered in Georgia, South Carolina, and New Jersey, the latter being those who died at Fort Delaware.

Forty-four officers perished in their imprisonment, including thirteen who were buried in unmarked graves at Fort Pulaski.

In *Immortal Captives*, a history of the "Immortal Six Hundred," author Mauriel P. Joslyn writes of the last surviving member of the Confederate prisoners. Lieutenant William Epps was eighty-seven when he was interviewed about his war experiences by a Charleston *News & Courier* reporter in 1930: "I am not untrue to my country. Every drop of my blood is pure American, and today, if America needed me, I should gladly give the few remaining years of my life to her service. The American flag is my flag. My fore-fathers followed it to the end of their lives. My heart still thrills to see its beautiful folds unfurl, but with that thrill comes an unspeakable sadness; for it was the Stars and Stripes that floated over Morris Island, Pulaski and Fort Delaware."

Notes

I. Secession Fever—1860
1. Olmstead, *Georgia Historical Quarterly* (hereafter referred to as *GHQ*), December 1959, p. 383.
2. Charles C. Jones, Jr., *History of Savannah*, p. 357.
3. Lawrence, *A Present for Mr. Lincoln*, p. 3.
4. *Savannah Daily Morning News* (hereafter referred to as *SDMN*), December 3, 1859.
5. *SDMN*, February 4, 1860.
6. *SDMN*, May 15, 1860.
7. Olmstead, *GHQ*, December 1959, p. 384.
8. Myers, *The Children of Pride*, p. 25.
9. *Ibid.*, p. 29.
10. *Ibid.*, p. 37.
11. Lawrence, p. 9.
12. Charles Jones, p. 357.
13. Henderson, *The Oglethorpe Light Infantry*, p. 11.

II. 1861—"Our Flag Victorious!"
1. Henderson, p. 11.
2. *Ibid.*
3. Charles Jones, p. 359.
4. *SDMN*, January 3, 1861.
5. Charles Jones, p. 359.

6. Olmstead, *GHQ*, December 1959, p. 388.

7. *SDMN*, January 5, 1861.

8. Myers, p. 38.

9. *SDMN*, January 12, 1861.

10. *Ibid.*, February 1, 1861.

11. John Elliott to his mother, February 12, 1861, in Lane, *"Dear Mother,"* p. 2.

12. Burton, *The Siege of Charleston*, p. 22.

13. *SDMN*, February 20, 1861.

14. D'Antignac, *Georgia's Navy*, p. 8.

15. *Ibid.*

16. *Ibid.*, p. 10.

17. Robbins, "Maffitt," p. 46.

18. Andrews, *Footprints*, p. 16.

19. *SDMN*, March 22, 1861.

20. *Ibid.*

21. Schott, *Alexander H. Stephens*, p. 334.

22. *SDMN*, April 19, 1861.

23. Myers, p. 57.

24. William Howard Russell, in Lane, *Times That Prove*, pp. 34–35.

25. *Ibid.*

26. *Ibid.*, p. 38.

27. *SDMN*, May 22, 1861.

28. William Howard Russell, in Lane, *Times That Prove*, p. 35.

29. Myers, p. 51.

III. "Never Give Up the Fight"

1. Lawrence, pp. 29–30.

2. *Ibid.*

3. *Ibid.*

4. *SDMN*, August 1, 1861.

5. Chesnut, *A Diary From Dixie*, pp. 86–87.

6. *SDMN*, July 24, 1861.

7. *Ibid.*, July 15, 1861.

8. Lawrence, p. 105.

9. W. H. Russell, in Lane, *Times That Prove*, p. 36.

10. Derry, *Confederate Military History*, p. 58.

11. W. H. Russell, in Lane, *Times That Prove*, p. 36.

12. *Ibid.*, p. 38.

13. Myers, p. 145.
14. George A. Mercer, in Lane, *Times That Prove*, p. 40.
15. *SDMN*, November 11, 1861.
16. George A. Mercer, in Lane, *Times That Prove*, p. 41.
17. Myers, pp. 146–147.
18. *Ibid.*

IV. R. E. Lee in Savannah

1. Olmstead, *GHQ*, March 1960, pp. 63–64.
2. Myers, p. 152.
3. Wert, "Lee's First Year," p. 42.
4. Olmstead, *GHQ*, March 1960, p. 67.
5. William Basinger, in Lawrence, pp. 114, 267.

V. "Repel the Invasion!"

1. George Mercer, in Lane, *Times That Prove*, p. 41.
2. Andrews, p. 10.
3. Myers, p. 160.
4. Bryan, *Confederate Georgia*, p. 67.
5. *SDMN*, November 29, 1861.
6. *Ibid.*, November 6, 1861.
7. *Ibid.*
8. Myers, p. 179.
9. *SDMN*, December 30, 1861.

VI. "We Shall Soon Have Some Hard Fighting"—1862

1. King, *Sound of Drums*, p. 83.
2. Olmstead, *GHQ*, March 1960, pp. 63–64.
3. *SDMN*, January 10, 1862.
4. Myers, p. 189.
5. Alonzo Williams, *The Investment*, p. 46.
6. Derry, pp. 85–86.
7. King, *Rebel Lawyer*, p. 48.
8. *Ibid.*
9. Lawrence, p. 53.
10. Buel and Johnson, *Battles and Leaders of the Civil War*, vol. II, p. 2.
11. Harwell, *Lee*, p. 159.
12. Merrill, *GHQ*, June 1959, pp. 205–207.
13. *Ibid.*

14. *Ibid.*
15. *Ibid.*
16. King, *Rebel Lawyer*, p. 70.
17. Derry, p. 17.

VII. "PULASKI FALLEN!"

1. Henderson, p. 22.
2. King, *Rebel Lawyer*, p. 71.
3. *Ibid.*
4. Buel and Johnson, vol. II, p. 1.
5. Bryan, p. 72.
6. Buel and Johnson, vol. II, p. 9.
7. King, *Sound of Drums*, p. 85.
8. *Savannah Republican*, April 12, 1862.
9. Buel and Johnson, vol. II, p. 9.
10. *Ibid.*
11. *Ibid.*
12. *SDMN*, April 12, 1862.
13. *Savannah Republican*, April 15, 1862.
14. Chesnut, p. 211.
15. Myers, p. 229.
16. King, *Rebel Lawyer*, p. 76.

VIII. "MAMMA, IT WAS TERRIBLE TO LOOK AT"

1. George Mercer, in Lane, *Times That Prove*, p. 67.
2. *Savannah Republican*, April 17, 1862.
3. Andrews, p. 10.
4. George Mercer, in Lane, *Times That Prove*, p. 67.
5. Myers, p. 243.
6. *Ibid.*, p. 245.
7. George Mercer, in Lane, *Times That Prove*, p. 67.
8. King, *Ebb Tide*, p. 15.
9. Melton, *The Confederate Ironclads*, pp. 171–172.
10. Buel and Johnson, vol. II, p. 6.
11. *Savannah Republican*, September 17, 1862.

IX. COMPLETION OF THE IRONCLADS

1. Still, *Savannah Squadron*, p. 6.
2. Melton, p. 172.

3. Myers, pp. 316–317.
4. George Mercer, in Lane, *Times That Prove*, p. 69.
5. King, *Ebb Tide*, p. 15.

X. ARRIVAL OF THE MONITORS—1863
1. Gordon Smith, *Chatham Artillery*, p. 52.
2. Wise, *Lifeline of the Confederacy*, p. 67.
3. Lawrence, p. 96.
4. Myers, p. 344.
5. *SDMN*, February 11, 1863.
6. *Ibid.*, March 6, 1863.
7. Myers, p. 344.
8. *SDMN*, March 6, 1863.

XI. EPITAPH FOR AN IRONCLAD
1. Still, *Iron Afloat*, p. 132.
2. Warner, *Generals in Gray*, pp. 226–227.
3. Still, *Savannah Squadron*, p. 13.
4. *Ibid.*
5. Melton, p. 178.
6. King, *Ebb Tide*, p. 22.
7. Still, *Iron Afloat*, p. 138.
8. Donnelly, *The Confederate States Marine Corps*, p. 32.

XII. "A GREAT CALAMITY HAS BEFALLEN OUR ARMS"
1. King, *Ebb Tide*, pp. 24–25.
2. *Ibid.*, pp. 34–35.
3. *Savannah Republican*, August 14, 1863.
4. Lawrence, p. 138.
5. *SDMN*, August 1, 1863.
6. Myers, p. 396.
7. King, *Ebb Tide*, pp. 85–86.
8. *Ibid.*, p. 103.

XIII. GLORY AND GLOOM—1864
1. Buel and Johnson, vol. IV, p. 671.
2. Commager, *The Blue and the Gray*, p. 925.
3. Nichols, *Story of the Great March*, p. 121.
4. Sullivan, "Leathernecks in Gray," p. 368.

5. Lawrence, p. 155.

6. Minor, *"Diary of a Confederate Naval Cadet,"* p. 26.

7. *Ibid.*, p. 27.

8. *Ibid.*, p. 28.

9. *Ibid.*

10. *Savannah Republican*, June 6, 1864.

11. Sorrell, *Recollections*, p. 21.

12. Hood, *Advance and Retreat*, p. 162.

13. King, *Ebb Tide*, p. 113.

14. Lawrence, p. 160.

15. Meaney, *GHQ*, Spring 1987, p. 19.

16. Donnelly, *The Confederate States Marine Corps*, p. 96.

17. Andrews, p. 148.

18. *Ibid.*, p. 151.

19. Hughes, *General William J. Hardee*, p. 247.

20. Roman, *Military Operations of General Beauregard*, p. 285.

XIV. "Give Sherman Hail Columbia"

1. Sherman, *"War Is Hell!"*, p. 129.

2. *Ibid.*, pp. 134–135.

3. Sherman, *Sherman's Civil War*, p. 355.

4. Sherman, *"War Is Hell!"*, p. 145.

5. Connelly, *Autumn of Glory*, p. 489.

6. Burke Davis, *Sherman's March*, p. 56.

7. *SDMN*, December 1, 1864.

8. Andrews, p. 151.

9. Roman, vol. II, p. 610.

10. *SDMN*, November 28, 1864.

11. Still, *Iron Afloat*, p. 215.

12. *SDMN*, November 29, 1864.

13. Roman, pp. 304–305.

14. Sherman, *Sherman's Civil War*, p. 369.

15. Nichols, p. 88.

XV. Besiegers and Besieged—December 1864

1. Sherman, *"War Is Hell!"*, p. 172.

2. Hughes, p. 258.

3. *The War of the Rebellion*, vol. XLIV, p. 940.

4. Roman, p. 317.

5. *Ibid.*, p. 312.
6. Sherman, *Sherman's Civil War*, pp. 369–370.
7. Andrews, p. 152.
8. *Ibid.*
9. *Ibid.*, p. 153.
10. Harwell and Racine, *The Fiery Trail*, p. 70.
11. Andrews, pp. 152–153.
12. Burke Davis, *Sherman's March*, p. 112.

XVI. Fort McAllister's Last Stand
1. Anderson quoted from "Historical Sketch of the Chatham Artillery," in Charles C. Jones, p. 378.
2. Warner, *Generals in Blue*, pp. 225–226.
3. Mosser, "Gateway to the Atlantic," p. 67.
4. Charles C. Jones, p. 378.
5. Sherman, *Sherman's Civil War*, p. 372.
6. Mosser, p. 67.
7. Sherman, *Sherman's Civil War*, p. 372.
8. Charles C. Jones, p. 378.
9. Cox, *Sherman's March to the Sea*, p. 54.
10. Burke Davis, *Sherman's March*, p. 105.
11. Lawrence, pp. 186–187.
12. Sherman, *Sherman's Civil War*, p. 376.
13. Lawrence, p. 187.
14. Hughes, p. 262.

XVII. "I Will Bombard the City"
1. Commager, p. 925.
2. Osborn, in Harwell and Racine, p. 72.
3. Sherman, *War Is Hell*, pp. 170–171.
4. Roman, p. 315. (General Hood's surrender demand to the Union commander at Resaca on October 12, 1864, included: "If the place is carried by assault, no prisoners will be taken.")
5. *Ibid.*, pp. 316–317.
6. Sherman, *Sherman's Civil War*, p. 393.
7. Infantryman Frederick Price, in Katharine Jones, *When Sherman Came*, p. 34.
8. Sherman, *Sherman's Civil War*, p. 392.

XVIII. "We Have Won a Magnificent Prize"

1. Roman, p. 623.
2. *Official Records . . . Navies*, vol. XVI, p. 481.
3. Burke Davis, *Sherman's March*, p. 112.
4. Donnelly, *The Confederate States Marine Corps*, p. 98.
5. *SDMN*, December 25, 1932.
6. Andrews, pp. 153–154.
7. *Ibid.*
8. Colonel Henry Barnum, in Katherine Jones, pp. 83–84.
9. Fanny Cohen Taylor, in Katherine Jones, p. 92.
10. Still, *Savannah Squadron*, p. 120.
11. Still, *Iron Afloat*, p. 218.
12. Sherman, *Sherman's Civil War*, p. 394.
13. Buel and Johnson, vol. IV, p. 680.
14. *Ibid.*
15. Osborn, in Harwell and Racine, p. 73.
16. Lawrence, p. 205.
17. Nichols, p. 100.
18. Andrews, p. 154.
19. Roman, p. 319.
20. Nancy Bostick DeSaussure, in Katherine Jones, p. 111.
21. Hardee to Jefferson Davis, in Katherine Jones, p. 83.
22. Charles C. Jones, p. 381.
23. Hughes, p. 270.
24. Lawrence, p. 205.

XIX. Lincoln's Christmas Gift

1. Sherman, *Sherman's Civil War*, p. 394.
2. *Ibid.*, p. 394.
3. *Ibid.*
4. Sherman, *"War Is Hell!"*, p. 188.
5. *Ibid.*
6. Lincoln to Sherman, in Katherine Jones, p. 84.
7. Frances T. Howard, in Katherine Jones, p. 90.
8. Lawrence, p. 219.
9. *Ibid.*, p. 221.

XX. Sherman and "The Negro Question"

1. Burke Davis, *Sherman's March*, p. 93.

2. Sherman, *Sherman's Civil War*, pp. 415–416.

3. *Ibid.*, p. 411.

4. *Ibid.*, p. 414.

5. *Ibid.*

6. Sherman, *"War Is Hell!"*, p. 195.

7. Sherman, *Sherman's Civil War*, pp. 416–417.

XXI. "The Army Is Acclimatized in Savannah"

1. Sherman, *Sherman's Civil War*, pp. 397–398.

2. Nichols, p. 99.

3. Fanny Cohen Taylor, in Katherine Jones, p. 95.

4. Sherman, *Sherman's Civil War*, p. 411.

5. Fanny Cohen Taylor, in Katherine Jones, p. 94.

6. *Ibid.*

7. Lawrence, pp. 212–213.

8. Osborn, in Harwell and Racine, p. 79.

9. Lawrence, pp. 212–213.

10. Nichols, p. 106.

11. Sherman, *Sherman's Civil War*, p. 403.

12. *Ibid.*, pp. 403–404.

13. Burke Davis, *Sherman's March*, p. 127.

14. Osborn, in Harwell and Racine, p. 79.

15. Frances T. Howard, in Katherine Jones, p. 91.

16. Emilio, *A Brave Black Regiment*, p. 299.

17. Lawrence, p. 232.

18. Harwell and Racine, p. 79.

19. Eleanor Kinzie Gordon, in Katherine Jones, pp. 97–98.

20. *Ibid.*

21. *Ibid.*

22. Sherman, *Sherman's Civil War*, p. 395.

23. Fanny Cohen Taylor, in Katherine Jones, p. 94.

24. Sherman, *"War Is Hell!"*, pp. 186–187.

25. *Ibid.*, pp. 189–190.

26. Harwell and Racine, p. 80.

27. Frances T. Howard, in Katherine Jones, p. 104.

28. Burke Davis, *Sherman's March*, p. 141.

29. Conway, p. 17.

30. Gattell, *GHQ*, December 1959, p. 429.

31. *Savannah Daily Herald*, January 28, 1865.

32. *Ibid.*

33. Frances T. Howard, in Katherine Jones, p. 104.

XXII. Arrival of the U.S. Colored Troops

1. Emilio, p. 299.
2. *Savannah Republican*, March 19, 1865.
3. *Ibid.*
4. Lawrence, p. 244.

XXIII. Death of the Confederacy—1865

1. Mrs. William H. Stiles, in Katherine Jones, pp. 105–106.
2. Nichols, p. 131.
3. Sherman, *Sherman's Civil War*, p. 439.
4. Lawrence, p. 242.
5. Olmstead, *GHQ*, June 1961, p. 153.
6. *Savannah Daily Herald*, April 19, 1865.
7. *Savannah Republican*, April 24, 1865.
8. *Ibid.*
9. *Savannah Daily Herald*, May 1, 1865.
10. *Ibid.*, May 2, 1865.
12. Burke Davis, *The Long Surrender*, p. 145.

XXIV. The Postwar Years

1. George Mercer, in Lane, *Times That Prove*, pp. 253–254.
2. Conway, p. 30.
3. *Ibid.*, p. 172.
4. *SDMN*, June 15, 1871.
5. Castel, "The Life of a Rising Son," p. 121.
6. *SDMN*, December 10, 1873.

XXV. Short Stories—1861–1865

1. Olmstead, *GHQ*, March 1960, pp. 61–62.
2. George Mercer, in Lawrence, p. 107.
3. *SDMN*, March 12, 1863.
4. *Ibid.*, March 6, 1863.

Bibliography

Albu, Susan H., and Elizabeth Arndt. *Here's Savannah: A Journey Through Historic Savannah & Environs*. Savannah, Ga.: Atlantic Printing Co., 1994.

Allardice, Bruce S. *More Generals in Gray*. Baton Rouge and London: Louisiana State University Press, 1995.

Andrews, W. H. *Footprints of a Regiment: A Recollection of the 1st Georgia Regulars, 1861–1865*. Atlanta, Ga.: Longstreet Press, Inc., 1992.

Beney, Peter. *The Majesty of Savannah*. Gretna, La.: Pelican Publishing Co., 1992.

Black, Robert C., III. *The Railroads of the Confederacy*. Chapel Hill: University of North Carolina Press, 1952.

Boatner, Mark M., III. *The Civil War Dictionary*. Rev. ed. New York: David McKay Co., Inc., 1987.

Booker, Simeon. *Susie King Taylor—Civil War Nurse*. New York: McGraw-Hill Book Co., Inc., 1969.

Bowman, John S., ed. *The Civil War Almanac*. New York: Bison Books, 1983.

Brown, Russell K. *To the Manner Born—The Life of General William H. T. Walker*. Athens and London: University of Georgia Press, 1994.

Bryan, Conn T. *Confederate Georgia*. Athens: University of Georgia Press, 1953.

Buel, Clarence C., and Robert V. Johnson. *Battles and Leaders of the Civil*

War: Being for the Most Part Contributions by Union and Confederate Authors. 4 vols. New York: Century Co., 1887.

Bull, Rice C. *The Civil War Diary of Rice C. Bull.* San Rafael, Calif.: Presidio Press, 1977.

Burton, E. Milby. *The Siege of Charleston, 1861–1865.* Columbia: University of South Carolina Press, 1970.

Carroll, John M. *Register of Officers of the Confederate States Navy, 1861–1865.* Mattituck, N.Y.: J. M. Carroll & Co., 1983.

Castel, Albert. "The Life of a Rising Son, Part III: The Conqueror." *Civil War Times Illustrated* (October 1979).

Channing, Steven A. *Crisis of Fear—Secession in South Carolina.* New York: Simon and Schuster, 1970.

Chesnut, Mary Boykin. *A Diary From Dixie.* Cambridge: Harvard University Press, 1980.

Commager, Henry Steele, ed. *The Blue and the Gray.* Indianapolis: Bobbs-Merrill, 1950.

Connelly, Thomas Lawrence. *Army of the Heartland: The Army of Tennessee, 1861–1862.* Baton Rouge and London: Louisiana State University Press, 1971.

————. *Autumn of Glory: The Army of Tennessee, 1862–1865.* Baton Rouge and London: Louisiana State University Press, 1971.

Conway, Alan. *The Reconstruction of Georgia.* Minneapolis: University of Minnesota Press, 1966.

Cox, Jacob D. *Sherman's March to the Sea.* New York: Da Capo Press, Inc., 1994.

D'Antignac, Munroe. *Georgia's Navy—1861.* Griffin, Ga.: The Goen Printing Co., 1945.

Davis, Burke. *The Long Surrender.* New York: Random House, Inc., 1985.

————. *Sherman's March.* New York: Random House, Inc., 1980.

Davis, William C. *Battle at Bull Run.* Baton Rouge and London: Louisiana State University Press, 1977.

————. *Duel Between the First Ironclads.* Baton Rouge and London: Louisiana State University Press, 1981.

————. *The Orphan Brigade: The Kentucky Confederates Who Couldn't Go Home.* Garden City: Doubleday, 1980.

Derry, Joseph T. *Confederate Military History, Vol. VI—Georgia.* Secaucus N.J.: Blue and Grey Press, n.d.

Donnelly, Ralph W. *The Confederate States Marine Corps: The Rebel Leathernecks.* Shippensburg, Pa.: White Mane Publishing Co., Inc., 1989.

———. "Personnel of the Confederate Navy." *Civil War Times Illustrated* (January 1975).

Emilio, Luis F. *A Brave Black Regiment.* New York: Bantam Doubleday Dell Publishing Group, Inc., 1992.

Fogarty, William L. *The Days We've Celebrated.* Savannah: Printcraft Press, 1980.

Fowler, William M., Jr. *Under Two Flags.* New York: W. W. Norton & Co., 1990.

Freeman, Douglas Southall. *Lee's Lieutenants: A Study in Command.* Vol. I. New York: Charles Scribner's Sons, 1942.

Gattell, Otto. "The Agony of Savannah." *Georgia Historical Quarterly* 43 (December 1959).

Gibson, John M. *Those 163 Days—A Southern Account of Sherman's March From Atlanta to Raleigh.* New York: Coward-McCann, Inc., 1961.

Glatthaar, Joseph T. *Forged in Battle: The Civil War Alliance of Black Soldiers and White Officers.* New York: Free Press, Macmillan, Inc., 1990.

Grimsley, Mark. "Robert E. Lee: The Life and Career of the Master General." *Civil War Times Illustrated* (November 1985).

Harwell, Richard. *Lee.* New York: Charles Scribner's Sons, 1961. Abridgement of Douglas Southall Freeman, *R. E. Lee,* 4 vols.

Harwell, Richard, and Philip N. Racine. *The Fiery Trail—A Union Officer's Account of Sherman's Last Campaigns.* Knoxville: University of Tennessee Press, 1986.

Henderson, Lindsay P., Jr. *The Oglethorpe Light Infantry: A Military History.* Savannah: Civil War Centennial Commission of Savannah and Chatham County, 1961.

Hood, John B. *Advance and Retreat: Personal Experiences in the United States and Confederate States Armies.* Secaucus, N.J.: Blue and Grey Press, 1985.

Hoole, William Stanley. *Four Years in the Confederate Navy: The Career of Captain John Low on the C.S.S. Fingal, Florida, Alabama, Tuscaloosa and Ajax.* Athens: University of Georgia Press, 1964.

Horne, Stanley F. *The Decisive Battle of Nashville.* Baton Rouge: Louisiana State University Press, 1956.

Hughes, Nathaniel C., Jr. *General William J. Hardee—Old Reliable.* Baton Rouge and London: Louisiana State University Press, 1965.

Jones, Charles Colcock, Jr. *History of Savannah, Ga., From Its Settlement to the Close of the Eighteenth Century.* Syracuse, N.Y.: D. Mason & Co., Publishers, 1890.

Jones, Katharine M. *When Sherman Came: Southern Women and the "Great March."* Indianapolis: Bobbs-Merrill Co., Inc., 1964.

Kennedy, Frances H., ed. *The Civil War Battlefield Guide.* Boston: Houghton Mifflin Co., 1990.

King, Spencer Bidwell, Jr., ed. *Ebb Tide: As Seen Through the Diary of Josephine Clay Habersham, 1863.* Athens: University of Georgia Press, 1958.

————. *Rebel Lawyer: Letters of Theodorick W. Montfort, 1861–1862.* Athens: University of Georgia Press, 1965.

————. *Sound of Drums: Selected Writings of Spencer B. King From His Civil War Centennial Columns Appearing in the Macon Telegraph-News.* Macon, Ga.: Mercer University Press, 1984.

Lane, Mills, ed. *"Dear Mother: Don't grieve about me. If I get killed, I'll only be dead."—Letters from Georgia Soldiers in the Civil War.* Savannah: Beehive Press, 1977.

————. *Times That Prove People's Principles—Civil War in Georgia.* Savannah: Beehive Press, 1993.

Lawrence, Alexander A. *A Present for Mr. Lincoln: The Story of Savannah From Secession to Sherman.* Macon, Ga.: Ardivan Press, Inc., 1961.

Luraghi, Raimondo. *A History of the Confederate Navy.* Annapolis: Naval Institute Press, 1996.

McDonough, James Lee. *Shiloh—In Hell Before Night.* Knoxville: University of Tennessee Press, 1977.

McMurry, Richard M. "On the Road to the Sea: Sherman's Savannah Campaign." *Civil War Times Illustrated* (January 1983).

Marszalek, John F. *Sherman—A Soldier's Passion for Order.* New York: Free Press, Macmillan, Inc., 1993.

Martin, Van Jones. *At Home in Savannah: Great Interiors.* Savannah: Golden Coast Publishing Co., 1978.

Meaney, Peter J. "The Prison Ministry of Father Peter Whelan, Georgia Priest and Confederate Chaplain." *Georgia Historical Quarterly* 71 (Spring 1987).

Melton, Maurice. *The Confederate Ironclads.* Cranbury, N.J.: Thomas Yoseloff, Publisher, 1968.

Merrill, James M. "Personne Goes to Georgia: Five Civil War Letters." *Georgia Historical Quarterly* 43 (June 1959).

Miers, Earl S. *The Web of Victory: Grant at Vicksburg.* Baton Rouge: Louisiana State University Press, 1984.

BIBLIOGRAPHY

Miller, Francis Trevelyan, ed. *Photographic History of the Civil War.* 10 vols. New York, 1911.

Minor, Hubbard T., Jr. "Diary of a Confederate Naval Cadet." *Civil War Times Illustrated* (December 1974).

Mosser, Jeffrey. "Gateway to the Atlantic." *Civil War Times Illustrated* (December 1994).

Myers, Robert Manson. *The Children of Pride: A True Story of Georgia and the Civil War.* Abr. ed. Binghamton: Vail-Ballou Press, Inc., and New Haven: Yale University Press, 1982.

Nichols, George Ward. *The Story of the Great March From the Diary of a Staff Officer.* New York: Harper and Brothers, 1865.

Official Records of the Union and Confederate Navies in the War of the Rebellion. 303 vols. Washington, D.C.: U.S. Government Printing Office, 1894–1922.

Olmstead, Charles H. "The Memoirs of Charles H. Olmstead." *Georgia Historical Quarterly* (December 1958–March 1961).

Patterson, Gerard A. *Rebels From West Point.* New York: Doubleday, 1987.

Perry, Milton F. *Infernal Machines.* Baton Rouge and London: Louisiana State University Press, 1965.

Phillips, Joslyn Mauriel. *Captives Immortal—The Story of Six Hundred Confederate Officers and the United States Prisoner of War Policy.* Shippensburg, Pa.: White Mane Publishing Co., Inc., 1996.

Pratt, Fletcher. *A Short History of the Civil War.* New York: Pocket Books, Inc., 1963.

Radley, Kenneth. *Rebel Watchdog—The Confederate States Army Provost Guard.* Baton Rouge and London: Louisiana State University Press, 1989.

Rauers, Betty, and Franklin Traub. *Sojourn in Savannah.* 6th ed. Savannah: Printcraft Press, 1984.

Recollections and Reminiscences, 1861–1865, Through World War I. 6 vols. South Carolina Division, United Daughters of the Confederacy, 1992.

Robbins, Peggy. "Maffitt: 'Magician' of the Blockade." *Civil War Times Illustrated* (November–December 1991).

Roman, Alfred. *The Military Operations of General Beauregard in the War Between the States.* Vol. II. New York: Harper & Brothers, 1884.

Russell, Preston, and Barbara Hines. *Savannah: A History of Her People Since 1733.* Savannah: Frederic C. Beil, Publisher, 1992.

Savannah Daily Herald, 1865.

Savannah Daily Morning News, 1860–1865.

Savannah Republican, 1861–1865.

Schmier, Louis. "An Act Unbecoming." *Civil War Times Illustrated* (October 1984).

Schott, Thomas E. *Alexander H. Stephens of Georgia*. Baton Rouge and London: Louisiana State University Press, 1988.

Semmes, Raphael. *Memoirs of Service Afloat During the War Between the States*. Baltimore: Kelly, Piet and Co., 1869.

Sherman, William T. *Sherman's Civil War*. New York: Crowell-Collier Publishing Co., 1962. "Selected and Edited from His Personal Memoirs, with a Foreword by Earl Schenck Miers."

———. *"War Is Hell!"—William T. Sherman's Personal Narrative of His March Through Georgia*. Edited by Mills Lane. Savannah: Beehive Press, 1974.

Sieg, Edward Chan. *Eden on the Marsh: An Illustrated History of Savannah*. Northridge, Calif.: Windsor Publications, Inc., 1985.

Sifakis, Stewart. *Who Was Who in the Confederacy*. New York: Facts on File, Inc., 1988.

Smith, Derek. "Bayard of the Confederacy." *Georgia Journal* (Spring 1991).

———. "Savannah's Forgotten Ironclad: The CSS Atlanta." *Savannah Magazine* (March-April 1993).

———. "The Stand at Ft. McAllister." *Army* (May 1989).

Smith, Gordon. *The Chatham Artillery, 1786–1986*. N.p., 1985.

Sorrell, G. Moxley. *Recollections of a Confederate Staff Officer*. New York: Neale Publishing Company, 1905.

Starr, Stephen Z. *The Union Cavalry in the Civil War*. Vol. III. Baton Rouge and London: Louisiana State University Press, 1985.

Still, William N., Jr. *Iron Afloat: The Story of the Confederate Armorclads*. Columbia: University of South Carolina Press, 1985.

———. *Savannah Squadron*. Savannah: Coastal Heritage Press, 1989.

Strode, Hudson. *Jefferson Davis—Confederate President*. New York: Harcourt, Brace and Co., 1959.

Strode, Hudson, ed. *Jefferson Davis—Private Letters, 1823–1889*. New York: Harcourt, Brace & World, Inc., 1966.

Strong, Robert Hale. *A Yankee Private's Civil War*. Chicago: Henry Regnery, Co., 1961.

Sullivan, David M. "Leathernecks in Gray: A Perspective of the War Through the Letters of Confederate States Marine Officers." *Journal of Confederate History* 2 (Fall 1988).

BIBLIOGRAPHY

Symonds, Craig L. *Joseph E. Johnston—A Civil War Biography*. New York and London: W. W. Norton & Co., 1992.

Taylor, Susie King. *Reminiscences of My Life With the 33rd United States Colored Troops Late 1st S.C. Volunteers*. Boston, 1902.

The War of the Rebellion: A Compilation of the Official Records of the Union and Confederate Armies. 128 vols. Washington, D.C.: U.S. Government Printing Office, 1880–1901.

Waring, Joseph Frederick. *Cerveau's Savannah*. Savannah: Georgia Historical Society, 1973.

Warner, Ezra J. *Generals in Blue: Lives of the Union Commanders*. Baton Rouge: Louisiana State University Press, 1964.

———. *Generals in Gray: Lives of the Confederate Commanders*. Baton Rouge: Louisiana State University Press, 1959.

Watkins, Sam R. *"Co. Aytch."* New York: Collier Books, Macmillan Publishing Co., 1962.

Wert, Jeffry D. "Lee's First Year of the War." *Civil War Times Illustrated* (December 1974).

Williams, Alonzo. *The Investment of Fort Pulaski*. Providence, R.I.: Providence Press Co., Printers, 1887.

Williams, T. Harry. *P. G. T. Beauregard—Napoleon in Gray*. Baton Rouge and London: Louisiana State University Press, 1955.

Wise, Stephen R. *Lifeline of the Confederacy—Blockade Running During the Civil War*. Columbia: University of South Carolina Press, 1988.

Index

INDEX